LONG WALKS IN FRANCE

BELOW *M. Rose in Le Saillant, Corrèze*

OVERLEAF *The Loire*

Adam Nicolson

*Photographs by
Charlie Waite*

LONG WALKS IN
FRANCE

Harmony Books New York

Acknowledgment

The production of this book was made possible
by a generous subvention from Elf Aquitaine
UK, to whom the Publishers wish to express
their gratitude.

Text copyright © Adam Nicolson 1983

Designed by Allison Waterhouse

First United States edition published by Harmony
Books, a division of Crown Publishers, Inc., One
Park Avenue, New York, New York 10016.
Harmony and colophon are trademarks of Crown
Publishers, Inc.

Published in Britain under the title *The Elf Book
of Long Walks in France* by Weidenfeld & Nicolson,
91 Clapham High Street, London SW4 7TA, England.

Manufactured in Italy

**Library of Congress Cataloging in Publication
Data**

Nicolson, Adam, 1957–
 Long Walks in France

 1. France—Description and travel—1975–
2. Walking—France. 3. Nicolson, Adam, 1957–
I. Title.
DC29.3.N5 1983 914.4′04838 83–6148
ISBN 0–517–55043–1

First American Edition

10 9 8 7 6 5 4 3 2 1

Contents

Acknowledgments

We owe enormous thanks to the following
people for all their help, encouragement and
company over the year it took to do this book:

Jessica, Romilly, Ella Bahama and Jessamy
Waite
Ron and Joanna Sullam
Nigel, Rebecca and Olivia Nicolson
Dido Merwin
Kildare Bourke-Borrowes, Montagu Don and
Michael Petch
Russell Ash and the outstanding Barbara
Mellor

and in France:

Thérèse Gahéry, Mme Viers, Pierre Pome,
Roger Moins, Mme Soulier, Raoul and Dick,
Gabriel Venteloux, Gilbert Renard, René Gras-
Boisson, and Henri Rose.

The photographs are for Jessica.

For Olivia Fane

Introduction

There are 30,000 kilometres of long-distance footpaths in France, the *Sentiers de Grande Randonnée*, about eight times as many as there are in Britain. This book chooses 1,600 kilometres of them, a thousand miles worth, in nine long walks of over 150 kilometres each. Four are in the northern half of the country – in Brittany, Normandy, the Loire valley and Burgundy – three in the Massif Central or on its edges, through Limousin, the volcanic hills of the Auvergne and following Robert Louis Stevenson through the Cévennes. The last two are in the western Pyrenees (the *pays basque*) and over the Cézanne landscape of Provence. Unlike the paths in Britain, which are engineered by the Countryside Commission, a government body that takes as much trouble and time as it would on a motorway, the *Comité National des Sentiers de Grande Randonnée*, which is private, uses local volunteers to paint the red and white waymarks and to write the small paperback *Topo-Guides*. They never depend on the creation of new rights of way, but use the ubiquitous and half-neglected sheeptracks and footpaths that net the French country-side. It is this admirable flexibility that has allowed them to develop the huge lengths of path in a couple of decades.

With so many, there is none of the overcrowding and erosion that has brought the Pennine Way such a bad name and which cancelled the proposed walk through the remoter parts of Wales. These French paths are astonishingly empty. On all of them, except for the inevitable crowds in famous places at weekends, I met no more than ten fellow *randonneurs*, most from Paris or Bordeaux, usually experimenting with this alien mode of travel and dressed in clothes and shoes your professional English rambler would disdain. On several of the paths I met no one but the local people, and the only sign of other walkers was the rare print of a boot in the mud.

But to walk in France is no solitary experience. Few people are more insistently welcoming, I have found, than the people of the French countryside. Their readiness to communicate and their lack of indifference should put the English to shame. No one here will accept unquestioningly, as Englishmen do, that you have just walked five days to meet them. You will constantly be shaken by the hand and told of your *courage*, a word that is endlessly repeated and works marvels for a drooping ego.

It is, besides, a fascinating time to be in rural France. For the past fifty years a revolution has been transforming it, turning the *paysan* into an *agriculteur* and pulling both him and the town-dweller's idea of him into the modern world. The *paysan* – meaning countryman without the derogatory overtones of 'peasant' in English – and his traditional style of life have always been a kind of political symbol in France, the foundation on which all the moral integrity of the nation is built. The protectionist measures brought in by successive French governments since the nineteenth century have been intended to shelter his worthy but inefficient way of farming. In 1920 the Minister of Agriculture gave medals to those *paysans* who could prove that they and their ancestors had farmed the same piece of land in the same way for 500 years or more. Those who could prove it for a thousand years were entertained to lunch. It was a world of minute holdings. One commune of some 2,000 hectares (5,000 acres) in the Loire valley was still divided before the war into 48,000 separate plots. It was also a life of great deprivation. Men drafted into the army from the towns were consistently taller than those from the country, while infant mortality, mental disturbance, alcoholism and suicide all ran at a higher rate in the country.

It is this which has been changing in the last few decades. There has been a massive exodus from rural villages into the towns, so that where half of all Frenchmen worked on the land in 1931, less than 8% do so today (compared with 25% in Greece, for example, and only 4% in Britain). You will pass many deserted farms on these walks. Invariably they are melancholy and romantic places, but each of them probably represents some personal escape from poverty and depressing toil. Although agriculture is almost all mech-anized now, there is still a profound wish in French policy-makers not to allow the land-scape of southern and western France or the French way of farming to become either East Anglian in style or capitalist agri-business in fact. The Mitterand government sees it as a choice between subsidized farming and

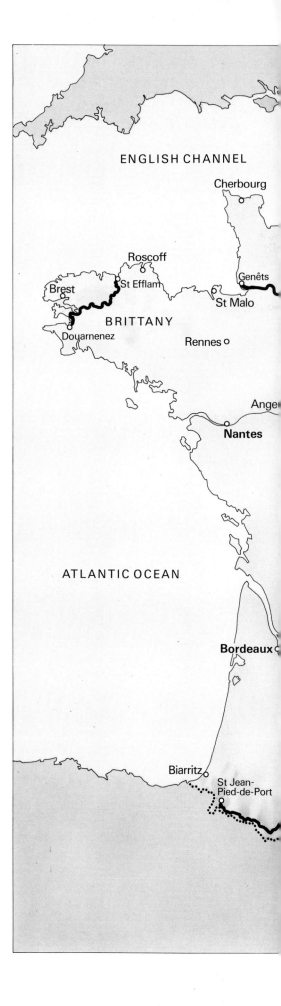

ENGLISH CHANNEL

Cherbourg

Roscoff

Brest
St Efflam
Genêts

BRITTANY
St Malo

Douarnenez
Rennes

Ange

Nantes

ATLANTIC OCEAN

Bordeaux

Biarritz
St Jean-
Pied-de-Port

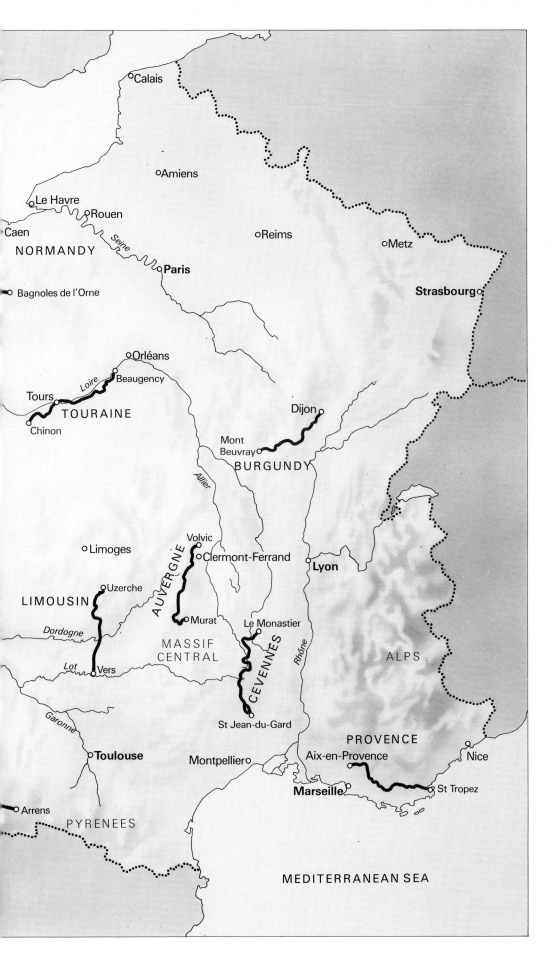

Calais

Amiens

Le Havre
Rouen
Caen
NORMANDY
Seine
Reims
Metz
Paris
Bagnoles de l'Orne
Strasbourg

Orléans
Loire
Beaugency
Tours
TOURAINE
Chinon

Dijon
Mont
Beuvray
BURGUNDY
Allier

Volvic
Limoges
Clermont-Ferrand
Lyon
A U V E R G N E
Uzerche
LIMOUSIN
Dordogne
Murat
Le Monastier
MASSIF
CENTRAL
C E V E N N E S
Lot
Vers
Rhône
ALPS

Garonne
St Jean-du-Gard

PROVENCE
Toulouse
Montpellier
Aix-en-Provence
Nice
Marseille
St Tropez

Arrens
PYRENEES

MEDITERRANEAN SEA

longer unemployment queues, with the added consideration that tourism itself depends on there being local farmers to participate in and shape the rural scene. Michel Débatisse, a small Auvergnat farmer who in the 1960s became the most brilliant spokesman for the *paysan*, summed up the dilemma and the aspirations as long ago as 1965: 'The farmer must keep responsibility for his produce – that is the basis of our *métier*. If he becomes a mere wage earner, tied to a firm, he will be alienated. We must try to stop farming going the way of industry in the last century and being proletarianized. But of course we believe in technical progress too, and we see the need for modern integrated markets and large-scale processing to serve the new mass-consumer needs. The only answer to this dilemma is for farmers to group together and take charge of most of the processing and marketing business themselves, in peaceful coexistence with the capitalists. But each farm will retain some individuality. The family or two-family farm offers the only sound moral basis; we don't want *kolkhozes*. What we do want is a new attitude to land-ownership. The *paysan's* implacable attachment to his own acres, even when he is no more than a tenant, must be replaced by the idea of the land as a common resource or working tool, as fishermen use the sea without owning it. The right to work the land must be divorced from the right to own it.' The Mitterand government had doubled aid to young farmers by the end of 1982, while the new President's first act was to save an area of beautiful limestone pasture in the Cévennes called the Causse du Larzac. It had been designated for military purposes and was saved partly for conservationist reasons, but primarily to protect the life of the sheep farmers who live there.

The French countryside today is full of the disjointedness brought about by any great change. High-wheeled wooden carts are hitched to Massey-Ferguson tractors too big for the ox-sheds that are meant to house them; self-conscious revivals of folk-dances are watched by grandparents wearing the clogs that the dancers affect only for the occasion; villages gradually emptied by the move to the cities are taken over by city dwellers as holiday-homes; men with the inevitable beret and lip-stuck cigarette boast the achievements of their technocrat children in Clermont-Ferrand or Grenoble. Ironically, the paths themselves – which are not yet protected by law, but for which the CNSGR is campaigning – are in many places threatened by the modern process of *remembrement*, a kind of Enclosure Movement in reverse by which the tiny fields of the west and south are regrouped in larger and more commercial units with the help of government grants.

Beyond the immediate changes, in the permanent substratum of life which neither politics nor social structure can affect, you will experience a kind of half-exoticism while walking in France, a repeated sensation that it is a hybrid way of travel, neither truly foreign nor domestic. So much is shared with England in the geology and botany, in the crops grown and the materials used for building, that at times you will find yourself thinking it the same as walking at home, only to be brought up against something unalterably French. You might be labouring up a muddy hill in Corrèze, wondering why you have substituted this foreign place for just as good a hill in Surrey, when underfoot you will discover one of those beautiful russet French slugs the colour of Devon earth, and the point of it all will again become clear. Downland walks will be transformed by the slip of lizards in the grass, three-tone cuckoos, the incessant asthmatic whirring of the crickets and the incredible abundance of butterflies in an unsprayed countryside. Your day will be made different by something as simple as the gentle handshake which is the standard greeting in Provençal bars, or as odd as a meeting like the one I had with a gang of Hell's Angels near Cahors in the Lot. They sported the Red Cross of Languedoc, seen nowhere else since the Middle Ages, professed it their intention to repartition France, and rather confusingly despised anyone who rode anything but a BSA, a Norton or a Triumph. French bikes lacked *courage*, they thought.

One other difference is crucial. France, or the Hexagon as it is called in newspapers, is bound to Europe on three of her six sides. It is this attachment to the continent that has dictated French history and has made of France, as you will see around you on all of these walks, a repository of everything Europe could give it. Since 1000 BC wide slices of the country have been ruled and shaped in turn by the Celts, Greeks, Romans, Britons, Burgundians (originally from the shores of the Baltic), Franks, Visigoths, Arabs, Vikings, Englishmen, Spaniards and Germans, not to mention the Basques who may have come from Georgia in southern Russia during the Bronze Age. It is cultural diversity on the American scale, something which can scarcely be grasped as a whole. Hazlitt thought that walking abroad 'like a dream or another state of existence, does not piece into our daily modes of life. It is an animated but momentary hallucination.' There is none of that sheet-anchor sense which you get in England of either belonging to or somehow owning the places you walk through, and instead you will find yourself quite isolated in the great width of this beautiful country, prepared to accept, I hope, the many pleasures it can offer.

The Loire

Chinon to Beaugency

187 kilometres

This walk along the Loire valley, not always by the river itself but always within the circle of its influence, goes through the heart of France. Clemenceau thought that here in Touraine more than anywhere else you could feel that the soil itself was French. But it is not the kind of irreducible Frenchness worn by the Auvergne: there is a *douceur*, a sweetness to this landscape and a comfort in its obvious well-being. Rabelais called his native Touraine the 'garden of France', and although it does not have the look of detailed care that we associate with Kent, the 'garden of England', it does have a style of self-assurance and certainty, of being an adjunct to the great houses which are gathered within it.

Its park-like lay-out and its profound wholesomeness have made Touraine one of the great holiday places of Europe. The large numbers of people who come here (although, in fact, I met not one other walker on this path in June) do not destroy it as they might Snowdonia or parts of the Alps, since Touraine is designed for crowds. It is ridiculous to imagine, for example, that the great palace of Chambord would be better without the public. The Michelin guide recommends you should visit it at sunset, as though it were Mont Ste Victoire, but to hope for solitude at any of these châteaux would be a mistake. The atmosphere of Touraine is gregarious now as it was in the sixteenth century. Look on the sweaty châteaux waiting rooms and their murmured conversations as historical experiences — a means of entering the crowded life of the Renaissance, where privacy was practically unknown and scarcely desired — and as something to be savoured after the long lonely miles of forest and cornfield in between.

Chinon to Azay-le-Rideau

28 kilometres

The town of Chinon exists because of the castle, the castle because of the bridge over the Vienne, and the bridge because the river is divided in two here by an island. The castle sprawls along the ridge like a leopard on a

Travel in the Loire valley, near St Dyé.

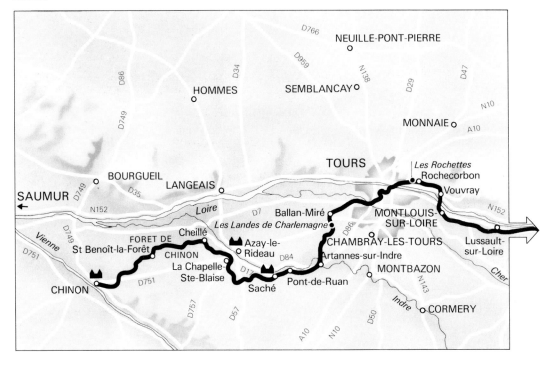

sofa, the houses below it are terraced like a Welsh mining village and beneath them both flows the Vienne, where the punts of the town's fishermen are tethered. The hierarchy is medieval, and Chinon embodies the Middle Ages more than any other place on this walk until Beaugency, at the end, where another unadorned fortress guards a bridge over a river. Between these two rather grim medieval bastions the Renaissance erupts into palaces.

The castle at Chinon, built on the site of an Iron Age camp and a Roman fort, was the scene of two emblematic moments in the Middle Ages, the one remarkable for its heroism and brutality, the other for its cynicism and simplicity.

The entrance is under the extraordinary clock tower, the shape of an upright book, 33 metres high, 20 wide and only 5 thick. Go straight through the Château du Milieu – the middle ward – and over an internal moat into the Château du Coudray, almost all of which was rebuilt by the French king Philippe-Auguste after he recaptured the castle from the English in 1204. Its circular towers, the continuous parapet-walk and the stairs within the thickness of the walls, spiralling alternately from right to left and from left to right at each floor, are all the products of a twelfth-century revolution in military architecture. Stimulated by the Arab castles discovered by the Crusaders, it was fostered by reading of the Roman classics on the military arts and by an investigation of the many Roman remains still standing in France at the time.

It was in the Tour du Coudray that the 160

principal Knights Templar were imprisoned in 1307. The order had been founded in 1119 to defend the Holy Places against the Saracens. Each knight took a vow of chastity, poverty and obedience and was forbidden the kiss of any woman, even mother or sister. By 1260 there were 20,000 knights, and in the two centuries the order was in existence the same number died in Palestine. But austerity and purity deserted the Knights Templar, as it did the Cistercians, and by the thirteenth century they had become corrupt and were in open warfare with the Knights Hospitaller. In 1306 Pope Clement V, under instructions from Philippe le Bel, King of France, told the Grand Master to leave his headquarters in Cyprus and bring the vast treasures of the order to Paris. A year later the wealth of the Templars, including very large estates all over France, was seized for the Royal Exchequer, and the knights were imprisoned here. They were collectively and quite wrongly accused of the denial of Christ, of spitting on the Cross, of holding black masses, of sorcery and of sodomy. Fifty-four of them spent two and a half years in this prison before they were burnt alive; others four years more. This remote story is brought to life by the inside walls of the Tour du Coudray, covered in graffiti carved by these innocent and arrogant men – the coats of arms of their friends or their own, simple board games like Nine Men's Morris and draughts, but, since knights as a class were almost illiterate, no words.

The second great focus of the castle is in the Château du Milieu, overlooking the Vienne

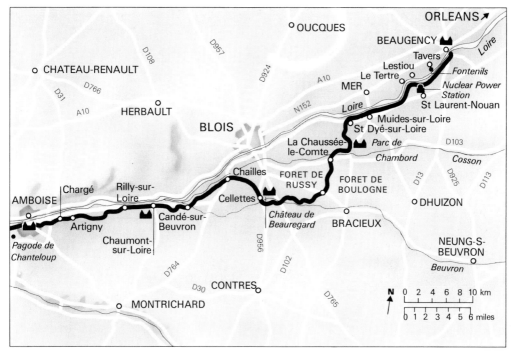

The castle at Chinon, on the site of an Iron Age camp and a Roman fort, is strung out along a ridge above the river Vienne. The famous meeting between Joan of Arc and the Dauphin Charles occurred in the room with large windows immediately above the church spire.

17

The seventeenth-century Hôtel du Gouvernement in Chinon. A comfortable atmosphere appropriate to the birthplace of Rabelais.

and the grey roofs of the town. It was here, in a room which now survives only as two walls and a large fireplace hood four and a half metres above ground level, that the famous meeting between Joan of Arc and the Dauphin Charles occurred in March 1429. The way in which Joan picked Charles out from among the 300 courtiers where he had hidden himself is too famous to recount here. Even in such ruin, the place is extraordinarily evocative of this symbolic meeting between a disillusioned, cynical regime and an enlivened and earnest conviction whose strength was its naïvety. The French court was still under the cloud of the defeat at Agincourt fourteen years earlier, when the French nobility had been slaughtered on a scale equivalent to the destruction of a generation in the First World War. Without Joan of Arc the French would not have won the Hundred Years War. It might well have dragged on into the next century, and peace – the primary condition without which the Renaissance could not have happened, without which trade could not have revived, without which Azay-le-Rideau could not have been built – might not

have come to France until decades later.

There are medieval memories in the town. In 1321 all the Chinonois Jews, 160 of them, were burnt alive on the island in the river under suspicion of having poisoned the wells. But in the pale limestone streets, where steep alleyways lead up to the gardens round the castle walls, the atmosphere is rich, ornamented and secure. With its good restaurants and comfortable hotels, it is no surprise that Chinon was the home town of François Rabelais.

His father was a lawyer, whose house probably stood on the site of 15 rue de Lamproi. As a younger son Rabelais was entered into the Benedictine order, and he spent the rest of his life, like his hero Erasmus, trying to escape from the monkishness and legalistic pedantry of his background. He replaced them with a plunge into limitless indulgence of his voracious appetites, and with satire at the expense of all those who were content with narrow certainties. The giants he created, Pantagruel and Gargantua, are perhaps the real embodiment of Renaissance Man. Thirst dominates their world. At night Pantagruel fills the throats of drunkards with salt to induce a craving for more, while at his birth 'when the midwives were waiting to receive him, there came out of the womb sixty-eight muleteers, each pulling by the collar a mule heavily laden with salt; after which came out nine dromedaries loaded with hams and smoked ox-tongues, seven camels loaded with salted eels; and then twenty-four cartloads of leeks, garlics and onions. . . . Some of the midwives said: Here is fine fare. We were only drinking slackly, not like Saxons. This is bound to be a good sign – these are invitations to drink!' Rabelais' work is a gospel of explosive freedom. In a marvellous Renaissance château he sets up the Abbey of Thélème with a single rule: 'DO WHAT THOU WILT, because men and women that are free, well born, well in-structed and conversant in honest Companies, have naturally an instinct and spur that prompteth them ever to virtuous actions.' Gargantua's colours are blue for heaven and white for joy, and although he is finely kitted out like a gentleman and knight 'His sword was not Valencian nor his dagger from Saragossa. For his father hated all drunken hidalgos, the devil's own infidels. But he carried a good wooden sword and a dagger of boiled leather painted and gilded as finely as anyone could wish.'

It is tempting to think that the overflowing beauty and generosity of Touraine played some role in making Rabelais. All that we know for certain is that large parts of *Gargantua and Pantagruel* are set among the farms around Chinon, where tiny hamlets are elevated into cities the size of Milan and village ponds into the Caspian.

The path leaves Chinon from up near the castle and heads east for two and a half kilometres along a nearly level track past a series of inhabited caves. These extraordinary troglodyte houses can be found all along the Loire valley. It is a kind of negative archi-tecture, in which to build you must remove stone. These houses have always been outside society – the town wall ran just below them – and were lived in by beggars and ex-convicts. Even now the poverty is appalling, with dogs and their droppings everywhere; as I passed one house a woman with a swag of greasy hair was smoking a pipe as she sorted through her mounds of treasured rubbish. Incredibly, the *municipalité* of Chinon still uses some of these dwellings as relief housing. Less surprisingly,

it has become rather smart to live in a cave, and one or two have plate glass windows behind which young couples light Real Coal Fires.

At the end of the row you come to the chapel of a saint from the Dark Ages, St Radegund, also cut into the rock. The chapel is connected to a series of rooms in which the priest and his animals lived, all of which are open to the public from time to time. There is a small museum of local objects and, best of all, a triangular sloping shaft sunk about eight metres into the rock with a well of pure turquoise water at the bottom. The roofs of the caves do not leak because the rock is not pure limestone, which is porous, but contains sandstone, which is not.

From the chapel it is about ten kilometres to the small village of St Benoît-la-Forêt, in the middle of the Forêt Domaniale de Chinon. After the first few kilometres through fields of lupins, poppies and walnut trees, you are surrounded by the forest of purple and orange pines, with islands of oak and beech. The path runs along the forest rides and for the whole afternoon, both before and after St Benoît, you are a slave to their geometry. Practical considerations do not dictate that a path should run straight for mile after mile – a cart is not an express train – and these lines are at least partly intended to demonstrate a control of nature. The landscape theorist Boyceau de la Baraudérie remarked in 1683, at the time these rides were laid out, that 'All things, however beautifully they may be chosen, will be defective if they are not ordered and placed in proper symmetry.' After Romanticism, such a feeling is hard to understand, but it shows how the seventeenth century was still suffering from a kind of communal claustro-phobia, a feeling that if an avenue did not extend endlessly into the distance, it was somehow restricting, or even an admission of failure. The axis, the *rond-point*, the hierarchy of forms – all these represented (with little difficulty, since it is easier to cut rides through a forest than to grow one) an intelligence and an order within which you could feel secure.

That is not the effect today. The attempt to make nature neat on a large scale only exaggerates the failure to do so in detail, where a great stand of rose-bay willow-herb breaks into the line of the track, or a spring has made it boggy and impassable, or a tree has fallen before its time, bringing half its neighbours down with it.

From St Benoît, a lagoon of maize and barley fields surrounded by the forest, it is ten kilometres to Cheillé, where you finally leave the trees and make your way towards Azay. In

St Benoît-la-Forêt, a lagoon of maize and wheat fields surrounded by the Forêt de Chinon.

Cheillé itself is an extraordinary and inexplicable sight: a fully grown oak tree springs from about ten feet up a church wall, with nothing to support it and no soil. For five kilometres beyond the village the path climbs high above the valley of the Indre, through fields of plums, apples, peaches, oats, barley, wheat and vines, with the white suburbs of Azay-le-Rideau constantly visible on the far side.

You come to the village of La Chapelle Sainte Blaise and cross the weed-choked Indre to Azay. The château is hidden behind willows as you circle it to arrive at the eighteenth-century stables, where you buy your ticket and cross into a world lifted from the illuminations in a Book of Hours and laid down on the river meadows of the Indre. Azay-le-Rideau is perfect: there can be few places where the elements of cultural history are concentrated so precisely. In 1518, Gilles Berthelot, a bourgeois treasurer to François I,

and his wife Philippe began work on this château, on the site of a medieval castle destroyed in a fit of anger by the Dauphin a century before. What now stands (except for one nineteenth-century tower) was finished by 1527. It was then that Berthelot was involved in a huge corruption scandal at court which forced him into exile, where he died. François confiscated the château on which his loyal treasurer had erected the royal badge, a salamander, and the King's motto *Nutrisco et extinguo*, I nourish and extinguish – a Renaissance announcement magnificent for its egotism and power.

The château is on the frontier between medieval and modern. In the last years of the previous century gunpowder had made castles redundant in warfare, but their towers, moats and machicolations were still potent symbols of status and nobility in 1518. For Berthelot, a newly risen and suddenly rich bourgeois, nothing can have been more important than to hoist these visual signals, and Azay has all of them. Somehow it had all become a game, a frozen ballet of extraordinary grace, a sort of refined joke in which the

Azay-le-Rideau – an illuminated image lifted from a Book of Hours and planted on the banks of the Indre.

wide-eyed dormer windows and the fine network of string-courses and pilasters put the 'castle' into a bridesmaid's dress.

The inside comes as rather a shock. All the rooms are huge and monotonously square, leading off one another (with no corridors and no privacy) with a kind of clumsiness in the organization. The huge stony fireplaces would have done little to heat the spaces around them, and would probably have smoked in most winds. The wonderful staircase is open to all weathers; draughts would have slipped in under every door; and the Indre flooded the kitchen several winters each decade until the floor was raised in the nineteenth century. It is sobering to learn that at the time Azay was built people actually put more clothes on when they came in from outside. Most of this would be dreadful for us – imagine the psychological effect of home always being cold – but perhaps comfort is a modern virtue. Would sixteenth-century people have minded doing without our modern conveniences?

Azay-le-Rideau to Tours

35 kilometres

You cross the Indre again and make a long loop up on to the plateau away from its valley as far as Saché, eleven kilometres from Azay. It is an area of rolling cornfields and woods, with cornflowers and glossy sweet chestnuts. Around the farms and the one village of La Vallée the apple trees have ladders permanently propped up into them. These wide cereal fields, with the slight contours that remove them from the billiard flatness of Beauce to the north, are true France. It has always been rich here. Roman villas of incredible proportions have been discovered near the Indre, one whose buildings alone covered 10,000 square metres, about 100,000 square feet. It was the centre of a huge cereal farm, a great deal of which may have been taken over from the indigenous Celts. The enormous Gallic wheat production (which

La Chapelle Sainte Blaise.

was harvested with a very efficient *wheeled reaper*) was an important factor in the speed of Caesar's conquest of Gaul. With so much local grain assured he had no need to waste his own resources on establishing or protecting supply lines.

You come down to Saché and an enormous lunch in the Café de Balzac. This is no place for austerity. On the edge of the village, behind a park wall, is the Château de Saché, a solid sixteenth-century block floored with cool tiles. It has an extraordinarily pacific air, but nothing would have been exceptional about it had Honoré de Balzac not spent large expanses of his time here in the 1830s. Balzac's room is still as it was when he used it for his daily sixteen hours of writing, beginning at two in the morning and lasting on nothing but black coffee and little buns until six in the evening, when he would descend for a few hours' conversation. It is a small, low room, and apparently he needed a tight enclosure for his genius to flower. The way in which it did can be seen in the amazing proofs on display downstairs. Printers refused to work on them for more than two hours at a stretch.

The way now follows the valley of the Indre, where poplars stand in square formations like blocks of soap and where the river itself runs under punts and pontoons. Pont-de-Ruan is three kilometres from Saché. There are several watermills here (none of them turning), some black-winged dragonflies and many waterlilies floating over the green river, where green weed waves like drowned hair. On the eastern end of the bridge is a plaque that says: *Ste Apolline. Les Practiciens de l'art dentaire à leur Sainte Patronne. 4 Juin 1950.* Why Pont de Ruan was singled out for this honour I do not know.

Another three kilometres along the river brings you to Artannes-sur-Indre, where a flour mill, with old cylindrical millstones outside it, turns the air floury in your mouth and nostrils, and where you leave the Indre to make the long flat crossing to Tours, eighteen kilometres away. Most of it is over wide, flat cornfields – *les grandes cultures* – where nine-tenths of the world is sky, and on a bright day a sun-hat is a necessity.

Mills on the Indre at Pont-de-Ruan.

As you come to within a few miles of Ballan-Miré you enter an area known as Les Landes de Charlemagne. According to many scholars it was here, in 732, that Charles Martel defeated the great Arab army under Abd-er-Rahman ibn Abd'Allah el Ghefiki, the *wali* of Arab Spain. The Arab invasion had been two-pronged: in the east they landed from ships in Provence and penetrated up the Rhône valley to Burgundy, where history loses sight of them; in the west they crossed through the Pyrenees – by the Vallée d'Aspe – and fought their first battle with Eudes the Visigoth on the Dordogne. This bloody encounter was a total defeat for the Christians, and after it Abd-er-Rahman decided to make for Tours to pillage the famous basilica of St Martin, enriched by pilgrims' offerings. Eudes begged the help of his one-time enemy, the Frank Charles Martel. Outside Tours, on the Landes de Charlemagne (the Arab chronicle says), the two armies sat facing each other for seven days and seven nights. When battle was finally joined, the Franks used the *cuneus*, a Roman formation which they called *svinfyl-king* – the boar's head. This was immensely effective. The Arab chronicler said it was 'like a rampart of ice' slipping from the grip of the Muslim army. By the end of the day 375,000 Arabs had been killed, among them Abd-er-Rahman, who died at nightfall. Charles Martel was ready again the next morning, but the Arabs had left in the night.

It was the northern limit of their advance in the west, matching their defeat in the east a few years before under the walls of Constantinople. It has been argued that the true Arab intention was to circle the Mediterranean and take Constantinople from the rear, and that Martel's victory was thus the most important in the history of Europe. But others point to internal dissension in the already over-stretched Arab cause, and say that this battle (erroneously called the Battle of Poitiers) was the limit of their natural swing, and that defeat was inevitable. What would have happened if the Arabs had won, and whether their victory would have harmed or benefited Europe, is impossible to say. Maybe their store of ancient learning from Byzantium

23

would have brought about the European Renaissance seven centuries earlier. It is fascinating to speculate on what would have happened in the great confrontation between an Arab Europe and the Vikings.

You pass some cherry trees heavy with black fruit and then the Château de la Carte, a demure residence which has a medieval gate romanticized in the eighteenth century. You will be exhausted from the hot afternoon's walking as you make your way through Ballan-Miré, embarking on the last eight kilometres to Tours. I must have been looking half-paralysed with boredom, since a girl whispered into my ear as she cycled past: 'Il faut faire du stop pour aller plus vite.' I put the devil behind me. You come across a pony hire

centre – only the most desperate will interpret this as temptation – and then a reservoir. You drop to cross the D 270 and then an old bridge takes you over the tiny Vieux Cher. A little more than a mile brings you to the edge of the Cher itself, a Limpopo-green and poisonous river running past allotments. In the distance are the welcome tower blocks of Tours. The city fills the gap between the Cher and the Loire, and after crossing the Cher you will find yourself accelerating to reach the great river itself. Through progressively older phases of the city, from concrete to stucco to parks, to the wedding cake Hôtel de Ville and its fountains, down the eighteenth-century *rue Nationale* (cut through an old quarter and seriously bombed in 1940 and 1944), you approach the Loire itself. Tours is famous for its pretty girls, but you will neglect them and the museums and cathedrals alike in this imperturbable need to arrive. You get there and find it a braided river, sandy, wide, with islands in it and as much potential for growth as a mountain stream, a continental artery pumping from the mountains to the sea.

The eighteenth-century Château de la Carte near Tours preserves a massive medieval gateway – slightly prettified – to add romance to its comfort. This is the eighteenth-century version of the meeting between medieval and modern that characterizes all the great Renaissance buildings along the Loire.

Tours to Amboise

33 kilometres

The old quarter of Tours is now full of restaurants and of restoration in progress on the slate and timber buildings. There are hundreds of little shops, the most faded of them – near the remains of the Basilica of St Martin – continuing to advertise 'Toutes les fantaisies des boutiques parisiennes', with one or two camisoles to show what is meant. But Tours is far from being in the shadow of Paris. It is a sharp-lit place which appears to take little notice of the hulks of ancient masonry moored in its streets. There is the Cathedral of St Gatian, begun in the thirteenth century and not finished until the sixteenth, when classical belfries were added to an exclusively Gothic building with no sense of impropriety. On the other side of town there are still one or two fragments of St Martin's Basilica in the streets near Les Halles. The fifth-century basilica which escaped plunder by Abd-er-Rahman was sacked a century later by Vikings who had sailed up the Loire. What is now left comes from a rebuilding in the eleventh and thirteenth centuries. In 1562 this building in turn was sacked by the Huguenots and for two and a half centuries was left like a bomb-site, until the nave was demolished in 1802. The residual limbs of the huge church – it was 107 metres long and 67 wide in the transepts – now stand carefully fenced off from the *pâtisseries* and sportswear shops around them.

Tours was home to Alcuin, the great Northumbrian scholar and Charlemagne's adviser, and to Gregory of Tours, the sixth-century Bishop and first medieval historian. But at heart it is the city of St Martin. He was born in the middle of the fourth century in Hungary but spent most of his early life as a legionary in the Roman army. When he was eighteen he saw a beggar shivering half-naked at the gates of Amiens, and cutting his own cloak in two gave half of it away. He became famous as a miracle worker and was the obvious choice for Bishop of Tours at the election in 371. His spiritual integrity was matched by a total lack of interest in personal hygiene: his appearance was so disgusting, apparently, that his election as Bishop came close to being nullified when the burghers of Tours found they had chosen 'a man so contemptible with dirty clothes and unkempt hair'. But spirit triumphed over flesh and Martin's episcopate marks the beginning of the second great stage of Christianity in France, when the gospel began to spread from the cities into the countryside. Martin was the first saint who was neither martyred nor said to be a martyr.

For nearly seventy kilometres the way now keeps within shouting distance of the Loire. You leave Tours on a pedestrian suspension bridge over the river, and on the far bank turn east to pass under the Bordeaux-Paris motorway. Leaving behind you the Abbaye de Marmoutier, founded by St Martin, you climb away from the Loire and up into an area known as Les Rochettes. It is the smartest suburb of Tours, where grand houses have tennis courts and names like *l'Ermitage*. Astonishingly, most of them are highly elaborated cave dwellings, their back rooms carved out of the limestone cliffs. The earliest were built in the mid-eighteenth century, when to live in a cave was the height of contemporary, Rousseauesque fashion. None of the chic has deserted it. As I was walking along the lane beside the high garden walls I came around a corner to find a crowd of ten upper-class girls, all with shiny, beautifully cut black hair, long noses and silk dresses. As I gaily said hello to them I was suddenly concious of my sun-hat and tourist air. Not one of them uttered a syllable in reply, but instead they looked at each other meaningfully and pretended not to have heard. On foot it is impossible to make a quick escape from your disasters, and it is the lot of a walker that triumphs and humiliations both last a very long time indeed. For the sake of pride I did not hurry to the next corner, but accepted as inevitable the everlasting gaze of collective contempt following me.

Rochecorbon is six kilometres from the centre of Tours, and Vouvray is five kilometres beyond that. After Les Rochettes most of the way is through vineyards high on the plateau above the Loire, with occasional trees standing in them. These vines produce the best white wine in the Loire valley, closely followed by those of Montlouis, just across the river. Famous in England as a dry sparkling wine, it is cheaper than champagne and tastes like it; but this is not the wine close to the heart of the growers themselves. The drink they treasure is much sweeter and stiller. Only small quantities are made and little exported. At least try the Vouvray *pétillant*, which is quite expensive but delicious, bubbling only very slightly and with a lemony edge to its grape.

From Vouvray it is twenty-two kilometres to Amboise, the end of a day's walk from Tours. The way crosses the Loire again, on a railway bridge, to Montlouis-sur-Loire, where common terns play on the river. Beyond, the

*The Pagode de Chanteloup is all that remains of the
château built near Amboise by the Duc de Choíseul in
the eighteenth century. Wheat is now grown on the
site of the* jardin anglais.

The Loire near Lussault.

Vines and a Spanish chestnut near Vouvray.

path runs across the roofs of more troglodyte houses. You would know nothing of them if it were not for their chimneys, excavated through the natural rock to emerge smoking through the turf.

A steady rhythm takes you along towards Amboise through a succession of woods and fields, one of which, when I was there, was cloudy with the smell of *fraises de bois*. It's a dry country, and water towers stand at the entrance to every village. Arthur Young hated it here: he was still enamoured of the Pyrenees and found the Touraine he had heard so much about little more than 'a dead level of burnt russet meadow'. The Loire was no better: 'For so considerable a river, and for being boasted as the most beautiful in Europe, it exhibits such a breadth of shoals and sand as to be almost subversive of beauty.' These beachy islands (*grèves*) and the streams (*luisettes*) that run between them are to my mind the Loire's real beauty. They also prevent it from being the working river which it was until the last century: the usual way for Parisians to reach their châteaux then was to drive to Orléans before embarking the coach on a raft and floating downstream to their particular palaces.

Beyond Chandon, a mile east of Lussault-sur-Loire, you at last catch sight of the château at Amboise, high above the town. Before making towards it – if you still have the energy on what can be a wearing afternoon – turn slightly aside and go about half a mile southwards to the Pagode de Chanteloup. This pagoda is all that remains of the Château de Chanteloup, ruined between the Revolution and the Restoration by one of the notorious Black Bands. These groups of revolutionaries bought up deserted châteaux for almost nothing and then set about destroying them, as if to erase the memories of a bad dream. Chanteloup was finally demolished by property speculators in 1823.

The château and the pagoda had been built by the Duc de Choiseul, a minister of Louis XV, whose Duchess was extraordinarily beautiful. Sent into exile here after a brush with Mme de Pompadour, he devoted himself to improving the estate. Large ornamental trees, now grown

Perseus reclines in Amboise.

neither asphyxiated nor catatonic but just a little sleepy. They shone torches into my eyes and felt my pulse and at last I was released to slope off towards the Ile d'Or where, under some poplars and next to a giant green statue of Perseus reclining on the Gorgon's head, I lay down and went back to sleep.

Amboise to Chailles

36 kilometres

Amboise is arranged like Chinon, but is a little neater and more compact. Architecturally the château – of which barely a quarter survived the Revolution – occupies a stage half-way between Azay and Chinon. It shows the Middle Ages ready to express the spirit of Renaissance but as yet without the means. The short stretch of royal apartments looking out over the Loire was begun in 1492, two years before Charles VIII's famous expedition to northern Italy, where he and the French nobility are said to have been so struck by the revolution in manners and art that they brought back the Italian Renaissance complete and unchanged to the Loire valley. When the King returned in 1496 he had with him twenty-two artisans, including architects, sculptors, decorators, marquetry workers, gardeners, tailors and perfumers, with which to transform his kingdom.

But that short stretch of apartments, with its big windows and flamboyant self-exposure, already had the air of peace and generosity which is the hallmark of all that was to come in the following decades. It is not quite articulate – it is slightly ugly – but it shows that Renaissance attitudes were already present in France before the Italian campaign.

On the other side of the courtyard is a tiny Gothic chapel, begun in the same year as the Logis du Roi as an oratory for Charles VIII's Queen, Anne de Bretagne, and dedicated to St Hubert, the patron saint of hunting. Whole worlds separate the two buildings. The Chapel of St Hubert was built at the very end of the Gothic tradition, and in its pointed little delicacies is closer to Horace Walpole's Gothick than to Chartres, displaying the total command of resources to be found only in works of art that risk nothing at all. It is a curious combination of charm and lifelessness. Its focus is the lintel above the door, which, below a Virgin and Child, depicts the Vision of St Hubert. Out hunting one day he suddenly saw a cross materialize between the horns of a stag and fell down in awe before it. Here is the stag, with an iron cross, St Hubert in awe, the hounds, little coneys disappearing

to maturity, surround the cornfield where the château once stood, and endless forest rides converge on the pagoda, which looks like a pile of Chinese tea-caddies, each one smaller than the one below. From the topmost, where there is room for nothing but the staircase, a view extends over the enormous forest and the valley of the Loire from Amboise to Chinon.

The Duke had intended it as a memorial to the friendship of those who had stayed loyal to him in exile, and on the first floor their names were carved on stone tablets. The Duke died in 1785, and when the Revolution finally broke four years later, some unseen hand quietly turned them face down to protect the names they bore. Even now they present dark, blank faces to the world. The disgruntled Arthur Young thought that this land should have been put to better use than hunting, and he grudgingly gave the Duc de Choiseul a single good mark: 'As a farmer, there is one feature which shows the Duke had some merit: he built a noble cow house,' but that too has disappeared.

You are within striking distance of Amboise. Its suburbs soon engulf you as the way comes down to the bridge over the Loire. When I arrived here at the end of a long June day I lay down in the shade of the bridge to recover. I felt myself cooling by the minute and fell asleep. I am not sure how long it lasted, perhaps half an hour, but I woke to find myself surrounded by two women, a bearded man and two youths with a stretcher, all of them wearing white nylon tunics. Oxygen cylinders bulked somewhere in the background and a blue light revolved on what I realized was an ambulance. Beyond the ring of professionals other interested parties gaped. I tried to convince them that I was

Near Tavers: the douceur *of Touraine.*

Willows at Muides-sur-Loire.

The Loire at Beaugency.

The chapel of St Hubert in Amboise is the final moment of the Middle Ages, in a Gothic closer to Horace Walpole than to Chartres.

into their burrows, and surrounding them all the forest, like bunches of parsley. It is typical of the building and of the self-contained attitude behind it that the little spire is decorated with a series of bronze antlers. The overall effect is of a face too carefully made up or of a paragraph rewritten too often.

You leave the river to wind back up through the streets of Amboise on to the plateau. At the south-eastern corner of the town you pass the Château de Clos Lucé, where Leonardo da Vinci lived his last two and a half years. He died here in May 1519, and bones which are claimed to be his are buried in the Chapel of St Hubert. There are models of some of his inventions inside the château. It is now twenty-one kilometres to Chaumont, the end of the next stage. There are small villages – Chargé, Artigny, Rilly-sur-Loire – but they are nothing to arrive at: you slide easily through them, no more than incidents in a drift. There is a small château like Clos Lucé in Chargé and a strange white statue in Artigny, but apart from that the world is flat, and quixotic fantasies will take you by the hand. Do not hope to hurry: accept your ice creams as you get to them and hold out for the eventual arrival.

The first part of Chaumont that you come to is the château stables, decorated with a frieze of panels showing a round hill spurting flame – a *chaud mont*. To reach the château itself you have to go the length of the village street and then climb back up through the English park of chestnuts and cedar trees. White and bulbous, its round entrance towers harbouring between them a small gate with a drawbridge, Chaumont plays the game of being a fortress more earnestly than any other

Renaissance château. In plan the building looks impregnable, but the pristine whiteness of the limestone, the delicate machicolations in the form of inverted stepped pyramids, and the collection of pointed roofs combine to emasculate it. The weirdest feature is the covered walk that runs around the top of the walls and towers. It was added in the late sixteenth century, when developments in artillery made high curtain walls more vulnerable than ever, and its construction (even during the Wars of Religion) cannot have been for military purposes. It is a sign that even so soon after the end of the Middle Ages, a nostalgia for the medieval crept in here, as it did in Elizabethan England: a longing for a simpler kind of life, a version of pastoral seen from behind the bars of Renaissance sophistication.

Eight kilometres beyond Chaumont, most of it up on the plateau before you come down again through woodland, is Candé-sur-Beuvron, where silver willows crowd the river edge. There are three hotels here, but this stage continues as far as Chailles, another seven kilometres. It is worth giving yourself the little extra mileage because it takes you through some of the prettiest fields on the walk, separated by large stands of poplars. Down on the valley soil more can be grown than the pure wheat which has surrounded the way since Amboise. At Madon and on the outskirts of Chailles are some of the smaller châteaux, either quite hidden behind their park walls, glimpsed through the woods around them, or, like the Château de la Pigeonnière, parked in the middle of a farmyard. All of these now seem more authentically sixteenth-century than the great showplaces.

Chailles to Beaugency

55 kilometres

Chailles is on the edge of the forest of Russy, and as far as Cellettes (eight kilometres) the path runs along the forest tracks. This is hunting forest, less regimented than the one near Azay, but with the same rational pattern of drives meeting in eight-point stars. All game is now dead or gone, but you can imagine how it was when the ordered structure of the paths actually made the wilderness between them, where the precious animals lived, seem still more exciting. One of the most treasured stories of the Loire valley describes an incident at Amboise when a wild boar somehow broke into the royal apartments, causing terror and panic. Disaster was prevented only when the young François I

Chaumont: the side of the château facing the Loire was removed in the eighteenth century to open the courtyard to the view. Mme de Staël longed for Paris when she was here.

The porcupine badge of Louis XII in Chaumont: a medieval habit turned to Renaissance individualism.

33

strode up to the raging animal, drew his sword like a king and spitted it. This is myth of the highest order and clearly shows the Renaissance conception of hunting as a manly confrontation with the forces of chaos, and their defeat. One of the reasons why the interiors of the châteaux are not more perfectly arranged is because the men spent most of their time outside hunting. Even when they came inside, the walls were covered in little but hunting tapestries. In this light, the urbane society of Renaissance France appears as no more than a thin skin of civilization, tightly stretched over the brutality it trusts to have left behind – but which it still fears, and which would erupt occasionally in conspiracies and mass executions. At the end of the century, in the massacres of the Wars of Religion, the skin would finally split.

You emerge near Cellettes, but before going down to cross the river Beuvron take a small detour eastwards to the Château de Beauregard, poised symbolically between forest and fields. The outside was remodelled in the seventeenth century, and of all the great châteaux on this walk Beauregard has the most modern appearance. All trace of castle has gone: even the corner pavilions, which by about 1540 had come to replace round towers in the ideal picture of the château, have here been absorbed into the single façade. But Beauregard's fineness – and this is significant in terms of social history – is inside. This château, in the comfort and human scale of its rooms, already belongs to the world of Molière – which somewhere like Azay (the inside at least) never could.

There are two rooms that matter: a long gallery and the Cabinet de Grelots. The gallery is lined with 363 portraits of great men (and a few women) arranged in epochs from the early Middle Ages until the reign of Louis XIII. This embodiment of the Great Man theory of history represents all the European conflicts over three centuries with portraits of their protagonists – most of them French, but also including one or two Ottomans and English captains from the Hundred Years War like Talbot and Henry V. From the Reformation, there is Thomas More but no Erasmus, these two men who were so alike having become, by several flukes of history, the one a Catholic saint and the other a hated and distrusted critic of the Roman church. The gallery is floored in small blue Delft tiles, each with a picture of a soldier on the march. Some are much brighter than the rest. They are not, as you might think, modern reproductions of old ones that had broken, but replacements from the stock of spares which was bought when

the floor was originally laid in the seventeenth century.

Next to the gallery is the Cabinet de Grelots, a small, late sixteenth-century room panelled in oak which has been carved, painted and gilded. Here at last is the intimacy so absent elsewhere, and the realization that wood is more pleasant to live with than stone.

For eleven kilometres after Cellettes (where a memorial on the Beuvron bridge commemorates a little battle in the Franco-Prussian War) your path traverses the rich dark green of maize and sunflower cultures as far as Rue de Meneuil, where you dive into forest again. Here, as you navigate the straight tracks, you will pine for the bicycle that would be the perfect vehicle for this walk. This is the Forêt de Boulogne, where you will find dispirited joggers padding their hearts out down miles of unsurprising path. Four kilometres from Rue de Meneuil you come across the high grey wall that surrounds the enormous Parc de Chambord. At thirty-two kilometres, it is said to be the longest wall in France.

At la Chaussée le Comte you enter the park, now a nature reserve, and after four kilometres of beautiful oak woodland, closed off inside a fence ten feet high to prevent the deer from grazing the wild flowers, you arrive at Chambord. It is like meeting Azay forty years on. A once-beautiful girl of twenty-two has become her mother, now desperately trying to make up in ornamentation what she has lost in grace. There is something sadly flat-footed about Chambord. Its enormous bulk – 150 metres long, 115 wide and 50 high – sits on the grass like a partially deflated hot air balloon, with all the pinnacles of the famous roofline only exaggerating its airlessness.

The château was the creation of François I, begun in 1519 on the site of a hunting lodge and continued for about twenty years with an average of 1,800 men working on it at any one time. There are 440 rooms and 365 chimneys, a stupendous double staircase, and, among the carved dormers and chimneys and lanterns, a roof terrace from which the court watched displays beyond the moats. It is in the staircase and terrace that the quality of Chambord resides, with their rich flowering of finely carved detail, the salamanders and fleurs-de-lis and slate discs and lozenges with which the masons decorated the architect's work. It is significant that those words, architecte and architecture, appeared in French for the first time in about 1539, just as Chambord was reaching completion. In its fortress plan, round towers and massive decoration (out of date in Italy as early as 1510) Chambord was a hopelessly unfashionable

building. It marks the end of a tradition: from here the increasing austerity of authentic Vitruvian classicism begins to take over, as the architect does from the mason.

From Chambord to the end at Beaugency it is only twenty-six kilometres. Through the park and then down across the cornfields to St Dyé you arrive again at the Loire, its sandy islands thick with osiers, and salmon fishermen waiting in their shallow boats anchored midstream. The path does not leave the river bank for any distance between St Dyé and Beaugency, now only twenty kilometres away. It is easy, gravelly walking as far as Muides-sur-Loire, where you cross to the north side of the river to reach the *digue*, an embankment above the cornfields. The two huge cooling towers of the nuclear power station at St Laurent provide the beacons as far as Le Tertre, where you embark on the last eight kilometres. They are among the best on the walk, the Loire as beautiful as your idea of it and the banks blocked out into poplars and meadows.

Pause at Tavers, three and a half kilometres from the end, to have a look at a small spring called Fontenils, where clear, grey-blue water

The cooling towers of the power station at St Laurent, a few kilometres from end.

bubbles up from the sandy floor of a pool. If you put your hand in the spot where the water springs from, puffing up mushrooms of sand, you can reach inside, feeling your way round its rocky walls like a womb.

The famous bridge at Beaugency soon appears, its long body trailed out like a millipede from side to side of the Loire. Each of the arches is small enough for the whole bridge to act as a dam, and upstream of it the Loire is held back in a calm reflective pool, which breaks in a kind of cascade under the bridge itself. This was the only medieval crossing of the Loire between Blois and Orléans, and as you walk from the end of it into the town, past the marvellous twelfth-century church, you will come face to face with the ruin of the castle designed to protect it, a sheer cliff of a keep built at the end of the eleventh century. It was once surrounded by double curtain walls, but these were destroyed in the seventeenth century. The keep remains, its only features some functional

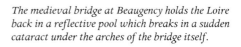

The medieval bridge at Beaugency holds the Loire back in a reflective pool which breaks in a sudden cataract under the arches of the bridge itself.

buttresses and the occasional niche, the nesting place of crows. It may be strange that only seven or eight lifetimes separate us from Azay-le-Rideau, but it is even odder that only eleven or twelve separate us from Beaugency.

DISTANCES (in kilometres)
From Chinon to:
St Benoît-la-Forêt 12; Cheillé 10; La Chapelle-Ste-Blaise 5; Azay-le-Rideau 1; La Vallée 6; Saché 5; Pont-de-Ruan 3; Artannes-sur-Indre 3; Ballan-Miré 10; Tours 8; Rochecorbon 6; Vouvray 5; Montlouis 5; Lussault 4; Amboise 8; Chargé 5; Rilly-sur-Loire 10; Chaumont 6; Candé-sur-Beuvron 8; Chailles 7; Cellettes 8; Clénord 4; La Chaussée-le-Comte 13; Chambord 4; St Dyé-sur-Loire 6; Muides-sur-Loire 4; Le Tertre 8; Beaugency 8

MAPS
I.G.N. 1:50,000 Numbers:
1723 (Chinon), 1823 (Langeais), 1822 (Tours), 1922 (Amboise), 2022 (Montrichard), 2021 (Blois), 2121 (Bracieux), 2120 (Beaugency)

GUIDE
Topo-Guide du Sentier de Grande Randonnée No. 3 (Loiret, Loir-et-Cher, Indre-et-Loire, Maine-et-Loire, d'Orléans à Saumur) C.N.S.G.R., Paris

LOIRE BOOKS
Jean Deriosse, *Charles Martel*, Tallandier 1978
Manuel de Dieguez, *Rabelais*, Seuil 1960
Lucien Febvre, *Life in Renaissance France*, Harvard University Press 1977
François Lebrun (editor), *Histoire des Pays de la Loire*, Privat 1972
Vivian Rowe, *Châteaux of the Loire*, Putnam 1954
François Rabelais, *The Histories of Gargantua and Pantagruel*, Penguin 1955

Burgundy

Dijon to Mont Beuvray

138 kilometres

This walk through Burgundy begins in the east at Dijon, the medieval capital, and after making its way down through the vineyards of the Côte d'Or turns west towards Autun, which at heart is a Roman city. From there the final stage is up on to Mont Beuvray in the Morvan, where the great Gallic capital of Bibracte rings the mountain with its ditches. To walk through Burgundy is an inescapably historical experience. It is layered with the marks of invasion – of the Celtic Eduens in about 800 BC, of the Romans in 58 BC, of the Burgundians themselves, in origin a Baltic people who came south as the Roman Empire disintegrated, and of the French.

The state of Burgundy has stretched and contracted over its history, at one time reaching the Mediterranean at Marseille and, under the Valois dukes of the fourteenth and fifteenth centuries, extending through innumerable small fiefs and counties to the North Sea. Artists and architects, new crops and farming techniques, have moved in from both north and south, defining Burgundy from the outside. Many of the roofs of Dijon and Beaune are covered in polychrome glazed tiles in a fashion that comes from the Low Countries, while the great school of Burgundian sculpture in the later Middle Ages was Flemish in origin. From the south, the vines that make Burgundy famous are of course a Mediterranean import.

The history of wine here is the history of the place itself. Sixth-century grape pips have been found in Provence, but none as far north as this. Nevertheless, the Celts were famous in the ancient world for their love of drink, and by the third century BC Greek and Etruscan wines were being transported up the valleys of the Rhône and Saône into Burgundy and the Franche Comté. This imported wine was a luxury, surrounded by the paraphernalia of a ritualized activity, the *craters*, sieves and spittoons, all of which have been found in graves on the Côte d'Or. Only well after the Roman conquest were vines planted here for the first time, probably not before the second century AD. They very quickly became successful and the Roman government was

The presses of the Dukes of Burgundy at Chenôve.

forced to bring in heavy protectionist measures to save Roman growers from too large an importation from the colony.

In Gaul itself, where the barrel was invented and quickly replaced the more fragile jars used by the Greeks and Etruscans, wine, often resinated and sometimes smoked, became the liquid staple. Although there are few records, wine production was probably unaffected by the end of Roman rule, and as the Dark Ages progressed the Burgundian vineyards fell increasingly into the hands of the Church, with a constant need for profit and communion wine. The chapter at Autun, for example, still owned half the vineyards at Chenôve near Dijon in 1789.

In the early Middle Ages Burgundy was scarcely drunk outside the area where it was produced, but by the beginning of the fourteenth century, as communications within France improved, it began to find favour with the nobility throughout the country. Together with Côtes-du-Rhone, it was the only wine which could last more than two years and was, besides, the best traveller. The boom stretched into the sixteenth century. but the Wars of Religion, and even more the Thirty Years War which in fact lasted from 1610 until 1660, seriously interfered with production. Only at the end of the seventeenth century, with the expansion that came with peace and the reduction of internal customs barriers within France, did the business revive. Dijonnais merchants bought up the vineyards of the Côte-de-Nuits, turning it into a classic capitalist enterprise and employing the villagers as paid hands. Of the 53 *vignerons* in Marsannay-la-Côte in 1760, for example, only three worked for themselves. Vengeance came with the French Revolution when the land was divided into the tiny parcels it is worked in today.

The acreage given over to vines on the Côte doubled in the two centuries up to 1850 and again in the century after it. The disastrous diseases caused by the fungus oidium in the 1850s, and a kind of Californian greenfly called phylloxera twenty years later (finally defeated only by importing resistant strains from America and grafting the French stocks on to them), nearly destroyed the culture; but it survived and in this century Burgundian growers have done better than at any time before in their history.

One final catastrophe was averted in 1944. Wynford Vaughan Thomas, a liaison officer between French, American and British forces during the Second World War, has told how the French general in command of the army coming up from the south had halted his troops near Beaune, and agonized whether or not duty compelled him to attack across some of the finest vineyards in Burgundy. He delayed and delayed. His allies steamed with frustration. At last a dispatch rider hurried into headquarters, his face radiant with joy. 'Mon Général,' he announced, 'the Germans are only occupying the inferior slopes!', at which the General, it is said, leaped to his feet with the cry of 'J'attaque!'

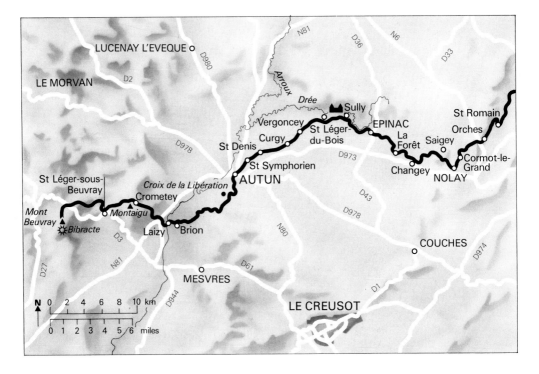

Dijon to Gevrey-Chambertin

15 kilometres

Dijon lies as a boss of accumulated stone beneath the hills of the Côte d'Or. Its buildings in a pale yellow limestone quarried on the Côte itself are carelessly crammed into an attic-like space, its streets and squares too small for their façades to be seen. Like Aix-en-Provence, Dijon was the seat of the regional parliament until the French Revolution and in most streets there is at least one *hôtel parlementaire*, built by one of the great legal or political families between the sixteenth and eighteenth centuries. The image of Dijon that stains the mind is of the dark arches of these *hôtels* cutting through the street wall into

Dijon: a sense of history.

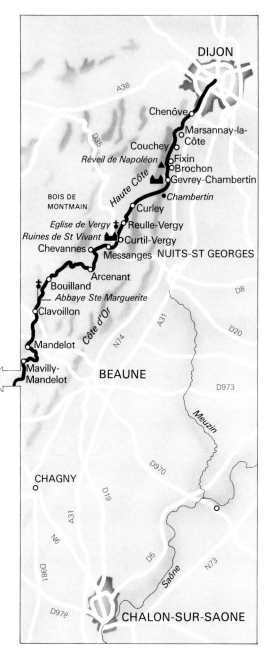

areas of lit and secluded privilege. It is an endlessly repeated formula of ambiguous admission, part-boast, part-concealment, and of a half-shared urbanity. Most of them are quite proper and straight in their façades, but occasionally, as in the sixteenth-century Maison Milsant and Hôtel le Compasseur, both the work of Hugues Sambin, a cabinet-maker and contemporary of Rabelais, Dijon bursts out into swags, lions, garlands and grotesques.

From the top of a tower that rises 150 feet above the Ducal Palace the impressions received of Dijon on the ground are confirmed. The city has teemed inside its container, only to have civilization, in the form of eighteenth-century streets, laid on the older haphazardry. The visual history is there before you, moving up from the hidden courts, through the classical semi-circle of the Place de la Revolution, designed by Mansart, to the bright new cars now splayed out there like a suit of hearts.

Around the tower itself is the palace, encased in an eighteenth-century skin but with a medieval core. Most of it is now a fine arts museum and right in the heart of it is the so-called Salle de Gardes, built in the middle of the fifteenth century by Duke Philip the Good. Protected by the walls of the city, the Duke's new building could boast windows as wide as a palace's, but the beautiful room is outshone by the monuments it now contains. These are the tombs of Philip the Bold (1342–1404) and of John the Fearless (1371–1419) with his wife Margaret of Bavaria. They were moved here from the Charterhouse of Champmol just outside Dijon in 1827. Larger than life-size effigies of the

41

two dukes and the duchess are laid out on black marble slabs, their feet resting on golden-haired lions whose tongues loll out and whose eyes are lifted heavenwards. Angels guard the other end, with gilded buzzard wings sprouting from their backs like flags. A miniature arcade surrounds each tomb below the black marble, and here there is a procession of foot-high alabaster figures in mourning for their sovereigns.

The whole of Dijon is gathered around these marvellous and extraordinary medieval objects. Each is an exact document of the phase and style of the Middle Ages at the moment it was created. At first sight there is little to set them apart, and it is extraordinary to find that the tomb of John the Fearless and his wife was finished in 1470, eighty-four years after its neighbour was begun. Nearly a century of change should have intervened, but you can easily imagine the prestige which the earlier tomb must have carried – much of it is the work of the great Flemish sculptor Claus Sluter – and understand the conservative wish to reproduce its glories. With this in mind you can begin to detect signs of greatness in the one and decadence in its copy. The angels' wings, magnificent above Philip, have grown even bigger over John, and questions of anatomical mechanics start to arise. The arcades above the mourners of John have a surfeit of spikes and curling tendrils, while Philip's are kept within bounds. Above all the alabaster mourners, which are Sluter's contribution to the earlier tomb, are astonishing cameos of the various reactions to death: from total withdrawal under the cowl of mourning, to an acknowledgment of death with a severe and graceful nobility – all this is copied by the later sculptors almost thoughtlessly and mechanically.

Just outside the Ducal Palace, pushed into one of the smaller squares, is the church of Notre Dame, whose western façade was heavily and excellently restored in the nineteenth century. Its three rows of false gargoyles were the subject of a particularly spectacular description by J.-K. Huysmans in his novel L'Oblat: 'The demons, with the familiar look of evil angels, their wings-butterflied with scales and their heads bristling with horns, harbour gorgon-masks between their legs; extravagant animals, lions crossed with heifers, beasts muzzled like a leopard and with the pelt of an ass, cattle with human features smiling in the grimace of a drunken hag who is eyeing up a bottle; nameless monsters, stemming from no known breed, grasping a panther and a pig, a Hindu dancing girl and a calf – the men, twisted into painful and comic attitudes, with their heads turned round on their shoulders and their eyes mad; others with pug-nosed faces and flared nostrils, their mouths hollowed out into funnels; still others with baroque cake-holes, with the look of salacious old burghers or mendicant friars who have had their fill ... and in the middle of all these demented animals and all these nightmare beings is an ordinary woman, praying and panic-stricken, her hands joined together in a look of terror and of faith, a distraught prisoner in this menagerie of half-beings, beseeching the prayers of those below, for her salvation and for grace.'

With all this, and much more, Dijon is nonetheless quite independent of its past. Between the limestone pillars, a whole series of international shops is packaged in brushed steel and plate glass as neatly and as chicly as bottles of scent. Trousers stop fashionably short of the ankle and the tourists (for whom there are 19,000 hotel rooms) are the ones who look provincial. This struck me as I was sitting at a café outside Notre Dame (you will find that a great deal of sitting in cafés occurs before you can persuade yourself to start on a walk) drinking a glass of white wine and cassis. This is the drink of Dijon, now known universally as kir after a former mayor, Chanoine Félix Kir, whose love of it was famous. I looked to the left and to the right of me. There were two sets of couples on either side, each of them reading the Michelin green guide, the husband declaiming to the wife on the exact provenance of Burgundian Gothic, and every one with a little glass of kir in front of them. You will never be alone in your admiration of Dijon and its drink. Instead, something like the communal air of self-congratulation at the opera – we were, we knew, doing the right thing – will hover over you and your fellow tourists. It was then, suddenly, that I found myself addressed by a marvellously bronzed American girl, with an equally marvellous head of bleached hair. 'What in God's name do people do in Dijon?' she shouted at me as though I were the far side of the Houston Astrodome. 'I mean, we were in Strasbourg yesterday which was pretty, you know really nice, and someone told us Dijon was ace too, so here we are,' and she looked across reassuringly to her companion, cosily encased in a thick brown sweater they had picked up in 'Edinborrow' three days before. 'Really I don't see much to it,' she said and waved her hand past the façade of Notre Dame. 'We were aiming to hit Nice tonight,' she went on, 'but the damn train was full so we're stuck,' and to emphasize 'stuck' she put

Chenôve.

her hands on her hips. I said something about the slow pace of Europe (the Michelin readers nodded on through the Renaissance) and felt I ought to apologize. The Americans thought it was a joke and went off to find what they hoped was the student quarter.

You will leave Dijon to the south and head out through the industrial suburbs which sprang up after the arrival of the railway in 1851 and where nearly all Dijon mustard is now made, towards Chenôve five kilometres away. You join the *Route des Grands Crus* through the suburbs which are built on what used to be the northernmost vineyards of the Côte d'Or. They produced a thin red Vin de Dijon which until the seventeenth century commanded a higher price than many of the more famous names further south. Here in the heart of the wine country it is strange to find large advertisements for beer at regular intervals along the roadside.

At Chenôve turn off the suburban pavement and up into what was once the street of a village separated from Dijon by open country. About 400 metres along it is a large white limestone barn which houses the presses of

the Dukes of Burgundy. Inside the air is sodden with the old smell of wine-soaked wood. As your eyes get used to the dark you will see along one wall a rank of massive barrels of which the total capacity is about 15,000 gallons. Wine from other vineyards is stored in some of them now. Those which are empty give a slight echo when tapped and those which are full none at all. Along the other side are the two presses themselves, built in 1238 with exaggeratedly massive oak timbers, and the same chunky and over-designed beauty as one finds in the earliest cast-iron monuments of the Industrial Revolution. Counterweighted with huge stones the presses still move quite easily by means of great oak screws to which capstan handles are attached. They were last used in 1928. Originally, weathered vertical planks were placed around the lowest level to make a temporary barrel which was filled with grapes. As they built up inside, their weight became enough to crush the fruit so that without any need for lowering the presses juice ran out of the gutter at the bottom. This unsolicited liquid, the first reward of the year's work, is known as *la mère goutte*, the mother drop, and, regarded as something apart, is never mixed in with anything less magically produced. Large pestles are next used to squeeze the grapes, and only then is the press itself lowered.

By chance, walking south from Dijon, you have arrived first at the last process undergone by the grape. From Chenôve the next ten kilometres of this walk is surrounded by vineyards and their intensely specialized landscape. In a shallow escarpment of exactly the same profile and proportions as the Cotswolds near Wotton-under-Edge, the limestone hills drop to the clays of the *pays bas*. The edge is incised by deep valleys called *combes*, the same Celtic word that is used in Wales and the English chalklands. It is a layered landscape. The vines themselves occupy little more than the slope itself. Above them are the stunted woods of the Haute Côte and below them the blond and tedious flatness of the *pays bas*, stretching out to the river Saône and beyond to the first hills of the Jura, over 75 kilometres away.

The contained narrowness of the vineyards gives the impression of a laboratory. Here in these few fields agriculture is most obviously a kind of chemistry, where the exact quantities of raw materials, accurate conditions for the experiment, and the care and knowledge of the experimenters will precisely determine the nature of the product. The history of maize does not appear in cornflakes, nor of wheat in bread, but it is the history of the grape's year, especially its last few sugar-generating weeks, that appears in the wine. When you drink a glass of Burgundy you experience the year's sun and rainfall and the quality of the earth. The grape and its juice are only the vehicle by which this information is conveyed, since for every great red wine in Burgundy the same *pinot noir* grape is used. (Lesser vineyards grow the more productive but coarser *gamay*.) It is in this sense that you can refer to 1969 or 1976 as being a good year for Burgundy. The wine becomes a kind of liquid geography, and your morning's journey a wine list. You will find yourself taking three hours to walk down this string of names – Marsannay-la-Côte, Couchey, Fixin, Brochon, Gevrey-Chambertin – which diners can read in seconds.

From Chenôve to the small hamlet of Fixin it is seven kilometres along small tracks, either of gravel or tar, through the vines. You might expect this landscape of pleasure to be as luxurious as its product, but in that alone the

Côte is disappointing. The ranks of vines, stretching either up and down the slope or along it, are rigid, brittle things. Their cultivation is the smartest kind of farming and these vineyards, occupying the Savile Row of viticulture, have the same stiff-collar look as wedding photographs. It is what the French call a *paysage conforme*, where the vine-grower's year is a pruner's lot, one of constant containment and attention.

As you walk from Chenôve to Fixin some of the many necessary tasks will be going on around you, of spraying, pruning, tying and weeding; of lopping off the tallest shoots to expose the grapes to the sun; of 'shoeing and unshoeing' the younger vines in times of possible frost. While the flowers are forming in May the vineyards are actually heated with fires or electric convector heaters. Occasionally, after four or five decades the vine-stocks, which make better wine but less of it as they grow older, will be torn up and new ones planted in their place. Then you will find the old roots dumped at the side of the track like the contents of an ashtray. Most of the yearly chores are nowadays done with the little grasshopper tractors with raised bodies that straddle the vine 'hedges'.

The lanes just touch the edge of Couchey and Marsannay-la-Côte, where a fine rosé is produced, and then move on towards Fixin. It is not quite a monoculture. There are strips of barley and maize, as well-nursed as the vines that surround them, and fruit trees which are occasionally pleached along wires like vines themselves. You pass the pretty yellow stone church at Fixey, with polychrome tiles on its tower roof, and head for Fixin through vineyards whose wine sells as Côte-de-Nuits-Villages, where scabious and stonecrop grow on the walls separating the *climats*, and where for butterflies you will find marbled and large whites, peacocks and red admirals in enviable abundance.

Above the village of Fixin, in the pine woods next to the Clos de la Perrière, is an extraordinary enclave called the Parc Noisot. Enshrined here is a statue by the Dijonnais François Rude of 'Napoleon Awakening to Immortality'. The laurel still firmly clamped to his head, the emperor lifts off his shroud before ascending to Elysium. He rests on a piece of Romantic landscape decorated with a few pillars from Fingal's Cave and the corpse of an eagle. Broken fetters and the neglected oak leaves of victory hang beside him as he gazes eastwards over the box hedges. Not far away in the trees is the grave of the Noisot who commissioned the statue. He is buried upright facing his emperor, a *Soldat de*

Napoléon 1er, as it carefully says on the plinth, distinguishing the Immortal from later, less worthy bearers of the name. The little pavilion in the park is full of Napoleonic memorabilia, including earth from every one of his battlefields in boxes, and a letter from Napoleon to Josephine addressed to: '*Grande Impératrice, pas une lettre de vous depuis votre départ de Strasbourg. . . . Les Russes sont partis. J'ai eu trève. Dans peu de jours je verrai ce que je deviendrai. Daignes, du haut de vos grandeurs, vous occuper un peu de vos esclaves. Napoléon.*' ('Great Empress, not a letter from you since you left Strasbourg. . . . The Russians have gone. I have called a truce. In a few days I will see what I shall become. Deign, from the height of your grandeurs, to take a little interest in your slaves. Napoleon.')

From the park it is two kilometres to Gevrey-Chambertin, one of the great wine villages of the world. There is no hint of rural decay or difficulty here. Wealth has gone into a rather insensitive repointing of almost every building and a repetitive geranium prettiness. Like the highest of *hauts couturiers* the wine

Napoleon (by François Rude) awakes to immortality at Fixin, clamped to a hunk of romantic landscape.

The château in Gevrey-Chambertin, the Savile Row of viticulture.

growers have small brass plaques next to their gates giving the name of the grower and his title – *viticulteur*. The great vineyards are beyond the village, clustering around one of the most sacred places of viticulture, the thirty-odd acres of Chambertin itself. Its neighbours, all classed as Grands Crus like cadet branches of some great ducal family, share the same prestigious name: Mazis-Chambertin, Chapelle-Chambertin, Griotte-Chambertin (said to be tinged with the flavour of cherries), Latricières-Chambertin, and prettiest of all, Charmes-Chambertin. Wine from the vineyard immediately north of Chambertin, the Clos de Bèze (first recorded as a vineyard in AD 630, six centuries before *Bertin* planted his *champ* in the thirteenth century) is thought to be so similar that it too can be sold as Chambertin. The two vineyards, covering only 28 hectares in all, are divided between about 75 owners.

There is nothing to indicate that this is a special place. Its distinction lies hidden underground. The low hills slide dully down to the plain over which farmers have planted vines for more than a kilometre, to benefit from the marketable name of their commune. As for the wine of Chambertin itself, it was Napoleon's favourite and followed him round the battlefields of Europe. In 1812 the sharper Paris wine merchants offered 'Chambertin *Retour de Moscou*' on their lists. The experience of drinking it is said to be like 'the Good Lord gliding down your gullet in velvet trousers', but at current prices that is probably a description to be taken on trust.

Gevrey-Chambertin to Meloisey

40 kilometres

The Côte-d'Or and its succession of famous vineyards pushes south to Nuits-St Georges and on past Beaune, but to continue in this hard-edged landscape would all too soon become dull, and here the walk leaves the Côte itself. You now climb up into the wood at the back of it and shadow the great vineyards on a line a few kilometres to the west of them in the more varied if less famous country of the Haute Côte. A stony white lane leads up from Gevrey through four kilometres of small, scrubby wood (the limestone prevents the oak and chestnut trees from growing more than about 20 feet high). Chestnut heartwood is said to be the best for vine-stakes and many of these trees or their ancestors may have been deliberately planted.

To emerge from the wood, which is in its way as singular visually as the vineyards you

have left, is to arrive at another Burgundy. The valley that greets you as you drop down to the hamlet of Curley is divided into arable and hay fields, darkened with islands of wood and here and there the occasional small vineyard. This is the Haute Côte, a limestone plateau divided into ridges, where there is none of the intensity of care that there is on the Côte d'Or, and broader, less frenetic rhythms can be seen in its agriculture. You will feel more relaxed here, as the landscape returns to a more human and fallible level. With relief you will find the earth a rich red brown, not white with limestone flakes as it is on the Côte, and there are sheep here instead of the ugly grasshopper tractors that characterize the vineyards down below. In Curley, five kilometres from Gevrey, there is no refreshment except for the spring which dribbles into the wash-house, nor at the slightly larger Reulle-Vergy two and a half kilometres further on. The path, which is now the GR7 from the Vosges to the Pyrenees, climbs a hill occupied in the Middle Ages by the village of Vergy. Everything but the twelfth-century church is now in ruins. Broken pieces of masonry stick through the vegetation on the crest, while the ivy-covered Tour St Denis is all that remains of the fortress from which the lords of Vergy (who also owned Gevrey) dominated this area until the sixteenth century. The castle was destroyed by the Huguenots under Henry IV. A little further towards Messanges are the more substantial ruins of the Abbey of St Vivant, in a dangerous state with the vaults held together by only the thinnest smear of mortar. You might well find a carpet of unpicked *fraises de bois* inside.

The village of Messanges, on the far side of the little Meuzin stream that turns the wheels in the Moulin Chevaillier (you can hear them grinding as you pass) is only two kilometres away, and has a good café-cum-restaurant but no hotel. There is a lovely washing-place, built in 1848, with two basins and a trough for the animals outside. It stands in the middle of the street like a town hall, the architecture on either side of it presenting a rustic echo of the *hôtels parlementaires* in Dijon. The structural arrangement of grand house, courtyard and entrance archway can be seen to have stemmed from the farm, its yard and the necessary gate. Here you find yourself in the back end of Burgundy, away from its prestige. The vine which has the Côte so entirely in its grip has up here loosened its hold to allow raspberries and blackcurrants a place in the sun. It is said that the idea of a *cru* has established so permanent a place in the

Arcenant, where static wages and increased prices have dramatically reduced the working population, leaving the village to the retired and the holiday-makers.

Burgundian mind that not only these fruits, but hops, onions and gourds are all graced, if not quite with an *appellation contrôlée*, at least with a sense of Holy Growth that would scarcely be conceivable in, say, the turnip culture of Norfolk.

From Messanges the path climbs two kilometres to the village of Chévannes, which appears round a corner with its red-tile roofs and the black spire of its church, cross-gartered in yellow, with one poplar beside it. You know you are in a different country because the tractors here are not the contorted little insects of the Côte, but four-square and manly. Over another hill, through woodland, you come down to Arcenant, arriving again at the sight of the roofs with their smoking chimneys collected in the valley below. The first building you come to is the church, with a life-size statue of St Martin of Tours with a beggar beside him in Renaissance style. The village spreads out from the church like the train of a wedding dress, its limestone streets often redecorated as second homes. It has a remote feeling, oddly like a mountain village. There is a small café-restaurant in the square, whose owner, rather disconcertingly, is an Alsatian desperately nostalgic for his homeland. He will serve you a typical Alsace lunch of *würstchen* and pickles.

For something more appropriate to Arcenant go and visit Mme Joännet who runs a large fruit farm at the bottom of the village. She produces jams and liqueurs in strawberry, raspberry, blackcurrant and cherry flavours, all of which are like nectar. Never mind the weight and buy at least one of her bottles to go in your rucksack. It will make you feel good when everything else is failing to do so. She told me that she is the only one left in Arcenant making liqueurs although there used to be many. The land no longer produced the revenue to support a family and now there are only 200 people living permanently in the village. She knew that things were different in England, and that what

French farmers really needed was a more effective Minister for Agriculture than Edith Cresson, someone strong enough to fight for their rights at the expense of overpaid office workers. Why should anyone be penalized for having been born into a rural life, which was hard enough from the start anyway? All that was needed, she told me, was a proper reward for important work.

The path from Arcenant to Bouilland is a distance of seven kilometres, at first along the banks of a small trout stream and then climbing into the spindly oak wood of the Bois de Montmain. This is the kind of untended, unused woodland which is common enough in France but almost never found in England, simply because there is less pressure on land in France. There is a sense in this wood, as you stumble along a path that wriggles over roots and under crooked branches, of a permanent landscape in which climate is the only agent of change, and which would have looked the same whether people had been here or not. There could be no greater contrast than this to the horticultural style of the vineyards, and

Stonecrop swamps a limestone roof in Bouilland.

The pale abbey of Ste Marguerite near Bouilland is now roofless but still nurtures fine details in its corners.

the effect of walking from one to the other, compared with the experience of the English landscape, is of an unbalanced, primitive country. The land is either man's or God's, with none of the compromise of the English field or of the inclusion within the human domain of a cultivated woodland which remains ambiguous and transitional.

You drop steeply to Bouilland. There is little to see, a café or two, some New Orleans-style balconies and a riotously expensive four-star hotel (eight beds only) with a selection of international limousines permanently parked outside. In the village the way turns south and climbs the side of the valley for two kilometres, with grey limestone cliffs above the fields to the east, until suddenly the ruins appear of a fourteenth-century abbey dedicated to Ste Marguerite. It is built in a creamy-white stone with ash trees growing round it, one of them filling the ruined east end like a window. Little but the bare cruciform structure has survived; here and there the remnants of leafy capitals cling to the walls, even where the attached columns have fallen away from below them. Nearby is the stocky gatehouse which straddles the way into the abbey precincts. It is hollow, and peppered with little holes for about 1,200 pigeons, all of which have flown.

Across the road is the farm of Les Buttes, owned by a Swiss from Neuchâtel. A vine is trained carefully over the building, a cart is aesthetically placed in front of the barn doors, and through the plate glass windows you can see scrubbed tables, pigtailed heads and the clear skins of children reared on yoghourt. A house embalmed in such perfection is a blight on the French countryside. There are now 800,000 second homes in France and some 6,000 rural communes (about 15% of the total) which double their population or more in the holiday seasons.

From the abbey it is about four kilometres to the village of Clavoillon through fields cultivated in curving strips of mustard, barley and maize. Some were left fallow, and in these the cowslips were so thick that at first I thought them a crop. Clavoillon is the opposite of Les Buttes. Mounds of real muck are everywhere, and running between them ugly strut-about chickens. Modern tractors are hooked on to tiny wooden carts, a reminder of the scale of peasant farming. You can see it too in the stunted size of the barns into which the modern machinery is somehow manoeuvred.

Only a kilometre beyond Clavoillon the path, now on a metalled lane, goes under the A6, the Autoroute du Soleil completed in 1970, and then climbs the embankment on the far side. For about eight kilometres easy stony tracks run between thick hedges, with occasional glimpses down to the east of the wide *pays bas*, and on the clearest of days over to the Jura. The hamlet of Mandelot sits in the prettiest of the valleys encountered on the walk so far. It is the image of a seigneurial village. The château, a rather stolid and sensible building, restored in 1882 *'par les soins de ses propriétaires Mr et Me Bouchard-Bréart'* as a notice says, is at the apex of the village's few streets. Outside the large stables there is a communal drinking-trough, presented by the same Théod. Bouchard and Ludov. Bréart for the health and well-being of their people. Another superbly Flaubertian plaque in Latin testifies to their generosity. It was full of weed when I was there, with three dead bees floating in the scum.

Meloisey is about six kilometres from Mandelot. This is one of the best sections of the walk; the combes spread tentacles up from the lowland, encircling the villages, which are comfortably spaced and marked by their typically Burgundian church towers, neither tall nor stumpy. The old mixed farming methods continue here, in a varied landscape that is a joy for the tourist but unrewarding for the farmer. The sheer pleasure of walking through these valleys will bring you comfortably into Meloisey, where the tiny Hôtel de la Renaissance will provide all that you need.

Meloisey to Epinac

29 kilometres

From Meloisey it is five kilometres along an easy lane to St Romain. This is the archetypal wine village of the Haute Côte. It received its own *appellation contrôlée* as recently as 1967 and produces both red and white wine. As you enter the limestone and red-tile village you pass the house of the *viticulteur* with the best name in Burgundy, M. René Gras-Boisson. He is an exceptionally friendly man and if you have already finished Mme Joannet's bottle from Arcenant you could replace it with one of his. The vineyards here are the highest in the whole of the Côte d'Or and St Romain is a light, fresh wine, best drunk when still young.

Go on into the village until you reach the church, where again you will find how important the cultivation of the vine is to this country. The walls inside are lined with the wine-pickers' baskets which are balanced across one shoulder when full. The stairs to the pulpit have carved vines climbing up

The twelfth-century church at Fixey is roofed in polychrome tiles imported from the Low Countries at a time when the territories of the Dukes of Burgundy stretched from the Rhône to the North Sea.

Gevrey-Chambertin – geranium prettiness and a sense of well-being.

them, with a giant cricket hovering near the foot, where the vine springs from a heart embossed with three small barrels.

St Romain is divided in two and as you drop from the *haut bourg* to the *bas* you will see, set like ruined buildings among the vineyards, the heaps of limestone that have been cleared to make the fields. The lower half of the village is the more sociable, with cafés and large blue signs saying *Buvez St Romain* fading back into walls on which they are painted.

From the streets in which planks are stacked in herring-bone piles, maturing more slowly than the wine they will one day encase, you climb westwards back on to the limestone plateau, where the extraordinary sight of a cliff-edge discothèque greets you at the top. It was unfortunately closed when I was there, but beyond it and beyond St Romain was the marvellous blue view eastwards, over one of the great European corridors, the plain of the Saône which extends the Rhône valley northwards away from the Mediterranean, the real *trait d'union*, as it has been called, the hyphen of France. To the west for the first time, as you make your way to Orches, appear

Vines at St Romain: the smartest farming in the world.

Chapelle de St Pierre in Nolay.

Saigey: after Nolay the path leaves the limestone and enters a wooded and poorer country.

the granite heights of the Morvan. Orches has yet more *Dégustation des Vins* to offer, this time a rosé, but unless you have resisted in both Arcenant and St Romain, it can be no more than a taunt to the walker. Besides, the end of the day is no more than seven kilometres away at Nolay. You cross the plateau to its edge, which is fretted into little pinnacles and chimneys, and then drop down to the valley of Cormot le Grand which leads straight to Nolay. You come into town past a pretty chapel under a red barrel roof and a bell turret with a lead Ali Baba hat. You will soon find yourself at the fourteenth-century market hall, which has a roof as good as the one at Martel in the Lot, made of limestone slabs weighing 800 kilograms per square metre. Its huge size shows that it was built before the Black Death and mid-century slump.

Nolay has the agreeable ambience of Ludlow transplanted to rural France. It is the birthplace of Lazare Carnot, who is a hero for Frenchmen but unheard of in England. Both soldier and strategist, Carnot was the logistical hero of the Revolutionary Wars, and his statue stands in front of the house where he

was born in 1753, one of eighteen children. It shows him pinioning a map with one hand and manipulating a pair of compasses with the other, as a winged figure of victory stands by.

As you reach the top of the hill above the town, at the beginning of the long traverse westwards to Autun, Burgundy undergoes another change. Here the limestone, on which all the vines have been planted and of which all the buildings since Dijon have been built, comes to an end. Mud surfaces underfoot, and green coppery strips appear in patches of exposed earth in the lane banks. The limestone wall above them doubles with a hedge for a while and then stops. In the field next to it you will find a small pond, unknown on the permeable limestone, but sealed here by the clay below it. In the meadows the cowslip hay grows thickly and in the woods the oaks are twice the height of their deprived limestone counterparts. Dozens of thick red slugs appear on the road. There is almost no arable farming here, just a few poor fields of oats thick with

Vines at Gevrey-Chambertin – a soil so valuable that the viticulteurs *wipe it off their boots when leaving the vineyard.*

Charolais at Saigey: boeuf bourguignonne.

unwanted sorrel; instead, acres of rich grazing are indolently chewed at by herds of the sweet-smelling Charolais, every one a walking creamery.

The next village is Changey, a place of scrawny brick barns, applied cement and faceless walls of grey plaster. There is a kind of scrubbed integrity to it, with nothing to offer save one or two shuttered holiday homes and a forsythia made brighter by its drab surroundings. There could scarcely be a more dramatic illustration than this of the effects of geology on prosperity. Here in Changey you are still in Burgundy but no longer on the limestone, and without its alkaline soil vines cannot be grown nor money made. The cattle farmers here wear bushy Nietzsche moustaches in a show of masculinity that in the more sophisticated wine country to the east would be considered naïve. In La Forêt I met a man mowing in front of his week-end house, which was, he told me, only four hours from his flat in Paris. Although his father had lived here before him, the locals remained aloof, he said, not because they were hostile but because they were shy.

Progress is easy through this back-country towards Epinac, which brings about another transformation. The town lies in the valley of the Drée, and as you come to the edge of the sandstone hills above it, the tall chimneys of the industrial buildings below protrude darkly into the surrounding fields. In the eighteenth and nineteenth centuries Epinac, along with several other towns in this basin around Autun of which the chief was Le Creusot, was the centre of both coal mining and steel manufacture, as well as glass- and tile-making. The town preserves the style of industry among farmland, with lengths of working-class lodgings rather arbitrarily arranged over a wide area. The newer buildings are a harsh red, but the older terraces are built in a good brown brick, laid in a French bond of headers only. The great monument of Epinac, now used only for storage, is the huge factory next to the station, in the finest nineteenth-century industrial style, of grubby brick with round-headed windows and grey keystones to the arches, dominated by a high pavilion. It is rusty, dirty and broken now, surrounded with old cranes, oil trucks and dumps of grit and waste in colours that suggest poison.

Epinac to Autun
24 kilometres

From the outskirts of Epinac, with its cafés and shops in the oldest part of the town, a sedgy and reedy track leads along the Drée to Sully, five kilometres away. A large dovecote at the very corner of the walled park is the first indicator of Sully's grandeur. You follow the park wall round until you come to the grand entrance. Two long service blocks with large hipped roofs and peach-coloured walls line the entrance court. At the far end of it is the grey sixteenth-century château. It is an ugly building: the façade is too long for its height, and the windows too mean for the decorative pilasters that surround them. The most interesting element is the chapel, enclosed in one of the towers on the southern side. Its window is a Gothic arch within which an attempt has been made to reproduce Gothic tracery using classical forms – circles, pediments, a coat of arms and small columns. It is the Renaissance dragging its feet. The most enjoyable thing about Sully is the name of its owner, which could have come straight out of a Barbara Cartland novel; the descendant of a nineteenth-century general and president of France, he is called the Duc de Magenta. I asked at the gate what the current Duke did for his living and was told that he owned his estates.

You will now head for Autun, which is the real target of this walk and only nineteen kilometres away. You tramp on along dead straight lanes, past St-Léger-du-Bois, and then over the track of the new Paris to Lyon high speed train, opened in 1981. At Vergoncey, six kilometres from Sully, you climb back on to a small ridge of limestone, where scabious reappears on the roadside like a pH indicator as the soil turns chalky. Autun appears in this Cotswold landscape, sheltering under its wooded granite hill to the west, and you drop down to the village of Curgy, where the dark

Vergoncey near Autun.

The name Autun is a reduced version of *Augustodunum*, which was founded in 15 BC by Augustus as the 'sister and rival of Rome', intended to replace the Gallic capital of Bibracte. The new city benefited from its position on the main road from Marseille through Lyon to Boulogne. At its height, with a population of 200,000, it covered an area of about 200 hectares, surrounded by a wall six kilometres long and eleven metres high, with four monumental gates leading into streets paved with morvandel granite. There was a forum, a capitol, a theatre for 12,000 people and an amphitheatre. It was a town, as Tacitus said, 'devoted to wealth and its pleasures'. It became in time proverbial for its degeneracy and sophistication, and even though the site was never deserted it shrank from its former 200 hectares to less than ten in the years following the Roman Empire.

grey Romanesque church houses twelfth-century ochre frescoes.

Between here and Autun the way continues along increasingly busy and suburban roads, unless you want to make a large detour through the forest on the southern side of the valley. I kept to the roads through St Denis and the suburbs of St Symphorien. Just outside St Denis a young man greeted me over a gate. I replied and asked what he did. 'Paysan.' And what did his parents do? 'Paysans.' And could he recommend Autun for anything? 'Too rich, too bourgeois. Nothing but paper-pushers. A couple of factories but nothing else.' He said I should go to Le Creusot, because it was more honest, less paper, more steel. He told me to look at the gates of the main *lycée* in Autun, and then I would see what kind of place it was, how hypocrisy and pretension were its *métiers*.

When, a couple of long hours later, I eventually arrived in the city, I found myself by chance in front of the *lycée* and its wide gates. Made of elaborately wrought iron, with tasteful gilding, they are late eighteenth-century and get one Michelin star.

The 'paysan' was too harsh. Autun is a unique place, a fact too well known by its inhabitants. One has to pare its modern skin of *crêperies* and antique shops to find the extraordinary Roman and medieval town underneath. If you plan to stay the night here you must also book ahead, since there is no chance of getting a hotel room otherwise. I had failed to reserve one and, travelling light without a tent, was forced to spend the night in the back seat of someone else's Mercedes. If this does happen to you there is one major compensation. The money you would have spent on a hotel room can go on the best dinner you have ever had.

Some of it still survives. The theatre is recognizable, if a little blurred, and it is worth visiting for the charming house built next to it, with Roman and medieval statues embedded in the walls – men on the ground floor, women on the first. Laundry is strung out to dry between the Corinthian capitals, and clematis laces itself around the funerary sculpture of 2,000 years ago. More complete are two of the gateways through the town wall, which are beautifully functional, rational pieces of architecture, imperial statements in white stone. They were designed for two-way traffic with a pedestrian door at the side.

These Roman remains had their effect on medieval builders in the city. You will find ordinary houses from the Middle Ages with their timbers fluted or grooved like classical pilasters and columns. This is something of which craftsmen throughout Europe were ignorant until the Renaissance. In Autun they can only have copied it from their local Roman monuments.

The great cathedral of St Lazaire, rebuilt in 1130–40 to honour the relics of Lazarus which had arrived here in the tenth century, owes a great debt to the architecture of Cluny, but it too has fluted pilasters rather than the clustered columns of the period. The triforium, the arcade over the main arches of the nave, is an exact copy of the arcade over the Roman gates into the town. It also contains some of the best Romanesque sculpture in Burgundy – the Last Judgement over the main west door and a fine series of carved capitals inside. In the Salle Capitulaire, where they are brought down to eye level, you will find, among others, the Three Kings asleep under a

BOTTOM *Arcenant on the Haute Côte – a more varied landscape than the monoculture further east.*

BELOW *Near Reulle-Vergy.*

St Romain: a clustering and sociability more out of choice – and a civilized habit of mind – than necessity.

Romanesque capitals in the cathedral at Autun: God tells Adam to work and Judas is hanged by devils.

single sweep of blanket, the Hanging of Judas, Cain with an arrow in his neck and, most sobering of all, a scene in which God commands a contrite Adam to work.

The best piece of sculpture in Autun is in the Musée Rolin just down the road. It is thought to have been done by Giselbertus, who carved the Last Judgement, and depicts Eve at the moment when she plucks the apple. Here the story is not the woman-hating myth it usually is, but the representation of someone in the contradictory grips of anxiety and desire. With one hand she wipes a tear from her cheek and with the other, looking away, grasps the apple. It is a reluctant fruit, the whole branch is pulled sideways from the tree, and the history of humanity is in that tension. Whether the apple will come or the hand will let go is still unresolved.

Autun to Mont Beuvray

29 kilometres

On the final day you will climb into the southern end of the Morvan, crossing from the Roman to the Gallic capital of Burgundy. To finish on Mont Beuvray is more of a poetic than a practical gesture – it is the neat antithesis of Dijon, no more than a few banks and ditches, far away from modern habitation and roads. It cannot be a true end unless you have arranged for a helicopter to take you from its summit. Otherwise, more prosaically, you can retrace your steps or, better still, head on northwards into the Morvan to emerge at the far side, either at Vézelay or Château Chinon, the one a high place of medieval art and Christianity, the other the constituency of François Mitterand. The choice is yours.

From Autun you climb immediately into the chestnut wood to the south of it, along sunken paths where the pale granite surfaces in boulders, to the first summit, crowned by the huge Cross to the Liberation. This is only the foretaste of what is to come. You descend again into grassy fields around Brion and Laizy, where the dozing Charolais sleep in the fields like giant daisies.

You cross the river Arroux at Laizy, which is like a garden suburb, and begin to climb again towards the blue-ridged horizon of the Morvan. The lane ascends continuously towards the hamlets of La Plante and Crometey. The country of these foothills is half-mountain, half-cultivated, with separate hamlets scattered throughout. There are buzzards everywhere in this naturally bosky landscape. One has only to cut holes in the woodland to make it a kind of *jardin anglais*. Only the pitiful thinness of the oat crops and the sight of a horse-drawn plough reminds you of its poverty. This, the Morvan, was famous for its two exports – the timber that was floated down the rivers to provide fire- and building-wood, and the *morvandelles* women themselves, for many centuries in demand as the best wet-nurses for upper-class Parisian babies. It was said that if only the Morvan was as fertile as its women the sorrows of life here would be over.

Through this intimate landscape of inter-locking fields and woods, you will arrive at St Léger-sous-Beuvray. I happened to come here on the day of the village fête. There was country dancing, with hoops, poles, clogs, drink and a faulty public address system. The sexual imagery of all the dances was quite overt, to the embarrassment of the dancers. The girls wore black lace hats and all the participants wore varnished clogs with sprays of flowers painted on the toes. Among the audience only the very old men wore clogs, scuffed, unvarnished and unpainted; they watched the dances as though foreign to them. One or two tourists like me enjoyed it more, if anything, than the locals around us. This is the modern form of *Bovarysme*, the mirror image of the nineteenth-century longing for romance.

Everything is much cheaper here than it has been. You can get a very good dinner in the hotel on the square, with the famous smoked Morvan ham, snails and the double luxury of cream cheese with cream poured on to it, food in the pluperfect, for twenty-five francs.

An easy ten kilometres from St Léger takes you through hazel and beech forest to the top of Mont Beuvray and the huge Celtic fort of Bibracte. Its ramparts are five kilometres in circumference, although in the woodland it is difficult to get any idea of them as a whole. There is a spectacular view to the east, but it is more beautiful to be here on a misty day when it is peopled by the ghosts of the Druids who undoubtedly taught here. This was the capital of the Eduens, and was the hub of a road

La Tour-du-Chapitre near Brion.

system radiating through eastern Gaul to Mâcon, Chalon, Lyon, Orléans and Sens. The rapidity of the Roman conquest owed a great deal to the quality of these roads. Bibracte's greatest moment came, ironically, in the last years of free Gaul. During a war with the Arvernes of the Auvergne, the Eduens asked Caesar for his help against them. In a great conference held on this hill in 58 BC he gave his support, conquered the Arvernes and in the joint Eduens-Roman victory established an important foothold in Gaul. In 54 BC, the great Gallic revolt took place, while Caesar was away in Britain. Its leaders were Dumnorix and Litavic of the Eduens, Draques of the Cadurci and Vercingetorix of the Arvernes, who, together with the tribes of the Eburones and the Seriones, raised Gaul against the Romans. Here again in Bibracte the general assembly gathered to unite its forces. It is reckoned that in these still forests 80,000 foot soldiers and 15,000 mounted troops collected to expel Caesar.

After a victory at Gergovia near Clermont-Ferrand early in 52, this massive force found itself, through the poor tactics of Vercingetorix, walled up for two months in the fort of Alesia (probably in the Jura) where after

heroic attempts to raise the siege the Gallic chiefs were led to total defeat and surrender. It has been suggested that, with the constant influx of goods from Rome, by the middle of the first century BC the idea of prosperity in the Celtic mind had become inseparable from Romanization, as Westernization may have done in some Third World countries today. If that is the case, Vercingetorix and his lieutenants were running against the tide, and the Great Assembly at Bibracte was no more than a futile gesture in the face of an empire and a culture whose mark has remained on France until today.

DISTANCES (in kilometres)

From Dijon to:

Chenôve 5; Marsannay-la-Côte 2.5; Couchey 2.5; Fixey 2; Fixin 1; Gevrey-Chambertin 2; Curley 5; Reulle-Vergy 2.5; Curtil-Vergy 2.5; Messanges 2; Chévannes 2; Arcenant 3; Bouilland 7; Abb. Ste-Marguérite 2; Mandelot 8; Meloisey 6; Saint Romain 5; Orches 3; Nolay 7; Changey 6; La Forêt 3; Epinac 5; Sully 5; Vergoncey 6; Curgy 4; Autun 9; Laizy 13; St-Léger-s-Beuvray 10; Mont Beuvray 10

MAPS

I.G.N. 1:50,000 Numbers: 3023 (Gevrey-Chambertin), 3024 (Beaune), 2924 (Epinac), 2825 (Autun)

GUIDES

Topo-Guide du Sentier de Grande Randonnée No. 7, Troncon de la Côte d'Or C.N.S.G.R. Paris 1976.

Topo-Guide des Sentiers de Grande Randonnée Nos. 13–131 C.N.S.G.R. Paris 1976

BURGUNDY BOOKS

Marie Bullier and others, *Visages de la Bourgogne*, Horizons de France 1950

Joseph Calmette, *The Golden Age of Burgundy*, Weidenfeld and Nicolson 1962

Graham Chidgey, *Guide to the Wines of Burgundy*, Pitman 1977

W.M.Crowdy, *Burgundy and Morvan*, Christophers 1925

Stephen Gwynn, *Burgundy*, Constable 1934

Gaston Roupnel, *La ville et la campagne à la XVII siècle*, Ernest Leroux 1922

Robert Speaight, *The Companion Guide to Burgundy*, Collins 1978

Charolais near St Léger-sous-Beuvray: every one a walking creamery.

Normandy

Bagnoles de l'Orne to Genêts

159 kilometres

Hardly a mile will pass on this walk along the southern edge of Normandy without your meeting a small and bored crowd of the famous Norman cows, as spotty as Dalmatians but furrier and with every other horn crumpled. They are one of the few Viking legacies to France. The breed was imported from Scandinavia in the eighth and ninth centuries and now makes up a quarter of all French cows, five and a half million of them, rivalled in number only by the Charolais, the pure white Italian cattle brought in by the Romans. Charolais have been made to work as draught animals, but the Norman cow, apart from its inevitable end as beef, has always been devoted purely to the dairy. Normandy grows no wine, but the role of *grand cru* is filled by the cheese and even more by the butter made from their milk. This is a cheese in itself and to eat it with Camembert or Livarot would be as gross as laying a slice of Stilton on one of Double Gloucester. At breakfast it is never given to you in sealed pats or little balls, but as a great pocked slab, thicker than a roofing slate and as wide.

It is a truism that an Englishman will feel both reassuringly and disappointingly at home in Normandy, which is no more than the Weald of Kent with a sea-change. But the strange effect of that shared geography is to throw the Frenchness of Normandy into sharper relief, in the same way that the subtle contours of a field are shown up only in first or last light. You will find the grammar the same, but the vocabulary different, so that at times Normandy is like England seen through a polarizing filter, its textures deepened and the glare removed. This is further complicated by the fact that Normandy plays the same part for Frenchmen (above all for Parisians), as it does for Englishmen, as an eiderdown of rural pleasures to which the drier, harder, emptier and higher parts of France can only aspire. One of Gide's parents was from the Cévennes and the other from Normandy, and this provenance, sharing the hard south and the rich north, automatically made him a kind of Universal Man of French culture.

Dorice on the estuary of the Sée near Avranches: an ancient design, narrowing at each end like a cupped hand.

The Normans themselves are of course aware of their role and the country's prettiness is usually by design. Defunct stone apple-presses are everywhere displayed converted into flower-beds and fountains, while the names of farms and parts of the countryside reflect not exactly what they are but what the Normans want them to be. Near Mortain you will find a group of farms called Val Fleury, Les Jolis Champs, Les Hauts Jardins, La Belle Prise (which is on land cut out of the old forest that still covers the heights, and has been *prise* or 'taken' from La Lande Pourrie, the Rotten Moor). The names are not descriptions but assertions.

From a fairly arbitrary starting-point at the spa of Bagnoles de l'Orne, this walk follows a ridge of hills as far as Mortain, where it plunges into the *bocage* country which until then it had only surveyed. After a couple of days deep in the lanes and hedges of the *bocage* (the term is distantly related to the word 'bush') the path emerges at Avranches on to the Bay of Mont St Michel; it then follows the northern coast of the bay for about fifteen kilometres to Genêts at the base of the Cotentin peninsula.

Historically two periods dominate the land, the one long and constructive, the other relatively momentary and cataclysmic in its

Normandy in February: a tendency towards the morose.

effects. For many miles the route coincides with the pilgrims' way from Paris to Mont St Michel, and you regularly come across relics from that time. At the other end of history, for a few days in August 1944, two months after D Day, this was the front line between the German Seventh Army and General Patton's American armoured divisions which were rapidly encircling it. It was the scene of some of the bitterest fighting in the war and not one of the towns on the way escaped without appalling damage. The *Guide Bleu* in 1947 listed in a deadpan way the state of the towns it hoped to lead its tourists round: 'Avranches 57% destroyed, Mortain totally wrecked except for the churches, Domfront 75% non-existent . . .' The damage has now been made good, and these places have the look of new shoes, rather foreign to their inhabitants, but of a good design which will improve with wear.

Midsummer was chosen for the invasion of Normandy because the English Channel was likely to be calm and because before April the Normandy mud would have been thick enough to bring any army to a halt. But in the summer the leafy *bocage* is a defender's paradise. No horizon is further than 100 metres away, and for the invader every hedge and sunken lane becomes a mental as well as a physical barrier. It is the time when Normandy comes nearest to the idea we have of it as upholstered and generous. But I chose to do this walk in February when, like a ski-resort without snow, Normandy appears unwrapped. Curiously, this stripped and primitive time of year is more forgiving to a country that has been mauled as deeply as this one. The replacement of thatch with corrugated iron, almost universal now, is not so ugly in this ugly time of year as it might be in June. The maltreatment of animals is understandable at a season when their owners are also knee-deep in mud. February has no humbug or facile prettiness. Instead it can occasionally give an unsuspected shapeliness to a valley, when an analytical light, emerging from under a cloud, investigates for a moment its sides and hollows.

Bagnoles de l'Orne to Lonlay l'Abbaye

32 kilometres

Bagnoles is inserted into Normandy rather oddly, like an inland Scarborough. It is a spa where circulatory diseases are cured in the cold mineral water springs. Royal patronage put the town on the social map in the sixteenth century, but the tone now is of 1910 perfectly preserved. The villas stand in rows, oblivious of each other, and all with vaguely Norman allusions in the stripes and cross-hatching of their stuck-on timbers. A half-genteel, half-squalid concentration on the body and its disorders grips the place. Only the additions of a casino and a cinema can divert you from this slightly shamefaced obsession. Like most spas that have failed to develop alternative attractions, Bagnoles is in financial difficulty. Doctors have become increasingly distrustful of the waters' efficaciousness, and the spas have been forced to look for customers other than the sick. But here they are caught in a trap. The ill need an atmosphere of purgative austerity, with menus geared to frail stomachs, but that is hardly what the more robust holidaymakers require. The obvious answer of a two-tier system, one for the healthy, one for the invalid, is apparently no solution. Tone is

Bagnoles de l'Orne – Norman allusions in the stuck-on timbers, but the dominant tone is 1910.

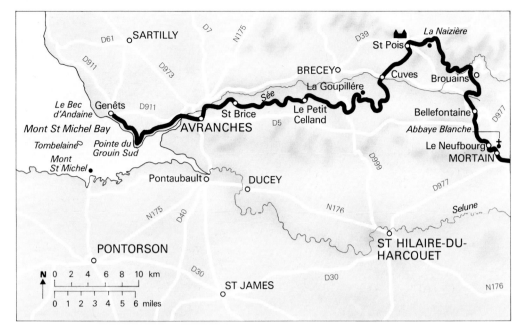

what matters in Bagnoles, and jollity has none.

From the lake next to the casino, drained in winter, go down the Allée Dante, through tended woodland, to the buildings that house the baths themselves. Here, where moss has crept out between the chips of gilt and turquoise mosaic, the ill were once soaked together. The iron-bearing water poured successively from one communal bath to the next, and it is revealing, if not entirely surprising, to learn that the first and cleanest was reserved for men, the second for women and the last for the unsegregated poor.

The *Route de Grande Randonnée No 22* leaves from opposite the baths (there is a small plaque to say so) and quickly climbs up on to the wooded ridge which forms the spine of the *Parc Naturel Régional de Normandie Maine*. The route follows the lip of the ridge for eighteen kilometres as far as Domfront, running almost all the way through forest of oak, beech, birch and pine. It is a Roman road of extraordinary straightness, without doubt on the line of an ancient ridgeway following these hills, which are pushed into Normandy like a narrow pier. The path is almost always surrounded by trees on either side, with only the keyhole prospect of the same path and the same wood for miles ahead. Occasionally, and this is signalled by the track underfoot changing from well-drained sand to glutinous mud, a field appears on one side of another, as though the flaps of the box had briefly been folded down. Then over the hedges of gorse and broom, the *bocage*, or a version of it, spreads wide to the south. It is nothing like as parcelled up here as the Cotentin country which delayed the Ameri-

cans for so long after D Day – by comparison, Patton said, it was like 'fighting in Indian country' – but nonetheless it is a divided landscape, where the green of the fields is filtered through a continuous web of hedgerow trees. This timber is a valuable resource which is culled in a great February shearing of the landscape, and then stacked in farmyards either as piles of brushwood or as great wigwams of poles laid up against the trunks of the apple trees. But, like the pigeons kept in the farms, the hedgerow timber of the *bocage* has always been thought by professional agriculturalists to have a harmful influence on the farming here. The deep margin of shade around any of the small fields severely reduces the cereal crop grown in them. In a country of acid soils, with the only accessible alkaline fertilizer the *tangue* or grey salt-mud of the sea-shore, many expensive miles away, this reduction of the food-producing capacity has at times been disastrous. But people here cannot do without wood, either for building or for fuel, while the property laws and immobile loyalty to particular patches has meant that one obvious solution, the grouping of trees in larger blocks with unshaded fields between them, has also been impossible. Only now are small farmers pooling resources, land and labour in cooperatives.

This is all to the south. On the path itself incidents occur from time to time. I passed a woman with a beagle on a twenty-five-foot chain, who explained that it had once escaped and killed three cats; two men furtively cutting the heads off chickens and then pushing both parts into a black plastic bag; a tumble-down dolmen on the side of the track

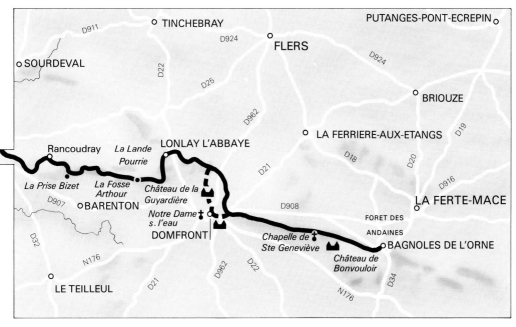

(proof at least of its antiquity) with the lid still hooked across the top of one upright, the other end on the ground. This, *le Lit de la Gionne*, is where a wicked fairy, La Gionne herself, was buried after a lifetime of eating little children lost in the forest.

The hill opens out again to the south and reveals the most extraordinary building in Normandy a few hundred metres away across the fields, the Château de Bonvouloir. All that remains of this fifteenth-century château are the chapel (now a farm), a large dovecote, a well and a kind of double tower, one of whose members is very tall (27 metres) and suggestively symbolic in outline. Cosmetically, official maps now call it the Phare de

The Château de Bonvouloir, erected by the seigneur *in gratitude to the mineral waters at Bagnoles for their restoration of his potency.*

Bonvouloir, as a miserable joke about an inland lighthouse. But there is a more interesting explanation. The Lord of Bonvouloir (a name to sum up all Norman place names, most of which express good hopes for the place) was for many years unable to father the enormous family he desired. Only after extensive soakings in the spring at Bagnoles did the wished-for fertility arrive, and from that moment his wife bore him a child a year for the next decade. In gratitude, as well as understandable pride, the seigneur had this stupendous monument erected.

The track pushes on straight as a railway towards the west, past a small restored chapel to the patron saint of peace and Paris, Ste Geneviève, where young girls in need of husbands would come to pray and scratch their names on the walls. Domfront eventually announces itself as something different with the enormous concrete spire of its central church, built in the 1920s and louvred like a ventilation shaft. Around it the town is now coherent again after the ravages of 1944. If anything it is a little too neat, with pedestrianized streets and cosy houses within the bastion towers of the twelfth-century walls. Domfront was one of the most important strongpoints in medieval Normandy. It belonged to the Bellême family, notorious over generations for their barbarity. Their castle on the edge of the Varenne gorge is more brutal than romantic. It had been built in about 1120 by Henry I, Duke of Normandy and King of England, as part of a thirty-kilometre-deep defence system to protect the eastern marches of his duchy against Louis VI of France. From

The Romanesque church of Notre Dame sous l'Eau at Domfront: a simple geometry of conviction.

the ruins you can look across the valley to the crag called Tertre Sainte Anne, from where, in 1559, during the Wars of Religion, the cannon of a royalist battery destroyed the ramparts of the castle in its last siege. Afterwards, only fifteen of the garrison of 150 Calvinists survived.

Below the town to the south-west (a direction opposite from the one you will eventually take, but the detour is worth it) is an altogether finer survival from the Middle Ages. The church of Notre Dame sous l'Eau is near perfect. It was built in small granite blocks by the monks from Lonlay l'Abbaye at some time between 1050 and 1100, in a Romanesque style of complete clarity and logic. It was once longer – four bays of the nave were removed in 1836 to allow for a widening of the Mortain road, to accommodate the newly increased pilgrim traffic to Mont St Michel – but you would not know it. Go to the east end, where you will find three apses that contribute curves to an otherwise rectilinear plan. Here the elevations rise, interlocking those same elements of the

Thérèse Gahéry.

rectangular and the circular in the arches of the windows and the blind arcades on the squared-off wall surfaces. This re-enactment of the plan in the elevation, and *vice versa*, is a simple geometry of conviction, and one of great beauty.

The path runs north from Domfront through a more bubbly landscape, more authentically Norman in the depth of mud in its lanes. They are thick with it, framed by stone and turf walls which are sometimes three metres deep. This is Normandy made dense, and walking along these lanes gives you the extraordinary sensation of going under between the farms, like a breaststroke swimmer sinking his head during each stroke.

The GR itself bypasses Domfront, but you can join it again by going directly north from the town, over the Varenne and then up past the Château de la Guyardière. The Normandy landscape is concentrated into its manor-houses and La Guyardière, not an architectural wonder, but charming and typical in its understated, Tolstoyan gentility, becomes on a sunny afternoon the modest heart of the country around it. It is a landscape that speaks of conservatism – the châtelain absent in Paris and his tenants here still playing the same old parts – and the immobility is somehow reinforced by the hedged structures around you. One French writer on rural France, Albert du Cayla, has recently defined civilization as the state in which each individual can learn more about how to live from the past than he need contribute himself. Significantly, this definition also embraces a state of complete stagnation.

It is fourteen kilometres from Domfront to Lonlay l'Abbaye. The lanes are too narrow for tractors and there is no central green strip between the wheel ruts as there is in every lane in England. Here the daily passage of cows, home and back, ensures wall-to-wall mud. At the farm called La Heyère Bidard, a mile or two short of Lonlay, Mme Gahéry, pitchforking manure into a cart, asked why I didn't wear wellington boots like hers if I insisted on dragging myself through the mud

La Foissonière, near Lonlay.

of the *voies anciennes*. I explained about blisters (for which the French word is a lovely one, *cloques*), but even so she thought I would have been wiser to have them. How could I arrive at hotels looking like that, she asked, pointing at the greaves of mud coating my lower legs. A small black and white puppy was playing near her feet. It was no more than ten days old. I asked where the rest of the litter was, and smiling, not with cruelty but in a matter of fact way, she said she had drowned them as they were born. The total absence of sentimentality over animals (even pets – this was to be a house dog) is very striking in Normandy. Every farm dog is permanently tied up, families of rabbits are kept in tiny boxes conveniently near the kitchen door, even pigeons are caged to provide a pretty sound in the farmyard. Several times I saw cows with a short rope tied to one horn and to an ankle, with the effect of bringing their heads nearer the grass so that they would eat more and be fatter for market. To my eyes the sight of a cow with its nose next to the ground but not eating was as pathetic as a schoolboy still presented with the cold meal he has previously refused, but to the farmer it must be like a typewriter whose ribbon will not go round. To speak of a nearness to nature in this agriculture is hardly more than a comment on the small scale of it. These men and women (there is no sexual division in the work to be done) look after their animals no better than most of us look after our cars: with neglect until they begin to go wrong. Factory farming is different only in its efficiency.

You come down towards Lonlay where behind a screen of poplars the tall abbey church sticks out into the meadow. Go down through the small town (all rebuilt since the war) to the square in front of the church. This is the site of a long nave which was demolished in the sixteenth century; all that is now left are the Romanesque transepts and a fourteenth-century chancel. Beside them, like a country house, are the living quarters of the abbey. The church was battered in 1944 (in the hall are some photographs taken on the day of Lonlay's liberation, when the town was like a demolition site, with almost every roof caved in and rubble like a year's rubbish in the streets). From the outside the restoration appears rather insensitive, but the inside is beautiful. The main body of the chancel is entirely surrounded by an aisle that curves round the east end and back again. Narrow stone columns are all that separate the two parts, while above them the simple tracery in the clerestory windows throws rich giraffe patterns on to the high ceiling.

Lonlay l'Abbaye to Mortain
33 kilometres

You leave Lonlay past the modern biscuit factory where *les Sables de l'Abbaye* are cooked. The factory has big glass windows and you can see the whole process happening inside. The fields around smell like a Saturday kitchen – but it is a false dawn, and for the first five kilometres back towards the edge which you left at Domfront, the country is as hard and as unsweet as it will ever be. The stone is darker than yesterday's and February has never been more dismal than in these damp woods and farms. Everything is in the colours of a French map – grey-green, grey-yellow and grey – and everything affected by the poverty of the season. Even the cows here seem to have small and pig-like eyes. The leaves of chestnut and oak turn up white underfoot after a winter's bleaching and the spring seems permanently unavailable. The fields are boggy and the only attempts at drainage were dug some time ago – shallow ditches in a herring-bone pattern, now silted up and thick with moss. The farms themselves are more patch than substance, with corrugated iron the ubiquitous material. To imagine that in style these separated farms have ever been different would be blinkered. The farmers' ignorance of new technology and their dependence on methods which for centuries were sufficient, only seems inadequate now because the world around them has moved on. They are still, on their own terms, as good as they ever were. More *echt* materials than those now used might satisfy the tourist, whether he is on foot or not, but both now and in the past cheapness

Broussailles *collected from La Lande Pourrie.*

On La Lande Pourrie: a pragmatic history of adaptation and addition.

has been the governing factor. In that sense corrugated iron is more historically authentic than thatch, which has become an expensive affectation. The depth, regularity and thickness of the field and lane boundaries that grid the spaces between the farms here symbolize a history in the landscape which can be effaced only with difficulty.

Arrival at the edge will show you what you have been missing. From the gorse, broom and heather of the ridge you look out over southern Normandy – the real Normandy it seems, away from the harsh deprivation of La Lande Pourrie – boasting green fields and a black haze of trees, regularly dotted with timber and clay barns. Buzzards nesting on the high ground cruise for food in the richer pastures below and, although the path keeps above it all, you too might want to drop down on to the low ground. Stay with the ridge as far as Fosse Arthour, about nine kilometres from Lonlay. This is the edge of two departments, and you now move from Orne into Manche and, rather more hazily, into the Avranchin, the hinterland of Avranches.

Fosse Arthour is not, as its name might suggest, a ditch, but a series of waterfalls. This is the first hint on the walk that Normandy is a Viking place, since the Danish for waterfall is *fos*. There are several fosses in Yorkshire too but, unlike the north of England, it is difficult to associate this country of orchards with the Vikings. Why the Norse connection is cultivated in England but almost neglected in France is difficult to say. Certainly that was the pattern historically. In England the links of the Scandinavian invaders with their homeland remained very close – in the early years of the eleventh century Canute was King of Norway, England and Denmark. In Normandy, however, the Vikings who first raided the coast north of the Seine in 841 and who were on the borders of Brittany by the second decade of the tenth century, turned east and south to mix with and gain from the dominant Gallic culture, which itself had retained a great deal from the Carolingian

Barn near Le Fosse Arthour: the Norman touch is to put a new door on a building near the point of collapse.

The counterbalanced gate, pivoting around a mortice and tenon on the right hand side. The Second World War broke into this country of primitive technology in August 1944.

empire of the previous century. The Viking energies were subordinated, within the Norman state, to a sense of society and civilization that stemmed at heart from the Roman. This was the source of the Normans' startling expansive power, colonizing and civilizing England, Wales, Ireland and large tracts of the eastern Mediterranean.

In the thick pelt of country south of Fosse Arthour and of the ridge leading to Mortain, barns are built of closely studded timbers with the very yellow clay stuffed so carelessly between them that in places you can still see the builder's fingermarks on the unsmoothed lumps. Timber dominates. The gates have no metal for their hinges. Instead, an enormous log is settled across an upright post at one side of the opening, and by a mortice and tenon joint revolves upon it, the gate hung like a curtain on one side and on the other the stump of the tree acting as a counterbalance.

The Second World War burst into this country of primitive technology at the beginning of August 1944. After the landings on 6 June the progress of the Allied forces

through the *bocage* had been slow and, to all but the highest command, disappointing. But from the start Montgomery's plan had been to fight the battle of Normandy as one immense waltz-step, consisting of the landing itself, the consolidation of the beach-head and, eventually, a rapid break-out. In a stately *pas de deux* Von Rundstedt, the German commander opposite Montgomery, was dancing to the same time, conceiving of his defence in terms of a crust, a cushion and a final hammer. The most important phase for both sides was the consolidation and the cushion, when each would try to destroy the enemy's resources while building up his own. The Allies were hampered by having to bring everything across the sea, and by a terrible storm which destroyed one of the artificial harbours, or Mulberries, each the size of Gibraltar, that were anchored off the beaches. Nonetheless they managed to land two and a half million men and half a million vehicles in the hundred days after D Day. The Germans meanwhile were under the impression, carefully fostered by Allied propaganda, that the Normandy landings were merely a diversion from the main invasion across the Straits of Dover. Not until 17 July were the first of the divisions stationed there moved south to the real battle in Normandy. On top of this the almost total destruction by Allied bombing of the railway network and marshalling yards of northern Europe made any mass movement of troops very difficult indeed.

By 30 July this 'crumbling' phase of the battle, as Montgomery called it, was over and the Allies had won. The Germans were threatened with a break-out at both ends of the beach-head, either at Caen in the north-east or at Avranches in the south-west, and were so stretched that they were unable to reinforce one of these corners without weakening the other. This impossible choice made it clear to the German commanders on the ground that Normandy, and possibly the whole of France, would have to be abandoned if the military power of the Reich was not to be destroyed in the *bocage*. To Hitler at his headquarters in East Prussia this conclusion was nothing but disloyalty and, replacing Von Rundstedt and others with more amenable subordinates, he insisted on a vigorous defence of Normandy. This intransigence was the background to the battle's last brutal phase, fought along the line of the walk.

As you make your way westwards, on or below the hills leading to Mortain with the church spires of southern Normandy standing up here and there like flags on a golf-course to your left, you will be tracing the front line of

Near Mortain.

this battle, between the Germans in the woods on the high ground to your right and the Americans in the fields and farm lanes below them. You would never have imagined from the land's present appearance that anything of such a scale had happened. As I was walking along an ordinary lane about nine kilometres beyond Fosse Arthour, near a farm called La Prise Bizet, I met a man who was cutting down a small chestnut tree with an axe. Beside him, unused, lay a chainsaw. I asked why he was bothering with the axe, when the saw would have saved him so much labour. He explained that it had broken down, and then that it was made in Germany. He shrugged a little and pushed his cap back half an inch. He would have bought a French one, but not a single chainsaw was manufactured in France nowadays. I asked the obvious question; had he been here in 1944? His first answer was a short exhalation through pursed lips, but he expanded on it: ' I was twenty at the the time and of course knew that the Americans were coming. Everyone did, but no one knew exactly when. I got up one morning and went over to see a friend who lived over there,' and he pointed south-west between the apple trees. 'I was going along the path I usually went on, when suddenly I saw them – the Americans, they had arrived in the night, and I have never seen so many machines, so much metal piled up together like that – it was like Paris had been built in our orchards overnight.' This was disorientating enough, but the following day three German Panzers came down from the wood and parked, one to the right, one just above and one to the left of La Prise Bizet, from where they conducted a duel with the Americans only two or three hundred metres away. During it this man and his family cowered under the tables in the farm. Of course he now knew the grand strategy that they had been caught up in, but frankly, he said, he still found it impossible to relate those neat diagrams in the histories with the noise and confusion and shock he had experienced nearly forty years ago. 'War isn't really arrows on maps,' he said to me, and pulled his cap back down.

From near La Prise Bizet it is still nearly fifteen kilometres to Mortain by the GR, which curves over to the back of the ridge and up to the small village of Rancoudray before approaching, again indirectly, the hills overlooking Mortain itself. With all the detours you may find it difficult to arrive at Mortain before nightfall, but it is worth every effort to do so. Above the town a small chapel crowns the tip of a promontory called Montjoie. Here, pilgrims making their way to Mont St Michel would have got their first sight of the journey's end, still, even as the eye travels, thirty-four kilometres away. In 1944 this commanding view, to the south as well as to the west, made it a pivot of the battle. From here in the first few days of August, after the gap had been blasted at Avranches with 60,000 tons of bombs dropped in two hours by over 2,000 Fortresses and Liberators, the Germans watched the twelve American divisions pour into Brittany and southern Normandy. According to General Hausser, whose headquarters were on this hill, 'The road down the coast was a sight to see, sixty miles of traffic bumper to bumper, it rolled south night and day. By day it passed under a net of protecting fighters; by night it was lit with the flares dropped by the Luftwaffe.' As early as 2 August Hitler had decided to cut off these divisions with a massive Panzer strike towards the coast at Avranches. The plan suffered from three fatal drawbacks. It was seen to be grandiose and inappropriate by the German generals, who knew that Eisenhower could drop 2,000 tons of supplies a day to the armies Hitler hoped to cut off. The Allies knew all about the plan as soon as it was formulated because, through Ultra, they could decode every German signal. And, most important, the Germans could gather only 180 Panzers for the attack, a force which could not do the job properly, but which was called, nonetheless, the Fifth Panzer Army.

The attack was made in the early hours of 7 August. Montjoie, which had been taken by the Americans only the previous day and renamed Hill 314, was quickly surrounded, and by six in the morning the Panzers had advanced fourteen kilometres and were within nineteen kilometres of Avranches. Then as the sun rose the protective morning mist cleared and the Typhoon fighter-bombers of the RAF, equipped with rockets, were able to bring the whole advance to a halt. By the end of the morning 81 tanks had been totally destroyed, 54 damaged and 26 left smoking. It was the first time in history that a powerful land offensive had been completely halted by air action alone.

On Hill 314 it was by no means over for the American soldiers. The 900 men on the hill, together with a few farmers, were cut off for the next week. They soon became hungry and parched in the beautiful August weather, since the only water was from a well covered by German snipers and the only food was raw potatoes and cabbages from the fields around them. Looking out southwards they could see their compatriots beyond the German salient, and that sight, as well as the few medical supplies and wireless batteries that could be lobbed in by their own artillery, kept them going. On the night of 13 August the Germans at last withdrew, threatened by Patton's flying columns already at Argentan to their rear. The relieving force found only 352 Americans alive out of the original 900, surrounded, as General Bradley later paid tribute, 'by a wall of German dead'.

It is only a kilometre or two down to the centre of Mortain. The town has been entirely rebuilt since the war, except in the very centre, where the collegiate church escaped damage. It has a big Romanesque door left over from an earlier building on the south side, and a marvellous early thirteenth-century bell-tower, in a strict Gothic which has more to do with 1920s power-station architecture than anything Ruskin would have recognized as beautiful. On his tour of Normandy in 1848 he came to Mortain and was sorry that this granite could not take the detail possible in the finer Caen limestone that is used in the north. Here, in granite, Romanesque really becomes Norman architecture, the version of Europe that was exported to England in 1066.

From this bell-tower on 3 August 1944 the liberation was prematurely rung out by two American NCOs who had driven up in a jeep, neglecting the German artillery on Montjoie above them. Canon Blouet, whose church it was and who himself had hesitated to ring the bells for fear of reprisals, heard them after four years of occupation with a flood of relief. 'The deep, beautiful sounds,' he wrote after the war, 'filled the valley with a sacred, grave and solemn joy.'

Granite door in the church at Mortain. In this material Romanesque architecture becomes Norman.

Mortain to St Pois

31 kilometres

From the middle of Mortain go north for about two kilometres to the large black buildings of the Abbaye Blanche, a twelfth-century monastery named after the undyed habits of the Cistercian monks. Most of the present structure is a nineteenth-century addition in the style of a prison block, but alongside it is a short length of reconstructed medieval cloister with zebra stripe shadows thrown across its floor. The church, consecrated in 1206, is severe and cold, embodying the stripped ideals of Cistercian Christianity, hovering on the frontiers of the puritan and holding the difficult line between simplicity and mere restriction.

The Abbaye Blanche is on the edge of the steep little valley of the Cance, where the river drops down the Grande Cascade, once painted by Courbet. The path crosses below the waterfall, and after passing through the middle of Le Neufbourg (new in the eleventh century) comes to the Petite Cascade, which was painted in an altogether less masculine way by Corot.

From the Abbaye Blanche to Bellefontaine it is eight kilometres, all of it (after the cascades) in mud-thick lanes to be savoured by connoisseurs. Some of them are twenty feet from the top of the bank to the surface of the mud, with a semi-liquid foot or two below that before you reach dependable earth. It was over this ground (in summer) that the tanks of the Fifth Panzer Army made so much headway in August 1944, reaching Bellefontaine by one o'clock on the morning of the seventh. In the mud it will take you maybe as much as two and a half hours to get there. When you at last arrive you will find the welcome of a café and a shop.

Bellefontaine is a dispersed village, of a pattern which is typical of Viking settlements, but which probably derives here from being cut out piece by piece from the surrounding woodland. Here you are on the edge of a change of country. The path makes a tall loop northwards, reaching its apex at St Pois, over

The reconstructed cloister of the Abbaye Blanche in Mortain demonstrates the austere ideal of Cistercian beauty.

country that is underlain by rocks at least 600 million years old. They were broken into by large granite intrusions during a great mountain-building period between 580 and 550 million years ago. These pre-Cambrian rocks are not as hard as the slightly younger granite ridges between them, and they have been cut up into small hills and valleys that are worlds away from the sandstone and granite monoliths around Mortain. It is suddenly as though the lilo of the country had been slightly inflated, and as you turn up the small valley of a tributary of the Sée, the river which reaches the sea at Avranches, Normandy suddenly becomes Swiss – neater and less trammelled than before. But the Swiss neatness is improved by the French predilection for mess and there is none of the airlessness of Switzerland here. Great cabbagy primrose plants with leaves like lips hedge the lanes and the black streams. Wood

is everywhere, arranged in stands on the valley sides, in the sweet sappy smell of woodsmoke, in the repeated bite of an axe as it slows rapidly down into a log. Beside houses covered in silver oak shingles whole trees lie sliced into discs like *andouillette maison*, or into long slivers to be used untrimmed in fences. The style of gate changes from the primitive pivot on the farms near Fosse Arthour to a more sophisticated and familiar design, in which an extended diagonal bar reaches up at the hinge end to a high curving side-post.

The way climbs the nose of another granite intrusion. On the highest point of it is the rather uninteresting Chapelle de Montfort, but from there you drop quickly down to the valley of the Sée, meandering brightly in rattlesnake curves below you. As you descend, the small village of Brouains is to your right on the far side of the valley. Its church tower, like many in Normandy, is closed off at the top with no more ceremony than a carton of orange juice. There is a small shop but no café in the village.

You cross the Sée next to a closed-down sawmill with stacks of cut timber maturing in the fields beside it, and the path then turns to follow the river valley. The Sée, surrounded by poplars with dark polka-dots of mistletoe in their branches, performs the most spectacular meanders here. Why does a stream not head straight for the sea, but instead wander through its valley, doubling or tripling the distance it has to cover? The answer lies in the principle that water will be acted on by gravity only if no other course is available to it. By oscillating so beautifully the Sée is reducing its subjection to gravity and lowering the gradient of its bed to almost nothing. In other words the meander is the river's attempt to become a pond. It is an effort that will always fail because the river, as it eats at the outside of the bends and on the inside drops sands and gravels, reaches a stage of such baroque elaboration that the process short-circuits and water breaks through the swan's neck at the base of the curve.

You move on away from the river and up over the snakeskin hills divided into scales of

Logs sawn and separated to mature in the open air, near Brouains in the valley of the Sée.

green fields by black and regular lanes. Here and there lime has been scattered on the grass in dusty alkaline lumps and occasional patches of purple polyanthus look vulnerable against the shales and granites. In the farmyards wood is stacked to geological depths, rotting in the mossy pile before it can be burnt. The path drops steeply into the valley of the Ruisseau Pierre Zure, and then gradually comes back out of it to arrive at another big outcrop of granite. It is somehow appropriate that where granite is the base the human contribution to the landscape should be massively over-designed. Barns and houses are enormous and permanent here. Fences made of granite slabs stand like rows of tomb-lids next to the path. The delicacy of the hills after Bellefontaine has been replaced by something broader in the beam and harder. Boulders lie in the fields like slaughtered horses. A GR sign at a crucial turning in the hamlet of La Naizière was deliberately

79

The beech avenue leading to the château at St Pois brings the relief of organized landscape after miles of incoherence.

smeared over with mud to hide it (almost the only place in the whole of France where I have found this) and electric fences are strung across the path with enough current running through them to motivate a corpse. Soon after the horrible experience of walking into one of these I passed a woman carrying pails of milk from a wooden yoke across her shoulders and felt an urge to ask her about it, but one look from her squashed the idea.

About eighteen kilometres from Bellefontaine and only one or two short of St Pois the walk suddenly lifts itself. After many miles of country arranged by expediency you at last arrive at something done with a purpose beyond mere survival. This is a bit of seigneurial landscape, a curving avenue of beeches a kilometre long, planted about 150 years ago, to judge from the size of the trees, in a double row on either side. The low light slashes wide interference bands of shadow across your path, until nearer the château to which the avenue is hinged more beech trees, planted like hop-poles in regular quincunxes on either side, cut out any direct light and sink you instead in damp orange shadow. The château itself is confidently undistinguished, withdrawn and grey. It is now only a mile down the road to St Pois, a single street with a hotel, several shops and an ugly church.

St Pois to Genêts

50 kilometres

I began at the grocer's in St Pois. When it came to her turn, the old woman ahead of me in the queue said, without pointing, '*Un fromage.*' After it had been checked for softness with a thumb, she was given one of the unboxed Camemberts on the counter. In the same way that people never refer to their own village by its name, but only as 'the village', cheese in St Pois is Camembert. For the rest of the world, too, Camembert is the essential French cheese, so much so that twenty per cent of all cheese now made in France is called Camembert, while imitations of it are fabricated from New

Jersey to Japan. This world conquest began at the end of the nineteenth century when the famous chipwood box was invented (it allowed the cheeses to travel further than the earlier paper and straw wrapping) and was boosted in 1910 when the process of sprinkling the young cheese with penicillin was introduced, adding the soft white bloom to the rind and replacing the rather unattractive grey mould with which it had previously been coated. Camembert's shape – small and flattish with a large surface area in relation to its volume – is designed so that the micro-organisms that ripen it can reach the middle before the outside rots. This delicate and delicious cheese takes only four weeks to ripen, compared with the three months a Livarot spends in an unventilated room before it is considered ready. Almost certainly it was a Livarot that Mrs Ruskin was offered in 1848. 'They gave us the cheese of the country,' she wrote in her journal, 'and how the people eat it is a marvel to me, for it is small, made of cream and kept until it is in the last stage of decay with the most disgusting smell possible.' There is a story that in 1944 some American soldiers blew up a small building in Normandy because the smell coming from it made them think it was full of rotting corpses. They then found themselves berated by the farmer for the destruction of a whole batch of his Livarots, which had been quietly making their slow way to perfection.

It is four kilometres from St Pois to Cuves, a flat stretch back down to the valley of the Sée. Trees sprout on distant hills and mud is pasted on to the roads. The fields are damp and undrained: with good management they could reach the glutinous efficiency of the Fens, but at the moment they are no more than a paradise for mosses and frogs. If you have been slow in the morning, the midday angelus will ring out from the church in Cuves as you approach it, each stroke swimming into the next. There are two cafés in the village and a nice *boulangerie*, which has delicious apple turnovers called *chaussons aux pommes*.

For three kilometres south of Cuves you head back towards the granite ridge which the path left after Mortain. Covered in chestnut woods and with farms at the point where the hill elbows out into the valley, it bears an extraordinary resemblance to the North Downs. The way keeps to the ridge – on top, at its foot or between the two – as far as Avranches, still twenty-six kilometres away. At La Tullerie you pass close by a forge where the farrier links two or three of the heavy rims of old cart wheels to make harrows.

The path moves again into the woodland

The farrier at La Tullerie makes harrows by linking together the rims of cartwheels.

along deep ditches of lanes that exactly recreate the scene at the beginning of *The Woodlanders*. Normandy often has the aspect of a Hardy novel, of an England enriched or frozen, preserving 1860 in its corners. It is no coincidence that Roman Polanski filmed *Tess* in the lanes and fields of Normandy. The floor of these tracks is orange with dead chestnut leaves, the sky grey with chestnut trunks and between the two the lane banks are covered in a marvellous moss, cat's eye green, blazing in February. The way, occasionally blocked by unused branches from the annual fellings, at last arrives at the scattered village of Le Petit Celland, where the café/shop/petrol-station provides the first refreshment since Cuves. Shiny orange clogs were on sale in the shop, stacked in various sizes. I had seen no one wearing them on the way (one visible difference between Normandy and Brittany) and asked the lady who looked after the many-branched business if people still wore sabots here.

'Of course!'

'For Sundays?'

'No, for the mud,' she said, and gave me a huge red smile.

Only a kilometre or two beyond Le Petit Celland, after the path has made yet another dip down and up the ridge, you come on to the best set of tracks the way has yet made use of, dry underfoot, direct, grassy – the very image of an ancient ridgeway pushing westwards to the sea. The river Sée is still with it, down to the right, thick and brown now, without any splashing, except for the occasional gulp on a bend like an intestinal juice.

Progress is rapid along here, past well-kept farms and a water-tower like a giant golf-tee,

*Near Le Petit Celland. Normandy in February has a
clarity that is smothered later in the year.*

through the small village of St Brice, with its
spired church carefully placed on the hillside,
until the urban thickness of Avranches coats a
whole hill in front of you.

Avranches is the capital we have been
heading for. It was the scene of the Third
American Army's great breakthrough at the
very end of July 1944, and there is a massive
monument to Patton at the spot where he
stood, spruce as a fighting cock, a pistol on
each thigh, personally flagging the 15,000
vehicles and 100,000 men through to Brittany,
all in the space of three days. There is now a
bright, nearly metropolitan air to the town,
which commands the whole bay of Mont St
Michel.

From the nineteenth-century granite cathedral of Notre Dame les Champs, as auth-
oritarian as a cliff-face, go down to the Jardin
des Plantes from where you can survey the
end of the walk and make your choices. There,
distant and chart-like, is the great grey spread
of the bay with the granite plug of Mont St
Michel, like the symbol for a town on an old
county map. The GR 22 heads around the
coast to Pontaubault and then faithfully
westwards to its programmed end. But, for
once, indulge the pleasure of wilful ignorance
and instead swing round to the north, keeping
the magnet of Mont St Michel at arm's length,
even if almost always in view, and avoid the
terrible disappointment experienced (among
many others) by John Ruskin. He had been
misled by Murray's Guide, which had pro-
mised 'something mysterious and almost
awful in the aspect of this solitary cone of
granite.' Ruskin found a small town 'surrounded by a flat of filthy sand, channelled by
brown and stinking rivulets of slow discharge
– and spotted by fragments and remnants of
filth and offal and street cleansings.'

From Avranches it takes a gentle morning
to go the thirteen kilometres to Genêts along
the estuary of the Sée and then along the north
shore of the bay. You drop down from
Avranches and cross the river for the last
time, here in its final manifestation as a
concrete-grey tidal river, shuffling dully out
to sea. Beyond it and after passing through the
yard of some *trotteurs*, with their pile of steam-
ing golden muck, you are out on the edge of *les
herbus*, wide salt-meadows grazed by the sheep
whose mutton, a speciality of Avranches, is
famous for its salty tang. These meadows are
half land, half water and invisibly, like a
lung twice daily filling with breath, the
high tides soak them with salt water.

83

It is eight kilometres to the Pointe du Grouin Sud, a promontory of higher ground that sticks out into the *herbus* and conceals all but the tip of Mont St Michel's spire. Hauled up next to your damp path, or temporarily stranded on the hard, grey salt-mud, you will find a succession of small clinker-built boats of a beautifully clear design, coming to a point at each end like a cupped hand. These are the fishing boats of the bay. I met a man painting the gunwale of one of them, who told me the design came from England, and after a long search for the name came up with the lovely word 'wurry', which is really 'wherry' made French. These wurries (I also heard them called *dorices*) ride high on the water, in effect skimming it, making them manoeuvrable and very light to row. The oars have a long shaft and a narrow blade, like those on the east coast of Yorkshire and in the Orkneys and Hebrides, and in all four places the design is a legacy from the Vikings. Whether these lovely boats are themselves descended from the Viking *faerings*, and whether they are the most tangible link we have with the longboats

Near Genêts at the base of the Cotentin peninsula.

that conquered Normandy in the ninth century and England in the eleventh, is far more difficult to say.

At the Pointe du Grouin Sud, Mont St Michel appears in full, five kilometres away across the mudflats. There is something grossly immodest about its profile, like a hopelessly elaborated German helmet from the Great War. To the right is a little stunted repetition, a kind of parody of its splendour. This is the island of Tombelaine, which the English occupied in the seventeenth century as second best and where the remains of the fort they built for the wretched garrison can still be found, overrun by rabbits.

As you walk the last five kilometres to Genêts, past the occasional *dorice* drawn up miles from the sea in its private slipway, with the sky exaggerated over Dutch horizons, you will be able to witness the extraordinary and famous movements of the bay tide. At spring tides, when currents from the North Sea and the Atlantic meet, the water rises fourteen metres vertically and moves fifteen kilometres on the flat. Only one in three tides now surrounds Mont St Michel and in fifteen years the figure would be down to one in ten, if nothing were done. But commercial pressures are such that plans to build breakwaters are already in train, to ensure that for another few decades at least Mont St Michel remains, occasionally, an island. But whatever is done, there can be no doubt that in 150 years at most the Mont, like Mont Dol just over the border into Brittany, will be surrounded by land. Many think this a disaster, but the sea has invaded and withdrawn from this bay with dependable regularity for hundreds of thousands of years. Its most recent encroachment is a historical event and was recorded (ironically) as something of a catastrophe in October 709.

The time to be here is about an hour and a half before high tide. The sea will have slipped out earlier over small rapids in the mud, leaving bright water stripes between the tongues of grey sand where shrimp fishermen string out their nets. When the tide is down there is the constant noise, like distant traffic, of channel surf breaking on the bar nine miles away. The first sign of the approach of the new tide is the dulling of this sound as the tide comes in at about three or four miles an hour, visible as a creamy wake two feet high. Then, as the islands in the bay are gradually drowned and the grey landscape becomes muddy with water – it takes no more than twenty minutes – swarms of geese, pulling together and apart like wool fibres clinging and breaking away, move in towards Avranches, rustling the air beneath their wings like a stream. Every bird honks to its neighbour as they fly, until a shot from one of the *chasseurs* crouching in the *herbus* silences them all for a moment. Of the thousands of geese flying over, I saw not one brought down.

Genêts is a modest end to the walk. It has a few cafés in which Radio 1 is constantly playing, and a fourteenth-century church with a big barrel roof, but little else. There are two alternatives: either back along the path to Avranches, with its welcome repetition of all the morning's pleasure, or, if the temptation is too much, across the bay to Mont St Michel. The tides, sea-fog and shifting sands all make it lunatic to attempt this without a guide. Ask for M. Jugan anywhere in Genêts. He will lead you across in about three hours, starting from the promontory just beyond the village called Le Bec d'Andaine.

———

DISTANCES (in kilometres)
From Bagnoles de l'Orne to:
Domfront 18; Lonlay l'Abbaye 14; Fosse Arthour 9; Rancoudray 16; Mortain 9; Bellefontaine 10; Saint Pois 20; Cuves 4; le Petit Celland 18; Avranches 13; Genêts 13

MAPS
I.G.N. 1:50,000 Numbers:
1516 (Domfront), 1515 (Flers), 1415 (Mortain), 1315 (Avranches), 1215 (Mont St Michel)

GUIDE
Topo-Guide du Sentier de Grande Randonnée 22–22B, de Mamers au Mont St Michel C.N.S.G.R. 1978, Paris.

NORMANDY BOOKS
Michel de Baïard (editor), *Documents de l'Histoire de Normandie*, Privat 1972
E. Florentin, *The Battle of the Falaise Gap*, Elek 1965
Peter Gunn, *Normandy*, Gollancz 1975
W. G. F. Jackson, *Overlord Normandy 1944*, Davis Poynter 1978
J. G. Links, *The Ruskins in Normandy*, John Murray 1968
Nesta Roberts, *The Companion Guide to Normandy*, Collins 1980

Brittany

St Efflam to Douarnenez

209 kilometres

Brittany is as big as Denmark and this walk of over 200 kilometres does no more than clip one small corner off the peninsula. The size is important since it means that all the peculiarly Breton ways of doing things – of building churches, making clothes, eating, speaking and thinking – all these are not simply the charming mannerisms of a remote little *pays*, but in some sense *national* to Brittany itself. This peninsula is one of the few areas of France sufficiently big and coherent to have withstood the Parisian campaign to unite France waged since the seventeenth century. Balzac wrote in the 1840s that it was not necessary to go to America to see savages, 'The Redskins of Fenimore Cooper are here.' However concealed it might now be, the motive of the tourists here, or *kodakeurs* as they are called by the Bretons, is still the search for a primitive rusticity, or as the Michelin guide calls it *'l'originalité bretonne.'*

This country is different from the rest of France because it has had a different history. France is utterly soaked in a Roman heritage, but for Brittany Roman rule was only an imperial moment in a Celtic past. Like the rest of France it received its share of Celtic tribes in the Iron Age and yielded to Roman conquest in 56 BC, but except for about four decades in the ninth century Brittany remained independent of the French throne between about AD 500 and 1532, when Duchess Claude ceded it to her husband, François I of France.

The most interesting and formative phase of Breton history, still only partly known, is the change in name during the fifth, sixth and seventh centuries from 'Armorica', an old Gallic name meaning 'land facing the sea,' to 'Brittany', meaning 'land of the Britons'. The old orthodoxy was taken from Gildas, the British historian of the Anglo-Saxon conquest, who believed that the Britons, weakened by sinfulness and driven from their homes by a massive and destructive Saxon invasion, had fled overseas 'singing with loud lamentation beneath the swelling of their sails, not sea-shanties but the words 'Thou hast given us over as sheep for meats and among the Gentiles hast dispersed us.' On arrival they are

Metamorphic rocks on the Pointe de l'Armorique were transformed by the massive granite intrusions inland.

said to have fought the native Armoricans, winning the land from them.

For various reasons this account is not convincing. There is almost no evidence in British archaeology of a wholesale destruction by the Saxons, while evidence of continuous occupation through the fourth and fifth centuries is growing. Some Britons must have been ejected and some certainly went overseas – there was, for example, a British settlement in Galicia, northern Spain, in AD 569 – but sheer impetus from Britain cannot explain the scale of emigration to Brittany. Gildas's account would lead one to expect most of the immigrants to come from eastern England, where the Saxon pressure was most intense. Yet the Breton language is most closely allied to Cornish and not to the Celtic dialects spoken further east. Nor is it possible that Gildas's ragged bands of refugees could have defeated the organized Romano-Celts installed in Armorica, especially since the Saxons themselves had already tried to do so and had been repulsed.

There is a further strange anomaly which may point towards the right solution. Although the dialects of Celtic spoken in Brittany are from south-west England, most of the leaders were from Irish or Welsh royal houses. This illustrates the amazing coherence and interdependence within the Celtic world. Add to it the fact that there are few military stories connected with the coming of the

Britons to Armorica and that there are, on the other hand, tales of diplomatic negotiation and even of the legal purchase of land from its inhabitants, and the transformation of Armorica into Brittany takes on the aspect of a colonization at least as organized as that of the eastern seaboard of America in the sixteenth and seventeenth centuries.

Why did it happen? Western Britain may have been overpopulated; there was certainly a serious outbreak of plague in Devon and Cornwall in the fifth century, which may have forced people out. There may have been an invitation from Armorica itself, in need of repopulation after the many raids by the Saxon pirates and as a result of the Romano-Gallic population moving east. Certainly the Britons only colonized the western end of Armorica, and this is the origin of the tension between the two halves of Brittany, one Celtic, one Roman, which in a reduced way still persists.

Brittany and western Britain remained close. A tenth-century Welsh poem calls on Bretons for help against the Saxons, while in the twelfth century Gerald of Wales claimed that exactly the same language was spoken in both Cornwall and Brittany. Trade between the two was important at least until the sixteenth century and even in the 1800s pit props for Welsh mines were grown on the lower slopes of the Monts d'Arée. The special relationship eventually suffered as

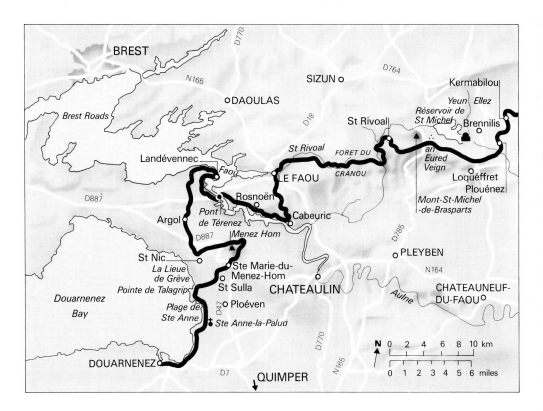

railway communications improved within the countries of which these were only the Celtic extremities.

The end of Breton consciousness has been forecast for 150 years or more. In the 1830s the young Jules Michelet, who was to become a great geographer and historian, paid a visit to a Breton bard in his hovel; 'I saw the poor old man lying back on a couch, with no children to look after him and no family, dying of fever between an Irish and a Hebrew grammar. He pulled himself together to declaim a few Breton lines to me, in an emphatic and monotonous rhythm, which was not, I must say, without charm. It was with a deep

compassion that I looked on this representative of the Celtic race, this man on the point of death harbouring a language and a poetry which were dying too.'

The separatist movement, begun in the nineteenth century, suffered a major setback in 1945 after its uncomfortably close association with the Nazis, but by the mid-1970s it had reasserted itself and in 1977 won some major concessions from Giscard's government, including the setting up of a Breton

Cultural Council and the teaching of Breton in the *lycées* and *écoles normales*. But the decline of Breton culture has reached such a stage that it is now more a question of reconstruction than of conservation, with the insurmountable problem that something to which one self-consciously returns cannot be the same, simply because one is returning to it.

A great deal of the Breton movement exists on the level of car stickers and folklore clubs, but it cannot be dismissed as trivial. A Breton organization called *Poing dans la Gueule* (Fist in the Face) has contacts with the IRA and in Quimper in 1976 it actually exploded a bomb. According to the PDG 'Brittany has been reduced to a training-ground for the army of occupation, a laboratory for the sorcerer's apprentices working on nuclear power, a tourist reserve and a reservoir of cheap labour.' But, sensational as this sounds, Brittany has not yet reached the plight of Bangor, let alone Bilbao or Belfast.

St Efflam to Huelgoat

73 kilometres

St Efflam is the perfect beginning. Get there on a windless wet morning, with the sea fog closing in on the sand, nobody on the beach and the Atlantic rollers pushing heavily on to the shore, and Brittany will be there in full. In 470, at the westernmost corner of the bay, an Irish prince called Efflam landed with seven of his countrymen. There to meet him was the most terrifying dragon in Brittany, which even King Arthur had failed to slay. But Efflam's countenance was so princely and so saintly (a familiar combination in the fifth century) that at the first sight of him the dragon threw itself into the sea and drowned. At the place of his triumph there is a chapel to Efflam and a well, roofed with a pretty stone canopy.

As you set off around the coast path, through the sprinkling of villas and the occasional puff-ball of a yellow mimosa tree, its colour reducing primroses to insignificance, you can speculate on the real meaning of Efflam's story. The dragon is of course the recurrent symbol of the forces of evil, but as a symbol it is peculiarly unspecific. The only hint of its significance in this story is that Arthur – the last defender of Roman values – had been unable to defeat it himself. It may well be that the story represents the final extermination by Efflam of a pre-Christian Celtic religion which the Romans had been unable – or had felt it unnecessary – to get rid of themselves. Roman Christianity had been

The sacred well at St Efflam is where Efflam, an Irish prince, cowed the Breton dragon which then retreated into the sea and drowned.

almost exclusively urban and the country people had continued under Roman rule with their old religion. The close association of rural with heathen still appears in the two words *paysan* and *pagan*, both stemming from the late Latin *paganus*, meaning countryman. The dragon's suicide when faced by Efflam may represent the voluntary extension of Christianity into the countryside precisely because the Celtic version brought over from Ireland was more congenial to the people of Armorica than the one propagated by the urban Roman hierarchy.

The ten kilometres around the Pointe de l'Armorique are very reminiscent of the Cornish Coast Path. Both of them climb and dip through gorse and the dark wet bracken. Both come across fields of early cauliflowers and artichokes growing on the sea-edge like transplanted sea-anemones. Both arrive at slate-blue bays banded by quartzite where the sand is poured between the stepped and shattered rocks like cream. Both were made in the early nineteenth century for customs officers to patrol the coast for smugglers. There is a single difference. On the Breton path now and then you find the concrete remains of gun emplacements, part of the so-called Atlantic Wall built by the Germans to oppose an Allied landing. It turned out to be an irrelevance as Patton's Third Army swept along the inland roads, taking only six days to cover the 320 kilometres between Avranches, where they had broken out, to the outskirts of Brest.

Through the small hamlet of Ste Barbe, its grey slate made even greyer by lichen, the path goes inland to Plestin-les-Grèves. You move past the new white villas on its borders,

on through the featureless sterility of bleak nineteenth-century houses, a ghastly combination of *Madame Bovary* and *Psycho*, finally arriving at the big, dark church in the middle of the town. St Efflam is buried here, commemorated by a statue of him with the dragon he cowed, but the outstanding objects in both church and town are the figures of the twelve apostles lining either side of the porch like the members of a committee, their serious, bearded faces reproducing Monet in old age.

From Plestin it is twelve kilometres to Trémel, through a landscape of neglect in which the modern fashion for electric fencing means there are no gates in any gaps, where ditches go undug and rubbish accumulates next to unused byres. For the whole time to Trémel I did not see a single person working in the fields, and the only activity centred on a pair of new houses with granite facings round the windows and breeze-block walls. The sullen, sodden taciturnity of the Breton countryside in February – *le mois noir*, as it is called – was one of the most forcible impressions left with the young Flaubert after his walking tour with Maxime du Camp in 1847: 'The mute landscape looks at you like a saddened face,' he wrote. 'It seems made for ruined lives and resigned sorrows ... On winter nights, as the fox glides over fallen leaves and tiles slip from the dovecotes, it is then, sitting alone by the last embers of the fire, listening to the wind howling down the sonorous corridors, that it must be sweet to draw from the bottom of your heart the despairs you have most cherished and the loves you have most forgotten.'

When the world appears unalterably depressed, walking has a way of pushing the

The Apostles in Plestin-les-Grèves: every one a Monet in old age.

The chapel of St Jagut near Lézormel: the unexpected pleasure in a sullen landscape.

pleasurably unexpected into one's path. After the scrap metal dumps of a garage, the Château of Lézormel appears over the fields to the south-east. Before reaching it you come to its little chapel. The tall triangular façade has a tiny *clocher* balanced on the top and at the very bottom a mousehole door, with uninterrupted grey granite in between. At the other end of a short avenue is the château itself, surrounded by empty barns with smashed windows, with a pair of cast-iron urns tilting on either side of the rutty drive. One wing of the main building is burnt out. The châtelain is a widower in his late sixties, whose wife died long ago in a car crash and who now lives alone with his daughter, behind the mossy stones of his half-ruined château.

Between Lézormel and Trémel the path meanders south-eastwards, making long detours from the direct route, first down into the valley of the Douron and then to the two *manoirs* of Trébriant and Kermerzit. Trébriant maintains the gentlemanly status it must always have had, but Kermerzit, built in the sixteenth century, is a sad disappointment. Contemporary with Chambord and Azay-le-Rideau, Kermerzit has failed to emerge from the Middle Ages. The gateway plays a small *jeu d'esprit* with a double pepper-pot tower, but otherwise the manoir is as sombre as the surrounding landscape. What makes the detour worth while is the degenerate state into which Kermerzit has sunk. Once quite grand, in a solid way, with even the occasional stone flourish around a door or window, it has now become a mucky farm-

A finesse rare for Brittany near Trémel.

The pale grey church of St Nicolas stands like a countess in a farmyard.

The new roof of St Nicolas.

yard where corgis slope out of corners to inspect your ankles. The preoccupied air of the current inhabitants preempts any inquiry. The corrugated iron scabs patching an old tower at the back and the blocked-in windows with glazing bars painted on them point to a Durberville history of carlessness and centuries of decline.

It is two kilometres to the village of Trémel and a further six kilometres to Plouégat-Moysan, over country that is more broken than before. Only two kilometres after Trémel is the best incident on the walk so far. In a small valley, where the river Yar curves out around a piece of flat meadow bordered by trees, is a church. If there was ever a village it has now gone and the church stands alone. You might expect a chapel, unadorned and rustic in such a damp corner, but instead this church is as fine as any in a market town. At the eastern end, as in many Breton churches, the nave divides into three, each branch with a steep gable, and with the tracery in every window spiralling into a rose. The west end, in another formula repeated all over Brittany, is surmounted by a row of open arches in which bells should be hung (there are none there now), with a staircase tower like a stumpy minaret clamped to one side. This rather clustered formation does at least give you the opportunity of climbing an unlit stairway to the roof, splayed out dark blue in front of you. Inside this marvellous building you will find that the roof is new, and when I was there the whole church space was filled with the moist, sweet tang of cut timber. The floor is of beaten earth and here the fifteenth-century experience of a Gothic church in its empty and beautiful newness is at least partly recoverable.

You push on to Plouégat-Moysan, where there is a café and a church equipped with a huge black pram on which coffins are deftly rolled in and out, but nothing else. Beyond it you cross the main Roman road from eastern Brittany to Morlaix, and soon afterwards begin to climb the first real hill of the walk. This Breton granite comes in two varieties, one with a fine grain and the other with large particles of older stone embedded in it like gristle in rough sausage. Above the rock the earth is the deep poisonous black of un-drained acid, with only brittle yellow grasses and gorse in flower growing on it.

The waymarks of the *Route de Grande Randonnée* have been very obviously obliterated or uprooted here. Local hostility to walkers has been roused recently by the loss of huge acreages of Breton moorland and forest in fires caused by tourists' carelessness. Between May and June 1978 over 4,000 hectares were destroyed. The resentment is understandable but the removal or deface-ment of signposts hardly seems the right way to prevent it happening again.

As you make your own way down the hedged lanes towards Guerlesquin, eight kilometres from Plouégat-Moysan, you will come across the first of the many standing stones on the walk which, along with Gauls in winged helmets, cider and *homard à l'armoricaine*, form such an important part of the Breton myth. These menhirs in various sizes can now be bought in horticultural stores all over Brittany as lawn ornaments, but this one, the Menhir de Guerlesquin, is authentically neolithic and has been standing here for at least 4,500 years, possibly as long as 7,000. It is just over six metres high, rough and slightly nicked on one side at the top. The most striking aspect of menhirs is the casual way they are positioned – not on the summit of a hill, or a meeting of two valleys or a great bend in a river but, as here, on a slight slope,

The seventeenth-century pavillon forteresse *in Guerlesquin dominates the sloping street and a nineteenth-century worthy.*

simply interrupting a line of barbed wire, as though the most ordinary setting was the intention of its erectors, an interestingly unhierarchical attitude to landscape. Explan-atory myths surround menhirs – this one is said to have been dropped one night by a witch in a fit of pique. But for us, the menhir's isolation as a fragmented signal from a forgot-ten code is irredeemably strange.

It is about four kilometres to Guerlesquin. On the way you will pass a small cross, said to date from 680, with the figure of Christ still faintly visible on the stone. Soon you enter the white outskirts of the town which boasts the most up-to-date chicken abattoir in Europe, with the infernal capacity to slaughter 80,000 a day. But Guerlesquin is lovelier than its proudest monument. It was founded in 1050 by a Welsh-sounding Breton, Ewen Gwen, and its situation at the corner of the three provinces of Trégor, Léon and Cornouaille ensured its prosperity.

The town is laid out as a long sloping market-place, tailing in at both ends like a canoe, and with good stone houses banked down either side. Lined up in its centre are the church, the market-hall and a tiny seventeenth-century prison, with four round corner towers stopping short of the ground and one small, easily defended door. The French for this unforbidding toy-like build-ing, *pavillon forteresse*, describes it exactly.

The old women in Guerlesquin wear wooden clogs, varnished black with black patent leather straps, indicative of the style of the place and the difference between it and the surrounding countryside, where it is referred to as *le bourg*. For the next fifteen kilometres, as far as Lannéannou, rural

Brittany is as hard-bitten and as solemn as it can get. Clogs in the country are worn for their insulation against cold and damp, encasing the farmers' feet like scuffed barges. As for the farms themselves, you are walking south and are always confronted by their north walls. These are windowless, turned against the cold wet winds coming from the north, and as you approach a hamlet your reception will be as cold as if you had entered the back of a theatre. The southern sides are far more open, with windows big enough to bring light to the far corners of the rooms, which of necessity stretch the depth of the house. Perhaps walking northwards would create a different impression of Brittany.

Ammoniac piles of muck are everywhere, either in the farmyards or being laboriously pitchforked on to the fields. Hay is not machine-baled but gathered by hand into loose-fringed haystacks, always on the point of collapse. Soon after crossing the river Guic I passed an empty house, prettily placed on its own in the valley, and on the path beyond it met the owner cutting trees. His parents had lived there, but when his father died a couple of years ago his mother moved *au bourg*. Not wanting to move from his own house on the other side of the valley, he left this one empty. I asked why he had not put it on the market, and his only answer was a kind of shrug.

It would be easy to think that a landscape as sombre as this would induce in its inhabitants a listless acceptance of circumstances. But according to Pierre Jakez-Hélias, the author of *Le Cheval d'Orgeuil*, a fascinating and often poetic autobiography by a Breton peasant who has experienced the changes of this century, mute acceptance of his environment is not the reaction of the typical Breton. He describes how the wind is nature's hardest agent here: 'The sea and the land are both subject to it; the men owe it all that is best in themselves. I don't think there is a single inhabitant of this area, either man or woman, who is not indebted to the wind – a west-north-wester or a south-wester – for that physical and moral exuberance which in Breton we call *startijenn*. Without it many of us would probably listen to the persistent voices of fate whispering to us, suggesting that we forsake all endeavours and sit under the gable of the house waiting for what may come. But the wind keeps us joyful and anxious.'

The path continues, with the occasional wide fronds of broom reaching out across it, past a pair of Bronze Age tumuli, the one covered with gorse, the other smooth. It keeps for the most part to muddy farm tracks, often very boggy, with dead vipers to be found on them, but regularly crosses wide tarred roads. It was on one of these that I waited while a huge double-trailered juggernaut boomed past me. Only after it had gone did I realize what it contained, as a few white feathers, sucked out by the back-draught of the lorry's progress down the road, floated slowly to earth in hesitant zig-zags, while half a day's cargo of 40,000 chickens was hurled onwards towards Guerlesquin.

About half-way between Guerlesquin and Lannéannou you cross the border of the *Parc Naturel Régional d'Armorique*, without a notice to announce it or any appreciable change in the country. This confirms the suspicions that are aroused by the shape of the park on the map – it has long thin extensions like an amoeba – that it represents more a bureaucratic decision than a geographical reality. It was inaugurated in 1969, at least as much to increase tourism as to protect the environment within its boundaries. M. Jakez-Hélias pours scorn on it. 'An Armorican Park has been created,' he has written, 'with entire farms restored to how they were in the good old days, which were not good and are not all that old. The whole thing smells like an Indian reservation.'

Lannéannou, after such a long slog through so much mud, is disappointing. There is a building with the notice 'Hôtel Restaurant' on the outside, but only bread and butter was available within, and even that at the cost of much muttering from the *patronne*. But beyond it Brittany improves again, with a more generous, rounded shape to the hills, and in the distant west the high summits of the Monts d'Arrée, where dark broken tors outcrop in the moorland grass. Paths are now cleaner and firmer, made in some places of pounded granite, and you can swing along where you only hopped and dithered before. This is much more the Brittany of large landscape gestures which its Celtic provenance should imply. Ten good kilometres' walking brings you south of Scrignac, signalled by a rare sight in Brittany: the church spire. There are shops, hotels and restaurants in the town, which the way bypasses to reach the valley of the Squiriou, following it almost as far as Huelgoat, nine kilometres away.

I did not hurry down to the valley. In one of the farms above it I knocked on the door to ask for some coffee. The couple who lived there were in their eighties, and their house had a gracious, friendly atmosphere. It was sound and clean, not elaborate, but equipped with a fridge, a gas stove and a television. They had lived there for fifty of their sixty years of

marriage. They had several times been to Paris and I asked if they had ever been abroad. 'Certainly,' he said, 'to Austria.'

'Why Austria?'

'It was during the war. I was taken there as a prisoner by the Germans and spent five years in a prisoner-of-war camp. My wife spent the whole time on her own here. We wrote to each other very often, and I got her letters, but she never got any of mine.'

There was a second home in their farmyard, newly done up and belonging to the son of the local landowner, while the red and white stripes of the *Route de Grande Randonnée* were liberally splashed across the yard. Neither of them expressed a trace of resentment at either of these invasions. Both had voted for Giscard d'Estaing at the last election, not for any community of interest, but because that *caste* of man, an aristocrat to his cufflinks, was in their eyes a born ruler. These gentle and generous people kept a herd of twenty cows, now looked after by their son, and the major change on the farm had been the introduction in about 1966 of automatic milking machines, which had transformed the drudgery of the woman's life to one of relative freedom and comfort. If there was to be any evidence in

Scrignac station in the valley of the Squiriou, trackless and trainless.

Brittany that the French language had not conquered every corner, it would surely be with people such as these. To my untrained ear the only sign that Breton was their first language was that occasionally one or other of them would fail to give a French noun its proper gender.

Another nine kilometres along the Squiriou is Huelgoat, following a deserted railway line which has been converted into a track for horse-drawn caravans, *roulottes*, which roll weirdly past the empty stations; the enamelled notices *Sortie* and *Consigne* are still fixed to the brickwork, but the station clock is now without hands. It is, of course, the flattest walking in the world, and fast because of it, but after a while the difference between your speed and a train's is detrimental to pleasure – incidents do not happen as quickly as you expect them to – and all you can do is push on to Huelgoat. The final approach to the pale grey buildings of the town is through a tall mossy pine wood and up the valley of a stream that curls round huge blocks of granite.

Huelgoat to Le Faou

54 kilometres

Nowhere is Brittany more ancient than in the filigree trees and pregnant granite around Huelgoat.

Huelgoat means the 'high forest' in Breton. It is in the middle of Brittany, surrounded by woods and famous rocks deep in the ancient forest of Brocéliande which once covered the central highlands and where the most retiring of Celtic wood-gods dwelt. There is nothing much of the ancient landscape left now. The pine woods around Huelgoat are all nineteenth-century plantations (the old forest was oak and beech). The town itself has gathered fringes of new white houses stationed round the lake, while *crêperies* fill the main square. An exquisite apple cider is the drink to be had in them, served up by the hectolitre to French tourists. For the English, cider is the product of the sweet, blossomy orchards of the south, but for the French it is a refreshingly naïve and northern drink, to be succumbed to when on visits to such remote places as Huelgoat. Proust loved nothing more than 'the bottle of cider drunk in the rough, cool kitchen of a farm.'

Above Huelgoat, on the pine-covered hill to the north, is the Camp d'Artus, one of the largest Iron Age camps in northern France. It has been claimed, rather oddly, that this is the site of Arthur's victory over the Saxons at Mount Badon in 520. The steep path up to it from the valley below Huelgoat goes through the pine wood between monolithic granite boulders, until eventually you arrive at the ramparts of the fort, 11 metres high in places, though greatly reduced from their original dimensions. They were built from stone blocks bound together within a timber framework, a kind of defence called *murus gallicus*. Caesar described it as one of the most effective he knew, and practically impervious to battering rams. This fort, covering 30 hectares, was excavated immediately before the last war by Mortimer Wheeler, who was hoping to find in Breton forts an ancestry for those in southern England. He failed to discover any connection. Instead, he concluded from its sheer size (which was far too large, given the poverty of the area, for it to have been the permanent capital of the local people, the Osismii) and from the single, narrow occupation layer, that it was the gathering place for a large number of people and their stock in time of crisis. The discovery of a single coin from the first century BC pointed to the Roman invasion of north-west Gaul in 56. In that year Caesar himself destroyed the power of the Veneti in southern Armorica, while his lieutenant Quintus Titurius Sabinus led three legions to victory against a confederation of tribes from North Armorica and Normandy, an alliance which would have included the Osismii. The south-eastern gate of the camp, Wheeler discovered, had been completely smashed soon after its construction. This demolition work was almost certainly done by Roman engineers to make the camp defenceless.

Only a kilometre beyond the end of the Camp d'Artus is the village of Kerampeulven. Hidden away behind some farm buildings is an amazing menhir, not as tall as the one near Guerlesquin, but smooth for its full height of five metres. It stands next to one of the natural granite boulders, in an obvious counterpoint of vertical male and brooding female, and if you examine the menhir you will find that it too was once attached at the corner to the mother rock, from which it has been chipped away. Very faintly incised on one of the faces are two little animals, a house and what might be a tree, all drawn in the most childish of hands. Such designs are undatable, but it is obviously an attempt to domesticate the menhir, in some way trying to emasculate its weird presence.

The ten kilometres from Kerampeulven to the small village of Plouénez is a passage almost devoid of landmarks. At one stage you pass an enormous new battery chicken plant, with red automatic feeders stacked outside and the carcases of inadequate performers tossed out among the rubbish. This is the middle of the Monts d'Arrée Parc Naturel and horizons are bigger and the dipping outlines of hills broader than they have been before. Here if anywhere you would hope to find the essence of Brittany. Instead the same wilfully undramatic rhythms continue. One's expectations of Brittany, I am sure, are derived at least partly from its place on the map, pushed out from the body of France into the Atlantic in an exaggerated meeting of continent and ocean. That the landforms themselves never fulfil that promise (except on the coast) is the disappointment of the place, ironed out as it is like Wales without mountains.

At Plouénez there is a ruined dolmen, or neolithic tomb. These megaliths bear no comparison with the single stone at Kerampeulven. They lie partly broken in a field next to an electricity pylon. After crossing a pretty stream three and a half kilometres further on, take a detour south from the path (which heads on westwards towards Loquéffret) towards the village of St Herbot, about three kilometres away. Before reaching it turn off towards the Château Rusquec. Ignore the warning *Taureaux méchants en liberté* and you will find yourself in a romantic and deserted near-ruin. Its romance lies in every part – the double gateway, the Renaissance doors and windows around the courtyard, the dovecote with granite blocks spaced between layers of slate, the curious cross-hatching of exposed timbers – all these remaining whole, while the whole of which they were part has collapsed. Isn't this the pleasure of ruins?

St Herbot, just down the road, is something different. Neither neglected nor restored, it is almost the first place in Brittany where there is evidence of a continuity in the care people have given it. Beneath a low hill crowned by beeches the few buildings of the village gather around an enormous and elaborate church. It has a Somerset air, and you will feel more welcome in St Herbot than in anywhere since St Efflam. The church is worth a close look. Cleverly, the square tower has been built half-way up the hill so that from one side it appears almost double its actual height. Below its near-perfect plainness the body of the church proliferates into a pinnacled and pavilioned extravaganza with small pointed turrets and ossuaries, all in a mixture of late curly Gothic and an unsure classicism. Inside there was a lady cleaning St Herbot himself. I asked if she could tell me when the saint had lived. She could not, but ventured that *en principe* his bones were buried below the effigy she was dusting, though of that too she was not entirely sure. He had been a hermit, she told me, who lived in the woods round here and in a Christian manner had been the friend of both wolves and cattle. I pointed out that his feet were resting on a lion and her only explanation was that lions probably lived in the forest at that time too. St Herbot's admirably eclectic patronage became more singular as time went on, and the medieval stone tables in the church were intended for tufts of hair pulled from cows' tails and brought here by the peasants to win the saint's protection against exactly such evils as wolves.

Outside the south door there is a calvary, typical of the great Breton school of religious sculpture (characterized by little stone figures

St Herbot: an elaboration in the architecture to compensate for the inarticulate landscape around it.

grouped together to form dramatic tableaux) which flourished in the sixteenth and seventeenth centuries. This calvary is a modest example, but the inclusion of human and emotive beings at the foot of the cross removes it from mere symbolism and translates it into a human event, easily comprehensible to the Breton peasant.

From St Herbot as far as the foot of Mont-St-Michel-de-Brasparts, nine kilometres away, the path skirts the great boggy depression known in Breton as *Yeun Ellez*, the Hell Marsh. It is a convenient irony for anyone with anti-nuclear sentiments that this great bog, one of the traditional mouths of Hell, which would devour any sinner who dared tread on it, is now the site of a nuclear power station and of the artificial lake needed to provide water for its cooling system. It has been here since 1966, but not until 1980 did a major confrontation occur (still talked about

with admiration in Loqueffret), when two coachloads of demonstrators from Paris were discouraged from anything too demonstrative by the sight of several battalions of CRS riot police formed up within the electronic gateways. Nonetheless several layers of anti-nuclear posters continue to clothe many of the prominent surfaces in the area.

As you tramp on along the good gritty track surrounded by gorse and heather, the buildings of the station and its chimney stand out alien against the surrounding moorland, which is mottled yellow and brown like the surface of a *crêpe*. You will pass a tiny menhir, about one and a half metres high, with a rubber *niveau général* clamped to it like a plug near the bottom. Further on, as you approach the round brown hill of Mont St Michel topped by its small pilgrimage chapel, you pass yet another megalithic monument, hidden unless you look for it, called *an Eured Veign*, the Stone Wedding. It is a short alignment of unshaped stones, but the explanatory myth (a fascinating if particularly joyless example of the Church's ability to turn local features to its own use) says that it is all

Stockpile of the essential resource in the Forêt du Cranou.

The perfectly restored (and empty) farmhouse at St Rivoal has drawn scorn from Breton nationalists who see it as an idealization of a difficult past.

that remains of a wedding procession which refused to bow down before a priest bearing the Eucharist wafer, and which as punishment was petrified on the spot.

The way passes to the south of Mont-St-Michel-de-Brasparts and continues westwards on a good dry path over the moorland, before threading through a pine wood and emerging on to a lane leading to the village of St Rivoal, five kilometres from St Michel. There is no doubting that you are in remote Brittany here. This village was the last stage on earth before the soul of a sinner sank hellwards in the great bog to the east. Every building is made entirely of slate, including the inevitable *crêperie*.

As you leave St Rivoal you pass the best thing in it, a farm built in 1702 and immaculately restored in 1968 as a sort of museum for the park. Along the ridge of the roof is a series of figures, each one cut out from a single slate, including the dates of building and restoration, a fleur-de-lis, some hearts and a whole menagerie of local animals – a stoat, a pig, a cow, a horse and a cock. The windows have no glass in them, only wooden shutters, and not a single piece of metal is used in the construction. It is all in chips and flags of slate, and oak pegs are used to hold the carpentry together.

The walk from St Rivoal to Le Faou, where the path meets the sea again for the first time since St Efflam, is twenty-four kilometres. You move off along the deep wooded valley of the St Rivoal river (it is a significant distinction between English and French habits of mind that in England places are often named after the river that runs through them while in France rivers are named from the places they run through) and then up across another strip of lion-skin moor before plunging into the marvellous Forêt du Cranou. For six kilometres the path runs through this beech and oak forest. The occasional holly finds a space between them, but for the most part the big forest trees stand in a dominant and perfect geometry. This is a 'climax vegetation' and there can be few places where the reality fits the term so precisely, embodying the incredible vitality of natural growth.

In Le Faou, a village with the air of le bourg.

As you make your way down to Le Faou, through the farmland that separates it from the end of the forest, the rock changes to red Devonian sandstone, the tracks rouge up underfoot and the unexpected gaiety of the mimosa appears again in the farmyards. The town itself is hinged at right angles to the top of a long arm of salt water lined with an empty quay. There used to be constant traffic in all kinds of necessities between Brest and Le Faou, with boats coming up on high water, settling on the estuary mud while they loaded and unloaded, and slipping out again with the next high tide. New roads to Brest destroyed the sea trade before the Second World War, and grey salt mud now gives the place a permanently derelict air. The street that leads from it is much more lively. Its slate-hung houses, each storey jettied out from the one below, have the pretty feature on the top floor of a kind of inset arch under the gable. Many of the slates are patterned, and the best are on a house at the top of the street, where each has been cut into a playing-card club.

Sunday lunch is the time to be in Le Faou. It is a moment of communal indulgence. In one

Le Faou: gift wrapping.

Slate-hanging in Le Faou.

hotel alone, the Relais de la Place, there were about 250 people in several dining rooms partaking of the 75 franc menu. I was seated between two old men, one a retired policeman who never laughed but whose eyes watered silently from time to time to indicate mirth, the other a retired teacher. I said I was amazed at how many people there were to lunch and the policeman agreed. 'The French eat too much,' he said and we all nodded. Only then did it emerge that the two of them ate there every day, one because his wife had died, the other because his wife was too ill to cook for him. The idea of him cooking for her was simply not acceptable. Breton had been their first language and they still spoke it between themselves. I asked if there were any people left who could speak only Breton, and they agreed that if there were, it would be *à la campagne*. (Le Faou is enough of a *bourg* for that phrase to make sense.) Even then, certainly not among their own contemporaries (they were both about seventy), but perhaps among *les vieillards*.

Le Faou to Landévennec

30 kilometres

A single ridge separates Le Faou from the deep valley of the Aulne, the great salmon river of western Brittany, whose name is really 'Avon' made French. Leave Le Faou to the south and climb towards the top of the ridge marked by television masts. A freezing south wind filled with hail was blowing when I was here. It slowly grew colder and more uncomfortable as I approached the crest of the ridge, until by the time I reached it my whole face ached with cold. Then, as I began to drop gradually down into the shelter of the valley towards the small collection of buildings called Cabeuric on the river's edge, the warmth began to return.

This stretch of the walk, not always down by the Aulne but following its wide deep valley westwards, is the prettiest (or at least the most Poussinesque) part of Brittany. Here there is an arrangement in the landscapes of woods, valley-sides and farms, in comparison with which the rest of the country appears *ad hoc*. It is eight kilometres to Cabeuric from Le Faou, and then about fifteen along to the great suspension bridge over the Aulne called the Pont de Térenez. On the way there you will find herons flopping lazily away from the reed beds, still cut in places and bundled for thatch; yachts oddly parked between hedges until you notice that a finger of the estuary has

In the valley of the Aulne, Brittany becomes its most acceptably pretty.

The Pont de Térenez over the Aulne replaced another destroyed in 1944.

The door of a small chapel at Folgoat near Landévennec.

crept up into the fields; rich brown ploughed fields stencilled out from the alluvial green and blocks of pines in squadrons. On the far side of the river is the dark bulk of Ménez Hom (the name means the 'worn-down mountain') which is the last great geographical monument on the walk, an intractable mass of ancient Ordovician rocks.

Once over the bridge, a replacement for the one destroyed in 1944, you are into the parish of Landévennec, which is still seven and a half kilometres away. In a sense, Landévennec is the goal of this walk. It is not only a peculiarly beautiful place, where the Aulne, before stretching out into Brest Roads, curves back on itself to make a doubly protected and warm corner of coast, lush in exotic vegetation. It is also, at least partly because of these favourable conditions, a place where the early Celtic history of Brittany and of its connections with Celtic Britain come to a point.

It is something to look forward to, but the walk along the estuary of the Aulne is not to be hurried. Like the Helford, the Fowey, the Yealm and many other rivers on the south coast of Cornwall, the Aulne here is a ria, or a river valley drowned by rising waters at the end of the last Ice Age about 10,000 years ago. In the thickness of vegetable growth on its shores and the damp warmth that such luxuriance always conveys, the two countries are here at their most indistinguishable. On forest paths you curl round small creeks where yachts stand on their keels at low tide, and past a chapel at Folgoat, which has a charming modern door carved with a kind of irregular tracery inspired by the interlaced branches of forest trees. Finally you round a corner to find, huddled in the shelter of the hook of land on which the abbey stands, a

graveyard of ships, one a rusting naval corvette, waiting for sale or for scrap.

Landévennec means 'the monastery of dear Gwennec', the nickname of St Guenolé, one of the great men of fifth-century Christianity. His parents, who with three of his siblings were also made saints, originally came from somewhere in Britain and settled near St Brieuc on the north coast of Brittany. When he was twenty-two, after six years' study, Guenolé came to this the most sheltered spot on the whole Armorican coast, where palm trees grow protected by the steep river banks, to found his monastery. It prospered, and in a reversal of the whole colonizing process churches were founded in Britain dedicated to Guenolé or Gwennec – at Llanwnog in Powys and at Gunwalloe and Landewednack, both on the Lizard peninsula in Cornwall.

But the history of Landévennec has not been sheltered. In the early ninth century Brittany was conquered by Louis the Debonair, the son of Charlemagne. Until that moment the monks here had followed the Celtic Rule of St Columba, in which they included the celebration, on 1 November, of the ancient Celtic feast of Samhain. On this day, marking the entrance to winter, the usual barriers between men and gods were suspended, and the ritual had been cosmetically Christianized as the Feast of All Saints. In 818 Louis, the son of the Holy Roman Emperor, forced the monks to abandon the Celtic Rule and adopt the Benedictine. This they did, but insisted, as one of the few concessions, that they retain the celebration of Samhain.

The abbey was destroyed by the Vikings in 913, and the Romanesque buildings which replaced it were themselves ruined during the French Revolution. There is a new abbey now, built in 1958, but go down to the remains of the old one, which are damp and untidy with cacti, aloes, agaves and bunched brambles flourishing in the special climate. It is worth poking round them for the two statues of Guenolé, one standing episcopal and lichened against a wall, and the other supine, with his head slightly higher than his toes as if he were reclining on a chaise-longue. Even in ruin the whole building speaks of a regular Benedictine propriety, until you notice at the west end a pair of capitals. These, like the Feast of Samhain preserved amid the less magical Benedictine practices, are carved with the exuberance of the Book of Kells, in a jungly intertwining of serpentine coils, the single reminder of Guenolé and his remote Celtic connections.

Landévennec to Douarnenez

52 kilometres

Leaving the villas and palm trees of Landévennec you move westwards along the front of the peninsula that faces the Brest Roads. The path stays above the sea for five kilometres, with the Roads broadening beside you, until after a long tongue of sand stretching out into them, called *Le Sillon des Anglais*, you turn inland again. The village of Argol is seven kilometres away, and when Flaubert and Maxime du Camp covered this stretch they found it *'une mousse rousse'* underfoot. Nowadays the way is almost entirely on stony tracks, coated here and there with a thin layer of grass. It is said that the land here is still some of the best in Brittany owing to the improvements performed on it by the monks of Landévennec. But as you make your way between the gorse and bracken in the lane-banks and climb in and out of sharp little valleys, it is hard to see this Brittany as different from the rest, or to reconcile any idea of rural gaiety with the permanent mud and wet of agricultural life here. The pleasure of summer in these farms and hamlets must be the enjoyment of a simple rarity.

Argol, a village of about 800 people, is ranged entirely around a triumphal arch leading into the churchyard. It is the best piece of classical architecture on the path, built in 1659 out of the local orange sandstone, which has natural whorls of a darker red looped within it. The arch itself has fluted pilasters, miniature bell-towers and, in the centre above the main arch, a small statue of King Gradlon, the mythical king of Cornouaille and of Is, the city which once occupied the Bay of Douarnenez. A folk-memory of the rising sea at the end of the Ice Age created the incomparable city of Is, which was drowned when Gradlon's daughter made love to the devil. The aged king was saved by his magical horse, and he is always represented mounted upon it. It is an animal partly descended from the Celtic horse god (famous in the form of the Uffington White Horse) and in some way connected with King Mark of the Tristan and Isolde story. *Marc'h* means horse in Breton, and it is significant that here the badge of the apostle Mark is a horse, not a lion, as it is everywhere else in the world. In the Argol statue, Gradlon's mount, in a miniature but magnificent example of the great equine gesture of the Renaissance, bends his neck down towards his chest in a tight and muscular arch. Even as late as the second half of the seventeenth century there seems to have been no difficulty in displaying such a pagan figure so prominently on the entrance to a churchyard.

It is eleven kilometres from Argol to the top of Ménez Hom, 330 metres above sea-level. The way is through a neatly folded landscape and small villages where tell-tale cleanness shows up holiday homes. The earth is an extraordinarily livid purple in the fields around the foot of the mountain, but Ménez Hom itself is brown and soft in outline except for a few outcrops of grey rock. The lower slopes are decorated in a strangely African way with single, spreading pines around which you expect to find a pride of lions and its kill. As you climb, the views to the west, south and north expand, until from the top, in good weather, there is a panoramic view – across the valley of the Aulne to the Monts d'Arrée behind it, Brest Roads and the Crozon peninsula to the west, and in the south the wide bay of Douarnenez, the first sight of the walk's end.

The path trails off the mountain to the east, arriving four kilometres later at the hamlet of Ste Marie du Ménez Hom, where there is a bulbous baroque chapel and a three-part Calvary in the graveyard. All the dark stone is coated in damp, green weed. A key from the café opposite will let you inside, where there is a sumptuous carved screen behind the altar.

There are only seven kilometres left to the sea, across wide swoops of farmland, divided into large fields and sustained by a strangely marine swell. The view from Ménez Hom showed how this western side of Brittany meets the ocean like two sets of fingers interlocking. The sea has difficulty in eroding the hardness of the Ordovician layer, and outcrops form promontories like the Crozon

peninsula, around which the sea excavates deep bays.

You arrive there at last – it is the beginning of the short final stage to Douarnenez – and find an incredibly beautiful width of sand in front of you, with long ribbons of distant breakers hauling themselves on shore. The enormous beach has a lovely name – *La Lieue de Grève*, the 'league-long strand'. Seventeen kilometres remain, partly on the sands, partly over the rocky promontories that separate them. The whole of Brittany points west, and to end here on this western shore is marvellous. You will be able, I hope, to ignore the fungus of villas that has sprung up on the seaside, indulging the impulse to gaze out to sea with a constancy that dulls the excitement of reaching the shore. For the young Flaubert his arrival here after too many miles of inland fields prompted a great overflowing of exotic speculation: 'Nothing stops here. Thoughts now run as fast as the wind and spreading and rambling and losing themselves on the ocean meet nothing but the swell; then, at the heart of it, truly in the heart of it, over there on the

Ribbons of breakers from the Bay of Douarnenez haul themselves on to La Lieue de Grève – the league-long strand.

dream horizon, they come to a wave from America, or perhaps from some islands still unnamed, some country where savages and humming-birds and red fruit are ... or to a wave from the great cities lit with coloured lanterns, or Japan where the roofs are of porcelain or China with its open stairways and pagodas with their gilded bells.'

The shore is an international place. There is none of the culture that has been imposed over many centuries on the fields inland. A marsh blocked off by a pebble storm-beach is the same here as it is in Pembrokeshire. Only the associations differ. The spire of the church in Douarnenez is visible long before you get to it, a beacon marking steady progress towards the end. Almost the only interruption, and you may be reluctant to make it, is a visit to the isolated church of Ste-Anne-la-Palud, shielded from the acid sea-winds by dark conifers. It is the scene of one of the most celebrated *pardons* of Brittany when, on the last Sunday in August, tens of thousands of people gather here. Ste Anne was a local girl transported to Nazareth by a team of angels to save her from the brutalities of her husband. There she gave birth to the Virgin Mary and was soon brought back to die in Brittany. Jesus came to visit his grandmother and made the barren rock spout water at the point where there is still a sacred fountain.

Douarnenez is a convenient end from which both trains and buses leave for Quimper, the city founded by Gradlon after Is had been drowned in the bay beyond. Douarnenez is famous for its shellfish, picked up with creels set among Gradlon's flooded halls. It is the place to have a final celebratory *homard à l'armoricaine*, lobster in a rich cream sauce, a dish whose history in a way epitomizes the ambiguous nature of Breton self-consciousness. Lobster prepared like this originates, in fact, in Provence. In about 1860 it was adopted by a fashionable Paris restaurateur, Noel Peters, and called, for reasons of chic, *à l'américaine*. Only in about 1915 did a M. Austin de Croze decide to call it *à l'armoricaine* and foster the rumour that *à l'américaine* was an ignorant corruption of the truth. Having one's own kind of food, as M. de Croze realized, is a long way down the road to being a separate community. A remark of Ernest Renan, the nineteenth-century historian, caps it: 'To forget, and, I will venture to say, to get one's history wrong, are essential factors in the making of nations.'

DISTANCES (in kilometres)
From St Efflam to:
Plestin-les-Grèves 10; Trémel 12; Plouégat-Moysan 6; Guerlesquin 8; Lannéannou 15; Near Scrignac 10; Huelgoat 12; Plouénez 12; Loquéffret 5; Mont St Michel 8; St Rivoal 5; Le Faou 24; Cabeuric 8; Pont de Térenez 15; Landévennec 7.5; Argol 12; Ménez Hom 11; Ste Marie du Ménez Hom 4; Lieue de Grève 7; Douarnenez 17.5

MAPS
I.G.N. 1:50,000 Numbers: 0615 (Plestin-les-Grèves), 0616 (Morlaix), 0617 (Huelgoat), 0517 (Le Faou), 0417 (Brest), 0518 (Châteaulin), 0418 (Douarnenez)

GUIDES
Topo-Guide du Sentier de Grande Randonnée No. 34 Tronçon des Côtes-du-Nord
Topo-Guide du Sentier de Grande Randonnée No. 380
Topo-Guide du Sentier de Grande Randonnée No. 37
All published by C.N.S.G.R., Paris.

BRITTANY BOOKS
Nora K. Chadwick, *Early Brittany*, University of Wales Press 1969
Gustave Flaubert and Maxime du Camp, *Par les Champs et Par les Grèves*, 1847
Pierre Jakez-Hélias, *Le Cheval d'Orgueil*, Plon 1975
Alan Houghton Brodrick, *Brittany*, Hodder and Stoughton 1951
Jack E. Reece, *The Bretons against France*, University of North Carolina Press 1977
Keith Spence, *Brittany and the Bretons*, Gollancz 1978
Mortimer Wheeler and K.M. Richardson, *The Hillforts of Northern France*, Society of Antiquaries 1957

Limousin & Que

rcy

Uzerche to Vers

160 kilometres

From the mountains of the Massif Central the rivers of south-western France cut rapidly west and south-west between the wrinkled hills of Corrèze and through the thick limestone plateaux of the Lot before slowing up in the vine-encrusted plains of the far west. Across this between-land, neither mountain nor lowland, the *Sentier Limousin-Quercy* takes a direct course to the south from Uzerche on the Vézère to Vers near Cahors on the Lot. It is a land that has been graphed by its rivers and the path in the course of about 160 kilometres crosses or follows the Vézère, the Corrèze, the Couze, the Dordogne, the Alzou and the Vers before finally arriving at the Lot itself. This is Aquitaine, the Roman province and the English duchy; the name means the land of waters, but the rivers are only the veins in a body which is, for the most part, high and waterless. For a week or so they form regular stage-marks on your journey south.

They are necessary markers. To anyone used to living in a narrow island in which the nearby coast gives an immediate set of coordinates, central France will seem vast. The beginning and end of any French walk away from the coast or the boundary mountains is destined to be arbitrary. Instead of the pleasure of domination, of knowing that you have walked from coast to coast or traced a major landform, you must indulge instead the luxury of submission. There is no possibility of satisfying an appetite for conquest here – there are no great climbs and the gradients are gentle – and you must leave yourself open to a different kind of pleasure. The *Sentier Limousin-Quercy*, especially in its southern half, is best taken as a drift through a landscape and a rural society which is unarranged and almost without structure. Karl Marx realized that 'the great mass of the French nation is made up of a simple addition of units bearing the same name, just as a sack filled with potatoes forms a sack of potatoes.' Nowhere is that more true than in Quercy, but with the added virtue that nothing in this unhierarchical society is valued more highly than the cohesive and gentle qualities embraced by the three adjectives *gracieux*, *serviable* and *brave*, which might be translated

Madame Soulier's favourite goat.

as affable, obliging and decent, all of them ringing the one word 'courtesy'. No walker could wish for more.

Uzerche to St Viance

35 kilometres

You begin at Uzerche in Limousin, high above the river Vézère, which curves round it in a flamboyant U-loop peninsula to the north. But the Vézère is almost irrelevant now to the town which is dominated by the N20, an arterial road full of trucks joining Paris and the north with Toulouse and Spain. The old part of Uzerche is islanded to the west of the road. It has a couple of bookshops selling postcards of cows emerging from mists but no local maps. Further up are many restored mansions from the Middle Ages and the Renaissance almost all of which, in this town that has been labelled 'La Perle du Limousin', have been given an air of alert antiquity. Uzerche's reputation and motto in the Middle

The Vézère at Uzerche, the first of the many rivers of Aquitaine that graph the walk.

Ages was 'Never Sullied', relying as it did on its unassailable site on the steep riverside, but that independence has now gone, sacrificed to through-traffic and the Syndicat d'Initiative's self-conscious sense of history.

Only at the top of the medieval town, where you can look out over the deep bend in the river, will you find a memory of the old Uzerche. The highest part of the steep slope down to the river has been carefully shaped and tended into small gardens, boasting young lettuce and hoed into weedlessness. This horticultural care within the town wall was the medieval image celebrated by Gaucelm Faidit, one of the greatest of the twelfth-century troubadours and a native of Uzerche. After years away at the Crusades, he wrote, 'it pleases God that I should return with a joyful heart to the Limousin I had left in sorrow. I must thank God deeply since he has brought me back safe and sound to this country where a little garden is worth more to me than all the riches and luxury of a foreign land ... The springs and clear streams, the meadows and orchards, they bring a lightness to my heart since everything here is good to me.'

Below the old town and edging on to the N20 is the Hôtel Bellevue, which is open all year. Judging from its clientèle when I was there, Uzerche is now wide open to outside influences. At the bar, regularly downing shots of Ricard, were some *pieds noirs* and a woman (with several teeth missing and a complexion like the Puy-de-Dôme) who claimed to come from Limousin but who everyone reckoned from her accent to be either Algerian or a gipsy. The *patron*, with a head like a Citröen Déesse, continued to wash up the glasses impassively as the attempts to prove the origins of the would-be Limousine became increasingly bawdy and rowdy with it. His indifference was matched only by that of the local drinkers. One woman, accompanied by an Alsatian dog who gazed at her lovingly throughout, had reached that stage of solitary drunkenness where the effect of each remark, as it worked its way down through the layers of the brain, was plainly visible on the features of her face. It would reach the intended destination, register, and the reply, once settled upon, would then begin to make its slow journey back up into the audible world, where it would surface at last as a slighly incoherent and muzzy burp. Once this was delivered and a new input received, the process would begin again. The brighter section of the gathering went on with its investigations unabated, taking no notice of the rest of us as we drank, ate and stared beside them.

Leaving Uzerche, you will find there is the sharpest of frontiers between the N20 and the country it passes through. You set off to the south and for a kilometre or two keep close to the main road, if not actually on it. Then the path breaks off to the south-west through a different country of grassy meadows full of cows like Jerseys, with their dark eyes and eyelashes, but more like Guernseys in their size and the milky brown of their coats. Almost every piece of land that is not wood is given over to pasture, which is left unsprayed and flowery. You will find yourself trampling underfoot whole forests of orchids, each one of which would be protected in England for its six-inch-high pagoda beauty, but which here in abundance can be treated as weeds. It was May and, as I was told when I reached Vigeois, nine kilometres from Uzerche, it rains in May. And although the downpour was not continuous there was a permanent dampness in

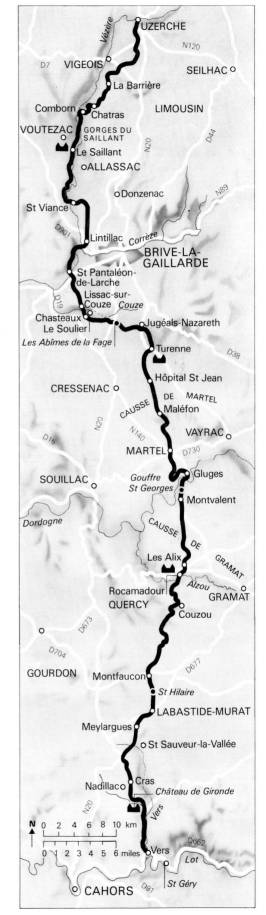

the warm air of these woods and meadows, as though I was walking through the fog of a laboratory culture specifically prepared to nurture mould. Walnuts, fruit trees, poplars and chestnuts all grow thickly around the farms and hamlets. Among the branches that have been cut or have simply fallen from the poplars you can find the ideal walking stick.

For Arthur Young, the professional agriculturalist who travelled all over France just before the Revolution and reported on what he saw in a way that often recalls Cobbett, these woody hills and valleys were the most beautiful that he knew. He had admired what is now the N20 as it left Uzerche as 'the finest road in the world, kept in the highest preservation, like the well-ordered alley of a garden, without dust, sand, stones or inequality, firm and level, of pounded granite.' As for the country itself, he was 'much in doubt whether there be anything comparable to it in either England or Ireland. It is not that a fine view breaks now and then upon the eye to compensate the traveller for the dulness of a much longer district; but a quick succession of landscapes, many of which would be rendered famous in England, by the resort of travellers to view them.' But, like Cobbett, a place was not good enough for Young if it was not properly productive, and the reliance of the people in this district on the chestnut ('the exact transcript of the potato in Ireland') and their failure to grow maize with which to feed their cattle disheartened him. He often passed the 'extraordinary spectacle for English eyes of many houses too good to be called cottages without any glass windows' and while the men wore both shoes and stockings the women and children usually had neither.

The landscape around the path between Vigeois and Comborn, ten kilometres further, has scarcely been disturbed since then. The places you come to – La Barrière, Le Theil, Chatras – are each a little bigger than the one before, but there is no real dividing line between farm, hamlet and village. Instead, there is a coherence both visual and functional, a sense of gradual accumulation with time, as sons have simply built next to the farms where they were born. The way never pushes straight through one of these hamlets, but is forced to curve carefully in and out among the houses and barns. These places are arranged not with a view to travel through them but to a life within them. The immediate effect on your own progress will be too many corners and an increased terror of dogs around them.

In La Barrière, despite a new roof of asbestos slates and a big new Massey-

La Barrière.

Ferguson tractor, half the buildings are empty and on the point of collapse. The roof of the largest house has developed the tell-tale cant which shows the *charpente* – the wooden framework supporting it – to be rotten underneath. It is impossible under the Code Napoléon to leave the family house to only one of several legal heirs, and if a single family is to continue living in it, all other claimants must agree to be bought off. Notoriously, families find it very difficult to make such agreements and while they squabble amongst themselves a fine old house, sometimes full of furniture, will rot into ruin. This may well have been the fate of up to a third of the ruins you will come across. But overriding all this is depopulation, now the controlling factor of the French countryside, at least in the south. Where 35% of the French people worked on the land before the war, this has now dropped to 13%. (It is worth comparing that figure with the 4% that do so in Britain and the 8% in the United States.) The reality of this is often loneliness and bachelorhood for those left behind. The suicide rate among farmers is higher than in any other profession in France, reaching the unhappy and hardly believable peak of one suicide in every nine farmers between the ages of 36 and 45. It is not difficult to pop the myth of the rural idyll.

You arrive above the gorge of the Vézère, Amazonian in the thickness with which the trees crowd the river edge, and find above it on the far side the ruin of a castle with a newer smarter château hooked on to the end. You drop down to the river, cross it and climb back up the far side. The oldest parts of the castle were built in the tenth century as the headquarters of a semi-independent fief which rivalled Limoges itself in the southern half of Limousin. This steep dense valley was the scene of almost continuous conflict until the thirteenth century when some kind of authority was finally established.

It is nine kilometres down the gorge of the Vézère to Le Saillant, on the edge between these slaty hills and the plain around Brive. The castle at Comborn has an entourage of *résidences secondaires*, their neat gardens strung out along the top of the ridge. There is an underworld darkness to the path along the forest gorge. The river, once a continuous, abrasive fall, has been tidied by hydroelectric works into a staircase of lakes and dams. Alongside it, filleting the valley in a spectacular piece of engineering that shoots the trains straight out of tunnels on to viaducts, is the railway from Limoges to Brive. It was finally pushed through here in 1893, eighteen years after the parallel route through St-Yrieux-la-Perche had already established the railway link. Can this line have been mere bravado?

As you come down from the hills towards Le Saillant a different world is spread before you: flatness and fertility, a blond plain of barley and wheat on the rich red sandstone that stretches from here to Brive. Le Saillant itself is in good shape with only one or two empty houses. As I sat down and ate my *pain au chocolat* next to the pretty bridge over the river an old man sat down next to me. He looked sourly and silently at the river for five minutes before showing any sign that he wished to communicate. It then emerged that he was a Parisian who had moved down here when his wife died, as his daughter had married a Limousin. He hated it. It was not the countryside itself – that meant little to him either way – it was the people. They would not talk to him. 'Les rustiques, they don't know how to behave,' he snorted. Was there anything that made it tolerable? 'At least,' he said with genuine pleasure, 'the mayors of all the villages near here are communist.' I looked around me, at the dignified château withdrawn behind high walls and the village deferent beside it, and did not immediately recognize a communist landscape. I asked about the château. 'Ah, the château. It so happens that the sister of Giscard d'Estaing lives there.'

'And does Giscard himself ever pay a visit?'

'Of course not, he doesn't need to. Don't you know he has four or five châteaux himself? They call him *la reine de la France* round here.' The Parisian, in a comprehensive bracketing of the political spectrum, had voted for Chirac in the first round of the Presidential election and Mitterand in the second. He claimed it was common enough

Henri Rose of Le Saillant, the descendant of an English soldier who came to defend Aquitaine in the Middle Ages and stayed.

among the local farmers, a simple *anti-Giscardien* gesture.

I set off across the plain for seven kilometres to St Viance. On the edge of Le Saillant, walking back into the village from the fields where he had been working, I met the medieval figure of Monsieur Rose, splendidly equipped with a huge crow-beaked scythe that would have graced a *danse macabre*. He was much gentler and more open than the Parisian. 'Do you realize,' he asked me with a smile, 'that the only reason I am called Rose is because of you English? No proper Frenchman would be called that – I'm a descendant of one of your English soldiers from the Middle Ages.' How true this was I could not say, but we shook hands to the memory of Eleanor of Aquitaine who brought this part of France to the English throne in 1152 when she married Henry Plantagenet, soon to be Henry II. Between then and 1453 the frontier between French and English possessions moved regularly back and forth across this countryside in a series of victories, treaties and treacheries. The people, one can be sure, cared only about the amount of tax levied, and hardly at all about the nationality of the exchequer it went into. Nonetheless, there is a residual, and perhaps necessary, French myth about it, that in the black moments of English occupation *'quand les lèvres avouaient les Anglais, les coeurs les répudiaient.'* Monsieur Rose and I have now made it up.

It is a gentle tramp to St Viance, most of it through buttercup meadows next to the river. There are one or two small vineyards and orchards of peach trees, even a tobacco field on the way, but most of it is through wide open fields. There are hints, with such a prestigious neighbour, that this has become an up-market area, with spreading lawns and swinging bench-hammocks under yellow striped awnings, as well as some spectacular new towers with pointed roofs. All of them add *standing*, the portmanteau franglais word that estate agents, ski-boot manufacturers and swimming pool salesmen all now use to indicate class. But in among these embellishments are the remains of what it was like before. The red sandstone, laid down about 200 million years ago, comes in two colours, either a very light pink or an opulent red, the colour of raw steak left too long in the air. The local habit has been to cut the stone into great blocks which are then bound with a mortar complementary to the colour of the rock itself. In this way you will find dark barns lightly gridded in pink and, often next door, their tonal opposite, with pale walls meshed over by a darker mortar.

St Viance is all built of this sandstone, some of it almost pure grey. The saint himself was a seventh-century hermit who performed more miracles dead than alive. His most famous act (it was a posthumous one) was the summoning of a frost solid enough to freeze the Vézère and allow a cart and its horses to drive over. In memory some horseshoes are pinned up in the porch of the church. There are all kinds of hotels, restaurants and shops in the village, which marks the edge of Limousin and Périgord.

St Viance to Turenne

34 kilometres

As you make your way south for the twelve kilometres to St Pantaléon-de-Larche on a track that keeps to a slight ridge between the Vézère and a little stream called the Clan, the influence of Brive, visible to the south-east, spreads into the countryside. The earthy or stony track is occasionally coated in tar and at one point you have to pick your way through a new housing estate. All this is plain enough: Brive, at the meeting of five railway lines and at a crucial crossing point of the river Corrèze (*briva* means bridge in Celtic) has become the commercial centre for the whole region and needs its dormitory suburbs. What is more interesting is the rural rhetoric of advertising that has leaked out with the commuters. There is a brand of garden seed on sale in these semi-urban villages called '*Le Paysan*'. It concentrates on the earthier plants, the turnips of this world. An enormous billboard occupies the entrance to a neglected field advertising

the new Citroën Visa with the symbol of an apple into which the Citroën logo, a pair of chevrons, has been carefully incised. Beneath it are the words '*La Qualité*', aiming to tap the virtue that is attached in our minds to that fruit. It is unfortunate for Citroën that almost all of the apples now grown on the plain around Brive are the American Golden Delicious, which have an unrivalled shelf-life but when it comes to taste are notoriously low on *La Qualité*. The growers themselves make a point of keeping one tree that produces the genuinely French, more perishable and genuinely delicious Reinette apples for their own consumption.

As you approach St Pantaléon yet another billboard advertises one of the new housing estates with a beautiful picture of a flock of sheep (not a house in sight) and printed over it the legend: '*Vivre au pays – c'est vivre. Vraiment.*' No one needed to be told that in La Barrière. The way crosses the Vézère, now gravy-thick with the silt it has pulled from the plain, just at the point where it runs into the Corrèze, another mountain river that was once uncompromising in its erosive force but has now slid gently into the sluggish obesity of a plain life. Once merged, they move off southwards together like a pair of company chairmen ready for lunch. You come to St Pantaléon-de-Larche (where you can get your own), the last of the red sandstone towns with a church which is at least a thousand years old and looks it. Here too you can inspect the *lavoir* built over the spring where the saint slipped as he stooped for a drink, hitting his head on a stone which, when rubbed briskly with a pebble, is said to produce a stream of blood with magical qualities.

The path now begins to climb the steep hill called Puy Gramont, over clay and the remains of last year's leaves. It is slippery and tiring, and almost the only entertainment is the regular appearance among the litter of some beautiful slugs, the colour, coincidentally, of the dark sandstone you have just left. As I was searching for another of these, I looked up to see a dog like a Dobermann Pinscher and its cylindrical owner, both of them bounding towards me. '*Il est méchant?*' I shouted, the standard question. '*Mais oui, bien sûr!*' he laughed. Only after the joke had been played was the dog restrained. It then turned out not to be a Dobermann at all, but a Bosseron, also known as a Bas Rouge. They are not at all ferocious, the man told me, despite their enormous bark, and in fact are very clever and gentle with sheep, cows and goats. The key to identifying them is the long tail; Dobermanns are almost always docked.

From the top of the hill, 350 metres above sea level and 250 above St Pantaléon, where there is an expansive view back over the plain of Brive, you drop quickly down to Lissac-sur-Couze. There is a pretty manor house at the top of the village and at the bottom a cemetery where the graves are half-hooded by their own greenhouses, decorated with iron scrollwork, like truncated versions of a railway terminus. Beneath them, on the bed of the graves themselves, the fashion is to crowd little marble books laid open at a page saying 'Regrets', 'Nous n'avons que nos souvenirs' or even 'A Notre Chauffeur.'

Passing an artificial beach on the shores of an artificial lake (made by damming the river Couze) with an old mill standing isolated in the middle of it, you are soon at Soulier Chasteaux, seven kilometres from St Pantaléon-de-Larche. The village fills the mouth of a tiny gorge where the Couze and a smaller tributary run out together into the valley now filled by the lake. It is the first outcrop of the limestone to which the way now sticks, uninterrupted, until Vers.

Turenne: the Hollywood image – of castle and houses trailed down from it – for once fits the reality. Turenne was an independent fief until the eighteenth century, raising its own taxes, minting its own money and boasting its own private nobility.

Streams are divided and channelled among the houses, islanding small garden plots between them. The buildings are old, with generous hipped roofs and against one of them, like digestives at a tea party, six fat mill-stones have been stacked, iron-bound and fuzzy with moss and ferns.

It is fifteen kilometres to Turenne. As you begin to make your way up the floor of a narrow valley, you reach a milky pool where the Couze resurfaces after a short passage underground. There is a tablet next to it to the memory of a pot-holer lost on 2 August 1970 while making 'une plongée souterraine'. By the pool itself a board announces that no one can explore the underground Couze without permission. It is dated 10 August 1970, a week too late.

The valley is dry beyond it. A narrow strip

of cleared land winds up between desiccated, stunted oaks and junipers like limp-wristed yews, with clover and trefoil thick around them. One or two fields have recently been cleared from the wood, with the scrub stacked like middens on one side. Mixed in with it are the limestone flakes that are picked up from each field, old and new, every spring. In sterile parody of the spring itself the earth sprouts them each year like a five o'clock shadow, churned and turned up by the winter frosts.

Past the point on the map called La Perte de la Couze, where the stream falls underground in a plug-hole spiral between mossy rocks, past a quarry and the N20 on its way south from Brive, and after the uneventful ruins of a château, you come to Les Abîmes de la Fage. Some of the most spectacular limestone caves in Europe are to be found in this part of France and many of them, like this one, are open to the public. Only here, where access is easy, can you get an idea of what lies beneath you on your way south to Vers. The limestone plateaux over which the path runs (they are called *causses*) are riddled with tunnels and adits, with reservoirs, lagoons and cascades which have been dissolved by the water in a system linked as intricately as the middle of a sponge. The earth's surface is no more than a fan-vault stretched tightly over them. It is easy enough to slip into the time-worn Gothic analogy for these caves and their huge accretions (who is not bored at the prospect of yet another Cathedral Cavern?) but the association is more than just a visual one. Gravity is the only physical force which can create the grotesqueries of a limestone cave – it is drip-architecture – which nonetheless assume the most weightless of forms. In the same way a manipulated gravity will alone sustain the spring of a Gothic vault, whose entire aesthetic purpose is visually to defy it. These caves in every way occupy a strange, amphibious position. Here, nature is both florid and sterile; the rock it seems once effervesced and teemed into jungly uncontrolled forms, but has now sunk back to the monotonous and uninterrupted tapping of drops from the roof. Algae and a few tiny plants grow in the electric light, but otherwise everything is dead. No place is so visibly in the process of either becoming or decaying; one cannot be sure if it is unfinished or rotten. In a few years it seems Les Abîmes de la Fage may well have been clogged or dissolved out of existence.

Eight kilometres on a slightly switchback course through woods and over meadows brings you to Turenne. Half-way, you skirt the village of Jugéals-Nazareth which was founded by Raymond of Turenne on his return from the first Crusade. He built a lepers' hospital, administered by the Knights Templar, and you can still visit the caves where the sick were quarantined. Four kilometres further, on a self-contained hill which controls the valley of the Tourmente, you come to the source of the money and the charitable impulse. This is Turenne, arranged in a perfect Hollywood image of a towering castle capping a hill, the dependent town trailing from it. It is a pretty place, with the walls all in limestone and the roofs in ordinary grey slate. Of the 150 houses all but 20 are now holiday homes and the permanent human population is easily outnumbered by the hundreds of snails to be found all over the castle. They are enormous, luxurious creatures which are, unfortunately, too rubbery to eat.

Turenne's history matches its appearance. From the early Middle Ages the Vicomtes de Turenne enjoyed a kind of independence from the state that in England had not survived the Norman Conquest. Controlling an area of over 1,200 villages, they minted their own money, raised their own taxes, sold off their own sinecures and created their own nobility of sorts. This nobility was housed in Collonges la Rouge, just to the east, a village built especially for them in the local red sandstone and consisting entirely of castles to ensure that nobody was jealous. The rights of the Vicomtes remained unaffected until an eighteenth century incumbent sold them to Louis xv for 4,200,000 *livres*, to pay off his debts. Almost certainly they would have gone earlier if the sixteenth-century Henri de Turenne had not been Henri of Navarre's chief lieutenant in the fight for the Protestant cause and the French throne; or if the greatest of them all had not been Louis xiv's most brilliant general. Even though he remained Protestant throughout his life, his service to the Catholic monarchy, from 1645 until his death from a cannonball thirty years later, guaranteed in large part the hegemony of Europe that his king required. To Henri de Turenne is attributed the cynical saying, understandable enough in the light of his career: 'Dieu est toujours pour les gros bataillons.'

Turenne to Rocamadour

39 kilometres

Turenne is only two kilometres from the boundary between Corrèze and the Lot. The change is more than just an administrative

Turenne, where six out of seven houses are now holiday homes and empty most of the year.

one. On your way south to l'Hôpital St Jean, five kilometres from Turenne, you get the first full-strength taste of what these limestone plateaux, the *causses*, mean. The stony paths are coated in places with a kind of reddish clay, which more often than not has been rippled like sea-sand by the hooves of the sheep which are driven backwards and forwards over them, night and morning. These sheep, called simply *brebis de causses*, are distinctive with their small black and twitching ears, two deep black lobes around the eyes, and a Roman nose. For their pasture, fields are cut from the low dry woodland – as near to Bahamian bush as you will get in northern Europe – so that from the air, or on a map, the land is pitted with them, like the miniature craters eaten into limestone slabs by centuries of rain. The human contribution to this almost skeletal landscape can only be intermittent, subject as it is to dryness and to the poverty of the soil. Strung between the random fields and farms – occasional remarks in the quiet of it all – is a network of lanes. One historian of Quercy has called them the '*lignes maîtresses du terroir*', the framework within

which human life on the *causses* must always have worked.

On these lanes (and to follow them is to know the essence of the *causse*, its moss-thickened stone walls and the brittle lushness of its dense dry woodland) you will come to l'Hôpital St Jean. On the edge of this one-street village I met a farmer and his wife standing in the middle of the road. She wore a pair of new glasses, each lens the size of a television screen, and he had a *papier maïs* cigarette, wet and mottled with nicotine and tar, stuck permanently to his upper lip. Both of them spoke in the accent of the south in which consonants stiffen into a fossilized rasp and a word like '*sûrement*' comes to rhyme with 'tang'. Their dog, called Bobby, sat by looking at us with one brown and one blue eye, an asymmetry which for some strange genetic reason most of the working dogs of Quercy are blessed with. She gave me a walnut from the tree shadowing the southern side of her house, which was delicious, oozing oil as I bit it. I thanked her and asked if people still found truffles here in an area that was once famous for them. The question tapped a vein and for the next ten minutes, in a litany that alternated praise and complaint, I heard the recent history of the fungus. The woods

The ewes of the causse *are famous for their Roman noses and black eyes and ears. They are the inescapable presence on the walk – the paths you follow were designed for them and every surface is rippled by their hooves.*

over to the west were once full of truffles but had been over-hunted with sows who became increasingly *perspicaces*, she said, and now they were almost gone. You could still tell if an oak tree had them attached to its rooots as it would begin the year slightly faded, its juices already sucked out by the underground parasites. But these truffles were more than average, they were *truffes grand cru*, and I was standing in the heart of their champagne country. Sadly, though, as the quantity began to drop a few years ago people began to mix the local products with inferior kinds from Spain and as soon as even a small proportion of the foreign variety was introduced the exquisite *parfum* was lost. 'Can you imagine what it's like,' she asked me, with her hands held out, palm upwards, 'if you even begin to dilute Bordeaux with Algerian?'

Her story of the improved rooting abilities of the sows was unfortunately not the true one, but the real history of the truffle in the last hundred years is nonetheless fascinating. It had always been part of the communal rights for any man to search for truffles in the woods with his trained sow or more rarely with a dog – which had the advantages of being able to travel further in a day and of not wanting to eat the truffle once it was discovered, but the disadvantage of paws that were less durable than trotters in the digging. It was an undatably ancient search and the mythology of the truffle is related to the deepest experiences of earth-given fruit. To present a friend or neighbour with a truffle is still considered a binding and significant gift, but only if still encased in the earth in which it was found. To give someone a truffle that has been washed is an open insult.

This ancient pattern was disturbed, or at least extended, after the phylloxera epidemic of the 1870s, which destroyed nearly all the vines in Quercy. Rather than planting the new, phylloxera-resistant and expensive vinestocks from California the Quercynois viticulteurs replanted their vineyards with *chênes truffiers*. It was an act of extreme patience and courage, since nine or ten years must pass before one of these oaks gives birth to its underground fruit. But then, between about 1880 and 1914, came the golden age of the truffle. Nearly 2,000 tonnes were produced in France 1889, 360 of them in the Lot and 160 in the Dordogne. The crop was extremely valuable: 40 kilograms were worth as much as a cow.

The hunting of the truffle was man's work, and the removal of men in the First World War dramatically lowered the volume gathered each winter. It was the initial impetus needed for an accelerating decline. The rural exodus that followed the war meant that the old knowledge needed to maintain the crop was not passed on. Truffles need light and a well-turned earth to flourish, but in the 1920s and '30s the ground over the fungus-bearing roots was no longer hoed annually, nor were branches for firewood cut from the trees themselves, and the shade beneath them deepened. The clear, stony fields and plantations of a few years earlier had tempered the potentially disastrous effects of late spring frosts by storing the heat of the day in their stones well into the early night, but, as the brambles and undergrowth began to invade the untended land, humidity gathered over the soil and the effects of frost were exacerbated. As these changes in the micro-climate reduced the number of truffles available, the persistent search for them resulted in a sort of over-fishing, so that by 1971 only 40 tonnes were produced in the Lot and two and a half tonnes in the Dordogne. Given that, the search is by no means dead, and a well-trained truffle-dog can still be sold for as much as 2,000 francs.

It is twelve kilometres from l'Hôpital St Jean to Martel, the capital of this block of *causse* which stretches as far as the river Dordogne. It is not the habit of the *caussenards* to gather together in social clusters. They have distributed themselves evenly over the available land and at regular intervals you will come upon their independent homesteads. It is not a communal society, nor are there any large estates. Instead, each of the farms establishes its own kind of nobility with an architectural gesture which is common to them all, but to which each particular farm has given its own interpretation. This is the *pigeonnier*. Pigeons have always been kept in France, partly for food (the very young birds, before they have even flown, are the tenderest) but much more importantly for their droppings, which are so rich in nitrogen and other nutrients that unless they are spread on the fields during a shower of rain (at least according to the sixteenth-century agriculturalist Olivier de Serres) they will burn the seedlings instead of nurturing them. In the north of France, where most of the land is grouped in large estates, the *droit de pigeonnier* was a hated privilege of the gentry – the birds would come and plunder the peasants' own tiny plots – and in 1789, less than a month after the storming of the Bastille, it was abolished. In the south, land has always been divided up between the children, and the smaller farms that have resulted (sometimes drastically smaller – Arthur Young came

The webbed charpente *of the market-hall in Martel supports a vast tonnage of limestone* dalles *which weigh 800 kilograms a square metre.*

across one in Quercy that consisted of a single peach tree) have brought a far less efficient agriculture, at least in financial terms, but a fairer society. The *pigeonnier* in Quercy was a symbol which almost everyone could display. The practice began in the valleys, where no other animals that could provide the manure were kept, and from there spread up on to the *causses*.

Sometimes the *pigeonnier* is simply a punctured wall, chequer-boarded with slots, one for each pigeon. From there they accelerate in elaboration, through no more than a dormer window in the attic space to the free-standing towers crowned by high finials, which are said to attract the birds back home, and the additional refinement of a stubble of tiles or slates standing proud of the roof itself, intended as personal shelves where pigeons can rest on the way in and out. Quite often the towers are tacked on to the main farmhouse and you would be forgiven for thinking at first that Quercy was extraordinarily full of churches with fat naves and stubby bell-towers. Only when you notice that the tower is perforated like a pepper-pot will you realize

that here, repeated over and over, is the Quercynois' statement of individuality and pride.

It is a fine afternoon through the *causse,* with the occasional sound of chainsaws in the distance, and past farms in which buildings are almost never joined together – the farmhouse, the *pigeonnier*, the barn, the granary on short rat-proof stilts, the *fournil* (a building where the dough is prepared and baked into eighteen-inch wheels of *pain de campagne*, in an oven roofed with limestone slivers called *dalles*) – all stand apart from each other around a small farmyard, with occasionally the great green roof of a chestnut holding the whole place together.

Sometimes Quercy is like a language made up only of auxiliary verbs, but Martel is different. It is a coherent, composite place arranged around its beautiful market-hall, built in the eighteenth century and with a webbed *charpente* supporting a huge country

121

The growth of the soil, near Martel.

estate of a roof. The town is said to have been founded by Charles Martel, Charlemagne's grandfather and the saviour of Christianity, a year or two after he had defeated the Arab army outside Tours in 732, pursuing them south into Aquitaine; somewhere near here he annihilated them. Certainly nothing of that era survives now. The church is a great fortified block from the fourteenth century decorated with Romanesque sculpture and surrounded with large *hôtels* from the late Middle Ages, when the town's prosperity depended on the lords of Turenne, of whose fief Martel was one of the chief ornaments.

It is six kilometres to Gluges on the Dordogne. You leave the outskirts of Martel through a strung-out housing development *à la Quercynoise*, built in the precisely informal way that makes it look like an excerpt from a planner's catalogue, *style du pays* by the metre. You soon escape into the *causse*. The dip of the Dordogne appears ahead, while the verges around you are rich with honeysuckle, creeping thyme, bladder campion, butter-cups, vetches, big daisies and orchids, and

The church at Gluges is pushed into a niche in the limestone cliffs which were once cut by the Dordogne. Orchards are now laid out on the alluvium brought down by the river.

with juniper, box, conifers and stunted oaks around and above them. It is a thin layer of exuberant vegetation enclosed and controlled by the drought of its surroundings. The landscape, like the paths through it, is neither patently cared for nor abused. It has kept its own rather difficult and unobvious beauty unadorned and undestroyed. There is none of the comfortable hierarchy of forms arranged around a particular point which usually constitutes our idea of a beautiful place. It denies that easiness in a way that has fascinated the American poet W.S. Merwin. He lived near here for many years and wrote of the *causse*:

The secret becomes no less itself for our presence
In the midst of it; as the lizard's gold-eyed
Mystery is no more lucid for being near.

You come down to the valley of the Dordogne.

The white limestone cliffs are stained black in stripes and orange in patches. They were once cut by the river, but are now protected from it by a buffer of silt brought down from the east, over which a pattern of orchards and fields has been neatly laid. Tucked into a crack in the overhanging cliffs is the village of Gluges, a rather smart place of brown-tile roofs and of ladies with both hair and shoes nicely lacquered, accompanied by their castrated pets. There is a discothèque in the village and the church has graphic representations of cardinal virtues and deadly sins inside.

The Dordogne is a beautiful and muscular river, as delicate and persistent as a vine. It is now no more than the great, lazy drain from the Auvergne to the Atlantic, lined with alluvium and creased into the calcareous masses around it. But from the earliest times until the beginning of this century it figured largely in the lives of men here as both vein and artery, pumping goods, supplies and information both seaward from the inland expanses of Aquitaine and upstream from the coast. Here in the upper reaches above Bergerac the trade

The rivers of Quercy are incised like open veins into the limestone causses *on either side. In summer the Dordogne was always too low and the Quercynois had to wait for October rains before trade could be resumed. Juniper berries for Dutch gin were shipped from this corner, the Port de Gluges.*

depended on the height of the river, and the coming in late September of the *eaux marchandes*, the commercial waters. After the three months' inactivity of the summer drought, these signalled a sudden increase in traffic, so that 40% of all river journeys were made in October and November. From the coast the necessities of salt, sugar and dried and salted fish, brought round from the warehouses in Bordeaux on the Garonne, were transported inland, while timber, quarried stone, and ores were all floated downstream on rafts and barges that were broken up and their timbers re-used on arrival. The trade in wine, which could have been promising, was made difficult by the protectionist measures taken by various wine-producing

*Rocamadour: perfection and
the common genius of rural
architecture.*

Coiffure in Martel.

Labastide-Murat: Hat shops, once common throughout rural France, are on the decline. Cars, hoods on tractors, fashion, depopulation and the acceptability of tanned skin have all cut into the demand for hats. Walkers, however, still need them. Make sure you buy one here.

A neon fly at Gouffre St Georges.

commiunes down the river, anxious that the cheap wine from upstream should not destroy the business for their own *viticulteurs*.

The river was the focus (there were no fewer than twelve local words for different kinds of river boat) and life in the valley was, in the words of its historian Anne-Marie Cocula-Vaillières, '*fertilisée et comme ensoleillée par ses eaux.*' The riverside communes were enriched by the mineral-thick alluvium it brought down, by the enormous amount of work it provided (until the beginning of the nineteenth century the barges were hauled upstream by teams of twenty or thirty men, rising to eighty or a hundred in difficult places) and by the access it gave to new markets. Here at Gluges and Montvalent, as at other 'ports' below the *causse*, one of the most fascinating and unlikely of trades was carried on. The junipers that grow so thickly and naturally on the *causse* provided a vast tonnage of berries for Dutch merchants who would transport them back to Holland to satisfy the enormous Dutch appetite for gin. In return, amongst other things, they would sell barrels of salted herring from the North Sea, the fish on which the Dutch Empire was founded.

You cross the river and for nearly five kilometres keep to the flat land of the valley, making for Montvalent above the cliffs on the far side. Underfoot a richer earth is revealed, and where you had walked clean-heeled before, mud now clings. In the words of the local proverb *buono terro, misson comi* – good earth, bad path. The best place in the valley, just below Montvalent itself, is the Gouffre St Georges. Here the water from the Gouffre de Padirac, the most famous and baroque of all the limestone caves, emerges after a journey of eleven kilometres underground. But the exit has none of the grandness of those entrances. At the point where cliff meets field, the rock curls its lip slightly upwards into a snarl, from which a milky-blue stream springs; never dry all summer, this oasis is surrounded by grass, and in the water itself flowers and green weed trail down to the Dordogne. Even though I knew where this water came from, its emergence was the image of pure creation. Such places fit our idea of a source far better than the boggy, indeterminate patches on remote mountains that are the true and rather dull origins of all rivers. I would not have been surprised to see a mossy river god here, asleep on his padded divan.

It is eleven kilometres from Montvalent to Rocamadour. On the back of a speed-limit sign just outside the village I read a poster, addressed to no one in particular, it seemed,

Raoul and Dick.

suggesting rather enigmatically: 'If you like the country, why not live here?' A hundred metres later, pinned to a tree, came the coda: 'Tourists! Settle in, we can sleep outside.' The distortions caused to the local economy (and hence society) by tourism, and the raising of house prices to catch the *résidence secondaire* market (thereby pushing houses beyond the means of young local couples) are among the worst effects of tourism, far more iniquitous than an occasional caravan. It is one of the profoundest ways in which tourism destroys what it comes to see. The new money that it brings does not find its way back to the ancient economic network on which the character and true meaning of places such as Quercy depend. Tourists and those who cater for tourists form a self-sufficient circle from beyond whose boundaries the older Quercynois can only look on powerless and unbenefited. This is an understandable source of anger.

Feeling slapped in the face by the message, I began to look at the Lot with a colder eye. The stone walls bordering the track, pretty though they were, had no tie-stones or throughstones in them, the vital constructional element which binds the two faces of the wall together. As a result they had often crumbled away and nowhere was there any sign of repair. Great ginger swags of juniper, with the berries shrivelled on them, had been used to block the holes. I passed a new barn made entirely of naked breeze-blocks and was on the point of condemning its ugliness when I realized that the limestone and the concrete were exactly the same colour and that the new barn was in fact a good building. It is the most revealing and fundamental fact about the Quercynois way of life that there is no attachment for its own sake to traditional techniques and materials – modernity, if affordable, is desirable – nor blanket commitment to the new. The single criterion according to which innovation or preservation becomes the right course is its *rentabilité*, its financial value. This is the Thrift Ethic on which the landscape is founded. However much you would like or dislike something, if it is not *rentable* it is not worth considering. In this way the farm will be improved before the house and it is by no means unknown, for example, for an automatic watering system to be installed for the animals in the barn while the human beings who own them continue to fetch their water in buckets. Where a house *is* modernized the reason will not be for more comfort or leisure but because modern materials and equipment allow more time in which to make more money. Personal comfort is not *rentable* and any indulgence in it is simply wastage. Austerity is the cardinal virtue and the patois of Quercy is filled with anti-consumerist precepts teaching a gospel in which what you have you keep and what you do not have you do not covet. *Cu tout jo bol, tout jo perd* – whoever wants everything, loses everything – one says, and another *Lou po dur fo l'oustal segur* – hard bread makes a solid house. Only in the great social gatherings of wedding breakfasts and banquets is this replaced by a massively expensive and alcoholic demonstration of solvency and a proud, ritual giving away of what in all likelihood has been nurtured and prepared by the hosts themselves.

After several kilometres of very stony ground, the way comes, near the village of Mayrinhac le Francal, to a beautiful passage of open grass, scattered with junipers like

In the eighteenth century Arthur Young thought that the well-being of any part of France depended on its ability to grow maize. There is a maize store on most farms in Quercy; it is fed to cattle.

debutante yews, their skirts spread widely around them and coming at the top to a narrow, alert head. Here the path is an old track, the pilgrims' way to Rocamadour, now only a kilometre or two away. At the top of a slight hill just north of Les Alix, small cairns mark the place where pilgrims, after the long hike south, first caught sight of l'Hospitalet, the medieval suburb of their journey's end.

Rocamadour reveals nothing of itself until it reveals all. Through l'Hospitalet you go, under a medieval arch, to the very edge of the gorge of the Alzou where you are finally confronted with the place which the French have decided, in a precise grading, is the second most extraordinary in France. (Mont St Michel wins.) And as you go down the road towards it, past an electricity sub-station made to look like a *pigeonnier*, you will indeed be amazed by the way in which a château on top of a cliff is almost met by the roofs of houses and church buildings struggling up towards it from the valley 90 metres below. This unnecessary verticality – it is no Manhattan, for open space stretches widely in every direction – is the source of its pleasure.

You could think of Rocamadour as an anti-functionalist manifesto, but of course it is nothing of the kind. Your arrival in its streets will show that it is certainly not free of gimcrack commercialism or a harsh exploitation of the quaint. The town, climbing up the cliff is no more than a cramming of buildings (both medieval and nineteenth-century) around what was, in those two periods, a spectacular source of revenue: a relic, dubious enough in its provenance, and a miracle-working wooden Virgin, probably from the ninth century. It is a place of hubbub now, as it has often been during its history, and you either like its miracles, waffles and three Michelin stars, or you don't.

Rocamadour to Vers

50 kilometres

The limestone walls of the deep gorge of the Alzou are layered where previous beds of the river have worn away scoops on the bends. Your way crosses its present course and just before it the trace of the *Route de Grande Randonnée No. 6*, a heroic transcontinental trek from the Alps to the Atlantic. Feeling parochial by comparison you will climb the side of the gorge, below one of the largest

Junipers grace the causse *near Rocamadour like debutantes sitting out a dance.*

131

pigeonniers in Quercy – a reflection of the wealth of the church in Rocamadour – and eventually arrive back on top of a *causse*. It is the same as before, as if nothing had happened, as if you could pull the skin together over the cut of the Alzou and no one would notice the difference. It is six kilometres to Couzou, around the rim of a large depression, 400 metres wide and 60 deep, called, like many of its smaller equivalents, *le cloup*. It is almost exactly the shape of a pudding bowl, just like the depressions left in the earth of the New Mexico desert after atomic weapons have been test-exploded deep underground. This is the first stage in the creation of a *gouffre* like Padirac or La Fage. Rainwater with carbonic acid in it has begun to rot away the limestone, destroying the structure of the rock by dissolving the carbonate of lime contained within it. The soil which results from this dissolution is rich in salts and gypsum, and the *cloup* becomes for a while a small pot of fertility sunk into the sterile *causse*. But this does not last, and as the water continues to work on the rock, deepening the *cloup* into a *sotch*, it eventually breaks open into a natural well called an *igue*, which is the same as a *gouffre* but smaller.

Surrounded by its flocks of sheep and some enormous chocolate-brown goats, you come to Couzou where you can get something to eat in the Hôtel de la Terrasse. The best thing to have is one or two of the small goat-cheeses called *cabécoux* (it means 'kidlet') which are made throughout Haut Quercy. They begin life mild and creamy, with a deliciously fusty smell, but as the *cabécou* grows older on the little straw fences where they are always laid, it dries out and sharpens into a bitter old age. Eat a *cabécou* with a glass of Vin de Cahors, a

Couzou.

dense, smoky red wine, and you will have tasted the essence of Quercy.

South of Couzou is the emptiest part of this walk. The commune is the least populated in the Lot, with a density of only four people per square kilometre, compared with an average of just under a hundred per square kilometre for France as a whole. It is fourteen kilometres to Montfaucon, the next village and almost the next inhabited place. But there is no wildness to it. Fields are ploughed and planted and flocks of sheep huddle together in the heat. I could not understand why until I realized their heads were in each other's shade. On the southern side only bottoms were turned out against the sun, splayed round like the spokes of a fan. The absence of people has meant the survival of red squirrels and partridges and even of a fox in the corn. But this, the Causse de Gramat, has not always been so empty. About five kilometres from Couzou you come to the deserted village of Rocabilière and five kilometres after that to the ruined hamlet of Crosse Basse, both of them deep in ivy and brambles. So complete an effacement of humanity from a site that not long ago housed a flourishing community is saddening and disturbing. The structures people struggled so long to maintain are easily and casually dismantled. The last person left Crosse Basse ten years ago, one of the four million Frenchmen who have exchanged the country for the city since 1945. The disastrous decline in rural population has for the moment slowed down, but the number of births, in the Lot at least, continues to drop, from 2,500 a year in the early 1960s to a little over 1,500 now, a 40% reduction in the active population of the years to come.

As I approached Montfaucon, on a rather more open and richer land, an army lieutenant came along the lane towards me, flicking sweat from his face with a folded handkerchief. He looked at my disintegrating shoes and the bit of poplar from Uzerche and we exchanged route histories. He smiled at mine and told me that he had come the forty kilometres from Cahors that day on foot. 'From Cahors to here in a single day!' I exclaimed in admiration.

'Half a day, actually.' Quarter of a mile down the track I came across his platoon, tanned and exhausted. I was aware that my face had got burnt in the hot day's walk over the *causse* and as I passed through them one of them broke into song, conducting the others with his cap until all of them together were soon singing *'Tournez, tournez mon tournedos . . .'* A corner and its trees provided relief.

Montfaucon is dominated by an enormous yellow hospital run by the Union of Post Office Workers for its members. It occupies an eighteenth-century building at the top end of the town which, in an amazing survival of thirteenth-century town-planning, is laid out in exact rectangles. Montfaucon is a *bastide*, in effect a medieval New Town. It is often claimed that *bastides* were built along the frontier between the English and French possessions in France, but that is not always true. Their function was primarily economic; they were fortified as a result of continual warfare, and only secondarily so that they could act as instruments in it. In an age that operated a system based on a kind of internal Brandt Report, where moralists preached kindness to the people for the practical reason that to inspire hate in them would only make the life of the privileged more difficult, the *bastide* was a very efficient example of mutual exploitation: the lord would guarantee to the new burgesses certain rights – a free market, freedom to marry their daughters to whom

An eighteenth-century house at Montfaucon embodies the nobility of Quercynois architecture. Two small towers with finials do all that is needed to make a farmhouse into a statement of quality.

The wash-place or lavoir *at Montfaucon, a focal point and sort of village hall.*

they pleased, and protection in time of war – in return for which he would levy a tax.

The protection was certainly necessary. The structure of feudalism was so rigid here that there was no social cohesion at all outside the direct line of power from the strongest of the barons down through their strings of vassals. These self-sufficient power-blocks situated side by side inevitably and regularly led to rivalry, disintegration and conflict. The church took its place alongside the others. Until as late as 1788 the Count-Bishop of Cahors (a significant title) had the right when he said mass to have helmet, sword and cuirass on the altar beside him.

It is six kilometres to Labastide-Murat, over a beautifully bumpy series of low hills with woods, farms and hedges spread over them. Labastide itself is pale grey and leafy. 'Murat' was added to the name in 1852 in memory of Napoleon's great cavalry commander and brother-in-law, who was born here in 1767 in his father's inn, now transformed into a museum. In the present hotel there was an English couple on holiday. It was not going well. They did not speak a word at dinner except to deal with his inability to understand the difference between *saignant* and *à point*, or to acknowledge that he would have preferred *bien cuit* anyway. He was wishing he was back in Minchinhampton, she was wishing he wasn't wishing it while wondering if she wasn't wishing it too. 'You're not quite in the Dordogne here, are you?' he suggested to me after dinner, as though I was slightly out of focus, and smiled understandingly.

The next morning, after the incident with the soldiers outside Montfaucon, I decided I needed a hat. In Labastide – amazingly – there is a hat shop just off the main square. I said to the old lady inside how extraordinary I thought it was to find such a specialist shop in such a small town. 'But don't you understand,' she asked me, 'that men working in the fields and on the vines need to be protected from the sun?' Or at least that's how it had always been, but times have changed and she was going to have to close down in the near future, simply because the trade wasn't there any more. What with the number of cars people had nowadays and the hoods on tractors and the simple fact of there being fewer people than there were, as well as all the changes in fashion, she couldn't sell enough to keep going. Umbrellas and cowboy hats were all very well – she offered me a 'ranchero' with a laugh – but it was all for nothing really. I bought a plain wide straw hat for twenty francs and left her with the hope that walkers in the Lot would come and boost her sales.

The last day, from Labastide-Murat to Vers, is twenty-four kilometres long, almost all of it high on the *causse*, with bland horizons in every direction and a long view to the blue south-west. I began the day in the company of a man with a row of silver teeth like a car bumper who said he was *Professeur des Lettres* in a typing school in Normandy. I asked him what exactly was meant by the term *lettres* in the context of a typing school but he didn't answer and complimented me instead on my new hat, saying it made me look a *routard de luxe* and asked where I got it. I told him, he turned round there and then and walked back into Labastide to buy one like it.

It is twelve kilometres to the village of Cras, balanced on the edge of the valley of the river Vers. The farms you pass on the way are like a museum demonstration of the styles of Haut Quercy – the entrance always on the first floor with an outside staircase to it, and a byre for the animals below; the walls caked in a kind of peach-coloured roughcast called *crépi*; small glassless oval windows called *yeux de boeufs* cut from a single stone block and intended for ventilation; and the roofs in a variety of tiles – the *tuiles plats* like English tiles, simple rectangles but of a particularly attractive grey-brown; *tuiles-canales*, the famous trough-shaped tile, each one half a cylinder, that are Mediterranean in origin; and the *tuiles-mécaniques*, the only machine-made style of the three, which is a kind of pantile, each one slotting precisely into its neighbour and with an ingenious protuberance on the underside which hooks over the roof-slats and makes unnecessary the wooden pegs usually needed for all flat tiles.

Villages interrupt the landscape and it seems inevitable that one of them will at some point swing into the line of your path. Cras dutifully obeys, a tiny place of only eighty inhabitants, but with a memorial to eighteen young men killed in the First World War. The present population goes up in summer, as the woman in the shop told me, with a family of Danes at one end of the village and a professor from Oxford at the other. The professor had recently bought his house from the people who lived next door; they themselves had bought it several years ago when the occupants died and their children left for Paris. '*La Spéculation!*' she said to me in triumph, wagging a finger in front of a smiling eye. Was it a bad thing? 'Oh no, not at all . . . they are all very nice.' There was, she had to admit, something of a problem with the language, but she was sure they would all get over it soon. Her shop was the only place of refreshment in Cras and it had nothing fresh

(except bread) for sale, only tinned ham, tinned fruit and bottled juices.

As you set off on the last twelve kilometres of the walk you begin a gradual slide down to the valley of the river Vers on a track which, when I was there in late May, was alive with neon-green dragonflies and the most beautiful butterflies – common blues and spotted fritillaries, huge black-veined whites and best of all white admirals, the smartest of nature's creations, with a firm, rhythmic flight pulsed into long glides and a black and white wing-pattern that would be noticed at Royal Ascot. The river itself is a trench, about three metres across and one deep, with a rocky bottom. Resist the temptation to swim until you reach the Château de Gironde about five kilometres from Cras. But there, under the limestone cliffs, succumb to it, as the river runs through a meadow flowery with scabious and Michaelmas daisies and beneath the neglected château, no more than an old empty tower with a big farmhouse attached.

Tuiles-mécaniques and tuiles-canales both stacked up; two kinds of tuiles-plates, old and new, on the roof. Tuiles-mécaniques are modern. The meeting of tuiles-canales (from the Mediterranean) and tuiles-plates (from the north) is marked by a definable if sinuous line across the middle of France.

A kilometre or two beyond the château, both the Vers and the path come out into a larger valley, along which the road runs from Cahors to Figeac. The perfection of the château and its meadow diminishes slightly on the six kilometres of track down to Vers, but the end-momentum will be strong enough for it not to matter much. You will be expecting a great debouching of the Vers into the enormous Lot, but that does not happen. The big river is itself constrained by a steep valley. Nonetheless, arrival at the Lot is spectacular. You have to go on through the town of Vers itself to reach its banks, where you will find it creaming a weir, wide and imperturbable, the

135

most masculine of all those rivers of Limousin and Quercy that you have crossed and followed, the river which W.S. Merwin identified as a 'great shining emanation of the whole terrain.'

———————

DISTANCES (in kilometres)
From Uzerche to:
Vigeois 9; Comborn 10; Le Saillant 9; Saint Viance 7; Saint Pantaléon 12; Soulier-Chasteaux 7; Les Abîmes de la Fage 7; Jugéals-Nazareth 4; Turenne 4; l'Hôpital St Jean 5; Martel 12; Gluges 6; Montvalent 5; Rocamadour 11; Couzou 6; Montfaucon 14; Labastide-Murat 6; Cras 12; Vers 12

MAPS
I.G.N. 1:50,000 Numbers 2133 (Uzerche), 2134 (Tulle), 2135 (Brive-la-Gaillarde), 2136 (Souillac), 2137 (Gramat), 2138 (St Géry)

GUIDE
Topo-Guide du Sentier de Grande Randonnée No 46 (Sentier Limousin-Quercy) F.F.R.P – C.N.S.G.R. 2nd ed. 1979

LIMOUSIN AND QUERCY
Alfred du Cayla, *Maisons du Quercy et du Périgord*, Hachette 1973
Alfred du Cayla, *l'Habitation rurale du Quercy*, 2nd ed., Editions Quercynoises 1979
A.-M. Cocula-Vaillières, *Une Fleuve et les Hommes*, Editions Tallendier
Charles Dartigue, *Histoire de la Guyenne*, Presses Universitaires de France 1950
Charles Higounet (ed), *Histoire de l'Aquitaine*, Privat 1971
Philippe Renault, *Géologie du Quercy*, Quercy Recherche 1978
Chanoine E.Sol, *Le Vieux Quercy* (2 vols), Bibliothèque de la Maison des Oeuvres
Freda White, *Three Rivers of France*, Faber 1952

The river Lot and, in the distance, the town of Vers at the end of the walk where the river Vers emerges into the Lot, the culmination of the journey and the terrain.

137

The Auvergne

Murat to Volvic

160 kilometres

The Auvergne is not quite in the middle of France. The exact geographical centre (and more than one commune claims it) is in the Bourbonnais, twenty kilometres to the north. But the Bourbonnais, a rich low-lying area of grassy meadows and streams, does not have the look of a core, and in the French mind the Auvergne replaces it. No sea is visible, even on the best of days, from the heights of this ancient block; from its edges the land mass of France spreads out over every horizon, like the white of a fried egg. It is symptomatic that the bank-notes of the Banque de France are made and printed in Chamalières just outside Clermont-Ferrand, a site chosen in the nineteenth century not primarily for the purity of its water, but for its distance from all frontiers and safety in time of war. At least part of the appeal of Giscard d'Estaing as Presidential candidate in 1974 was that he too was a *vrai fils de château* from the Auvergne, with a true Frenchness that a Breton or a Basque could not have shared.

This massive centrality is the overwhelming impression on the hundred-mile walk from Murat in Cantal to Volvic in the Puy-de-Dôme. At heart the country which the walk crosses is one of the oldest in France. It was raised in the mountain-building period called the Armorican Orogeny about 190 million years ago and has since gathered around it the great sedimentary deposits of limestone and sandstone that make up the body of the country. Two major convolutions have utterly changed this basic pattern. The first was about 35 million years ago when the collision that built the Alps, between the African plate and the mass of Eurasia, shook the foundation of the Massif Central; molten material from the earth's mantle erupted in two huge volcanoes, each of them at least fifty kilometres across at the base. Their remains, now deeply eroded and sitting like a pair of rosettes on the map of France, constitute the Monts du Cantal and the Monts Dore.

This walk climbs in and out of the centre of the Monts du Cantal and crosses to the Monts

Looking back at the Monts du Cantal from the Plateau du Limon. These mountains are the scene of a short but brilliant spring, delayed by the cold of altitude and soon burnt out by the southern sun.

Dore over a wide basalt plateau formed by the liquid lava flows. The final stage, from Saulzet-le-Froid to Volvic, is through a chain of small volcanoes called the Monts Dômes. These are the products of a much more recent vulcanism; most of them erupted about 8000 BC and none of them is more than about 35,000 years old. There may even have been a single volcanic explosion in the area as recently as about AD 1050.

Their history is not yet over. Borings to the depth of about 1,500 metres have revealed, as part of a programme spread throughout Europe, that the Auvergne is still one of the hottest places on the continent. Whereas south-east England, for example, is about 50°C at that depth, the Auvergne in places reaches nearly 200°C. There are two alternative explanations for the volcanic activity in the recent past and for the present heat under these mountains. The first, and more likely, is that one of the so-called 'hot spots' surfaces here; a plume of heat, generated by nuclear reaction deep in the mantle, makes its way to the earth's surface, both by conduction through the solid rocks and by convection in the semi-liquid mass of the mantle. The second, and more exciting, associates those volcanoes with vulcanism in the great fault of the Rhine valley near Strasbourg, and with a geological weakness in Europe that runs north-east from this fault into Polish Silesia. In this string of volcanic activity which stretches across the continent, there is evidence of an abortive attempt, only yesterday in geological time, to open up a new ocean. It is well known that about 200 million years ago the shores of the Atlantic began to move apart and are still doing so. The African rift valley, the Red Sea and the Jordan valley are also part of an equivalent crack in the earth's surface, in which the crusts on either side, driven apart by the convective forces in the mantle beneath them, are themselves at an early stage of forming another ocean. It is possible that the volcanoes in the Auvergne represent the overture to an attempt at splitting Europe in the same way. You may ask why it failed, but we cannot be sure that it has, or that we are not now witnessing the aching pause between moments of convulsion. However, pressure of an expanding Atlantic on one side and of a converging Africa on the other may have been enough to reclose the gap.

For Teilhard de Chardin, the Jesuit theologian and geologist who was born in 1881 at Sarcenat (just east of the path in the Puy-de-Dôme) and who grew up among these mountains, the volcano was the most obvious demonstration that the earth was not simply being but constantly *becoming*. When he was six he disappeared for a whole day, only to return at night to tell his parents that he had been 'to see what there was inside the volcanoes.' He conceived a lifelong passion for what he later called the 'Ocean of Matter' and for the great history of evolution; when he was five he had been deeply shocked by the idea of his own perishability when he saw a lock of his hair, cut off by his mother, burning in the fire. He later described his search for the essence of matter, sometimes to be found 'in a blue flame over the logs in the hearth, at once so material and so impossible to get hold of. More often in some transparent or brightly-coloured stone, crystals of quartz or amethyst and above all shining fragments of chalcedony which I was able to collect in my country of the Auvergne.' The cherished substance had to be 'resistant, unassailable and hard'. Compared with this rocks, flowers and insects were 'scandalously inconsistent and destructible.' Mineral, on the other hand, was 'planetary'. 'I woke up to the notion of the Stuff of Things and that famous Consistence, which I had hitherto looked for in the Hard and the Dense, began in a subtle way to emerge in the direction of an Elemental permeating all things – whose very ubiquity would make it incorruptible ... During the whole of my life there was but one thing which would irresistibly bring me back to the study of the great eruptive masses and continental shelves – that was an insatiable desire to maintain contact (a contact of *communion*) with a sort of universal root or matrix of being.'

There is an enduring caricature of the Auvergnat – attributable to the nineteenth-century geographer Jules Michelet – which represents him as closed up, embittered by circumstances, ungenerous of spirit and 'the inhabitant of a rough land grown stony in its image.' This depends on the basic and primitive idea that people come to resemble their surroundings if exposed to them for long enough: that city-dwellers will be grey and regimented and men from bucolic farmland rosy-cheeked and jolly. If anything, it is more true that people develop in contrast to their landscape and that a bedouin will be more generous because the country around him is not. In the week or so that this walk lasts, you will find, if not exactly open-door hospitality, at least a good and generous treatment from the people you meet. That was my experience without exception. Even the dogs (at least in the mountains) were less aggressively proprietorial than any I have met. But this must not be taken too far the other way: there is a

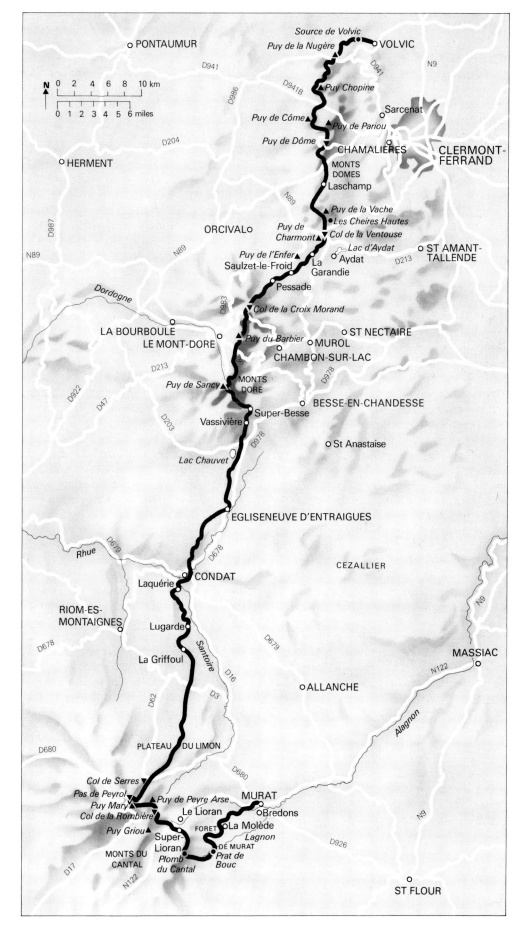

story told by Henri Pourrat, the novelist and historian of the Auvergne, of a peasant he knew in Cantal whose wife and only cow had both died within a month of each other. M. Pourrat commiserated over this double disaster, only to be told that it was no disaster at all: the new wife's dowry paid for a new cow.

The Auvergne has always been ruinously poor. It is said that God touched Cantal twice: once to make it and once to abandon it. Until the eighteenth century the expected ratio of grains harvested to grains sown was three to one. Even then land on the high ground had to lie fallow for up to five years before such a meagre crop could be grown on it again. Significantly the coulter on the Auvergnat plough only needed to weigh one kilogram compared with the five kilograms necessary in the richer fields of Languedoc. People ate almost nothing but bread – the incredible figure of 400 kilograms per adult per year. This malnutrition reduced the average height of the men to less than five feet four inches, the legacy of which can still be seen in the shortness of many of the Auvergnat peasants today.

From the mid-eighteenth century, agricultural techniques, static since the Celtic invasions two and a half thousand years before, began to improve. Spring wheat shortened the time that land had to lie fallow; the number of pigs in the Auvergne doubled between 1740 and 1790; and the growth of Paris expanded the markets while new roads made them more accessible. Selective breeding began to improve the red Salers cows, which became an increasingly important part of the rural economy.

As France slowly became industrialized during the following century the people of the Auvergne began to drain down towards the new sources of urban wealth. Migration, it has been said, is the main industry of the Auvergne, and even now there are thought to be more people of Auvergnat descent in the eleventh *arrondissement* of Paris than there are in the Auvergne itself. This depopulation was sealed by the First World War in which over 26,000 young men from Cantal and Puy-de-Dôme were killed. This removal of a generation made empty houses commonplace in every community, a situation exacerbated by the rapid growth of Clermont-Ferrand (almost entirely due to the large Michelin factories there), so that now it is quite understandable to refer to Clermont-Ferrand and the Auvergnat desert.

The effect of all this on the walker, at least on this path which keeps where it can to the heights, is of near-total isolation. You can spend a whole day and pass only two buildings, one of which will be empty. It makes these mountains cultureless and in a way removes them from France. Frenchness survives in fragments only, and most of these are gathered around the edges. You are pushed back into a natural world which is both dramatic and detailed, with a spectacular history, and which in May alone comes into a short and brilliant spring, delayed by the cold of altitude and soon burnt out by the southern sun.

Murat to Col de Serres

34 kilometres

Murat is on the edge between the mountains of Cantal and the valley of the Alagnon. It lines the crook of the elbow between the two, climbing up towards the Roche de Bonnevie that rises abruptly above it in fine, slightly curving, basalt columns. These were formed from a lava that cooled rapidly into regular, large-grained crystals. The rock was capped with a castle until 1633 when Richelieu, as part of the extension of royal power into the provinces, had it demolished – it took six months and six hundredweight of powder to do so. A white virgin stands there now surveying the roofs of the town. These show the transition from highland to valley, from the black and green slates, or *lauzes* (some of them in enormous slabs, as suitable for floors as for roofs) to baked-earth tiles at the bottom.

You leave Murat to the south-west, past the sawmills and *fromageries* on which the town depends, and on across the Alagnon, gradually leaving the buildings behind. High on the opposite side of the valley is the blocky silhouette of the eleventh-century church in Bredons, a village famous for its underground houses; most of them are now ruined except for one or two which are still used for cows. It is fourteen kilometres from Murat along the *Route de Grande Randonnée No 400* to the Col de Prat de Bouc, the pass of the mountain meadow, all of which is an introduction to the lower slopes of the great volcano through the Forêt Domaniale de Murat.

You begin climbing steeply through the pine woods, nearly all of them nineteenth-century plantations, and, as the day warms up, the air in the clearings thickens with their scent, but in the shadow stays clear and cold. The snow-patched heights are hidden except for the occasional glimpse and the track is ruined and runnelled by springtime melt-water which has brought large broken logs down with it. Underfoot, in the pebbles on the

Murat, on the frontier of mountain and valley, is dominated by the Roche de Bonnevie, a block of solidified lava from the great volcano of Cantal. A white virgin now stands on the site of a castle destroyed by Richelieu.

In the valley of the Alagnon near Le Lioran.

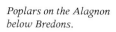

Poplars on the Alagnon below Bredons.

The track in the meadows near Murat: a sense of structure only inches below the surface.

path, there is evidence that this was once the scene of eruptions. Unlike the rock at Murat, this ridge is not made of basalt, which is essentially the liquid of the earth's mantle made solid. It is formed from an andesite, erupted from the volcano as a very viscous lava, with pieces of other material embedded in it. You will recognize andesite as a fine-textured grey rock, with black glassy chips dotted all over it. Next to these are the petrified remains of volcanic ash which was blown high out of the vent and sank back to earth, forming a stone with an airy, pumice-like structure riddled with holes. Many of these rocks oxidized and turned red when exposed to the air in a volatile state. Strangely, at about ten o'clock in the morning the rock from the lava flow is much colder than those with air trapped in them, which have already been heated by the morning sun.

After about eight enclosed kilometres, above the small hamlet of La Molède, the path opens out around you in a wide brown clearing and displays for the first time the blotched width of mountain ahead, penetrat-

ing the caustic blue of the southern sky. Looking east, in the other direction, the basalt plain or *planèze*, over which the lava flowed from this volcano, sandwiches a layer of colourless haze between it and the heights of the Haute Loire far to the east. The path now drops into a steep valley, climbs out of it, and drops again to another small stream, the Lagnon, before climbing the final mile to the Prat de Bouc. This switchback course is tiring but has its rewards. As a buzzard begins to cruise above you (the first of many), the way descends from the clarity of the high ridge into the increasing warmth of the valley. Suddenly from silence you drop into the cricket zone (they will only sing above a

A buron, or summer dwelling, below the Plomb du Cantal. The Auvergnat village remains tightly gathered in the winter, but in the early summer the cowmen move up on to the hills to their separate burons, *before coming together again in the valley at the first sign of snow. At least, this was the traditional pattern; motor cars have now blurred the edges.*

The roofs of Murat, where the walk beings.

certain heat and will even pause as a cloud passes over them) and to their accompaniment you will find yourself in a spectacular field of flowers, as densely packed as the dots on a half-tone print: orchids, crocuses and violets of an imperial purple; small wild daffodils, marsh marigolds, dandelions and cowslips; forget-me-nots, crane's-bills (the wild geranium), saxifrages and globeflowers whose yellow sepals fold in at the top; arnica or mountain tobacco, masses of tiny pale purple androsace, hairy lungwort and, if you are very lucky, the rare martagon lily.

You leave this battalion of bright life behind you and climb the far side of the valley to emerge on to a yellow moor which hints at things to come. A short climb up the valley of the Lagnon, in which old tree trunks split and bleach in the sun, brings you to the Prat de Bouc and its ski chalet (closed in spring and autumn) at the foot of the Plomb du Cantal. Here the preliminaries are over. The mountain rises to 1,858 metres ahead of you, 451 metres above the pass, and a mere three kilometres

away on the map. It is somehow friendlier and smaller in close-up than it was from above La Molède, but the climb, past still ski-lifts and the occasional piste-marker, is a long and hard one. You move on and off wide patches of snow, where the reflected sun burns up at you like studio lights, as you laboriously kick footholds with the side of your feet. There is no snatching at it, and only the slow plod, the patient climbing by accretion, will get you there. You reach a saddle with the lovely name of the Col de la Tombe du Père and as you rest beside the red rocks, the oxidized top layer of a lava flow, you get a long look down into what might be thought to be the remains of a crater, but is actually a valley cut by a stream over many millions of years after the volcano went cold. It is empty, its remoteness tempered only by the point of a small summer shieling, the Vacherie de Grandval. The whole of France lies beyond it, at first sight absolutely brown and empty, but a closer look

reveals tracks, barns, villages and an occasional movement.

The summit is still nearly 274 steep metres away. Almost all of it in May is on snow, with hidden gullies in the heather. The air thins and the climb becomes harder. Tiny purple and white crocuses and their giant relations, whose petals are covered in a fine golden hair, grow on those few patches not covered in snow. There are one or two butterflies up here, fritillaries and orange-tips, and, most incongruous of all on the snow, some lime-juice-green viviparous lizards. All these appear as strange and disconcerting incidents in the heart-draining climb to the summit. You will arrive there at last, your mind blurred by the exertion and lack of oxygen, to find a series of destinations expanding in front of you: tomorrow's mountains, as you look west across the breadth of the old volcano, from rim to core to rim, are broken, pointed and patchy; northwards, over the Plateau du Limon, are the Monts Dore covered in snow but dirtied by the haze and the distance, well

The Plomb du Cantal, 1,855 metres and 6,029 feet above sea level.

over fifty kilometres away. Their image, with occasional disappearances, is a constant and growing incentive on this walk.

Near the summit is a café and cable-car which comes up from the resort of Super-Lioran, visible 500 metres below. Both of them are open in winter and summer, but neither in spring. The way I went down – and I am not sure whether to recommend it – was a beautiful, running, avalanching gallop down steep mobile snow-slopes, zigzagging down like a skier without skis, the snow coming rolling down in cartwheels beside me, sometimes solid, sometimes with gaping doughnut middles, an exhilarating, careless swoop with gravity entirely in control. It made the mind-bending effort to get up there worth it, but I suppose it was not very wise. There is a careful, steady path down to Super-Lioran for those who would prefer it.

Even by the safe way you are soon down

into the curiously golf-club world of the lower pistes, neatly fringed by pine trees into a star of fairways all of which lead to the resort itself. The architecture declares it to be the rich playground it is – smart and well-finished in good materials, but shaped into Alpine points and cow-girl curls. It is a Disneyland that has taken one rather short step towards Le Corbusier. Super-Lioran is skiable for no more than three months of the winter, and again none of the many bars and hotels are open in spring.

Just below the resort, above the village of Le Lioran itself, are a pair of nineteenth-century tunnels, one road (1839) and one rail (1868). The older tunnel is nearly one and a half kilometres long and it is said that you drive in one end from the north of France to emerge at the other in the Midi. In 1944, this was the scene of a climactic incident during the war-long campaign by the Auvergnat Maquis. From the start the Auvergne had been the heartland of the Resistance, originally called for by de Gaulle in a broadcast from London in 1940. Three successive events, well after the beginning of the war, had combined to put the Resistance properly on its feet. The first was the invasion of Russia by Germany in June 1941, which allowed the French communists to put their full weight into fighting the Germans. The second was the German invasion of Vichy France in November 1942 and the demobilization of what remained of the French army in December. The decisive factor did not come until the beginning of 1943 when the Germans began a compulsory work campaign, in which suspected or known troublemakers were deported for work in other parts of the Reich. The scheme was largely a fiasco for the Germans and a boon for the Resistance. Many of those who guessed they might be up for deportation 'se sont évanouis dans la nature' – vanished into the undergrowth – as their historian Gilles Levy has described it.

Targets were urban, almost always in Clermont-Ferrand, hide-outs were rural and in a Swallows and Amazons way the myth of the ideal life in the countryside became meshed – perhaps necessarily – with sustaining morale in the harsh and difficult conditions. The winter of 1943–4 was the worst time. A few of those who were living in tents made of re-sewn parachutes defected, causing havoc and many deaths among those who remained. For the rest the hero continued to be Vercingetorix, the young leader of the Arvernes against Julius Caesar, who after courageous resistance in Alesia was captured, kept in a cell for six years, finally displayed in Caesar's Roman Triumph, and then privately strangled. One of his modern successors was the poet Paul Eluard. Cramped into a shepherd's hut in these mountains for that long winter, he was still able to write in a tight compression of personal and patriotic history:

J'aimais hier et j'aime encore
Je ne me dérobe à rien
Mon passé m'est fidèle
Le temps court dans mes veines.

Ideally each *maquis* – the word was taken from the wild scrub in the mountains of Corsica – consisted of twenty to thirty men, ten to fifteen kilometres from its nearest neighbour. As 1944 wore on, each of these Maquis received a liaison team of an English and a Free French officer, and a radio operator parachuted in by the RAF. There were two plans for the moment of invasion. The first, the Green plan, was to cut all communications, the electricity network and the railways. The second, the Red, was for a more general mobilization, to control roads, attack military objectives and establish a series of redoubts which would make the Auvergne an island of Free France ahead of the Allied armies advancing north from Provence. At 9.30 on the evening of 5 June 1944 the BBC broadcast the following message:

Sa robe a la couleur d'un tapis de billard.
Ses joues ont la couleur de la pomme d'api.

Both plans were on and there was a natural explosion of unfocused enthusiasm. The redoubts were established all over southern Auvergne, but the scarcity of small arms and, more importantly, the total failure of the British to supply the Resistance with any artillery, meant the fight against the Germans was hopelessly unequal. After only a few weeks the Resistance leaders decided to abandon the idea of the redoubts and returned to the guerrilla harassment for which they were much better suited. It was towards the end of this phase, as the German army began its withdrawal from the Auvergne, that the sour little battle of Lioran took place. The German garrison of Aurillac to the south, consisting of about 500 men, made its way towards Murat and was allowed to enter the tunnel before the French attacked and cut it off from behind. At the same time a crucial bridge was blown up further down the valley of the Alagnon. In theory this should have meant the isolation and destruction of the column, but reinforcements from Murat and strafing of the French by the Luftwaffe allowed it to escape – after two days' fighting in which about twenty men died. Eisenhower credited the Maquis with having contributed the effect of fifteen divisions to the Allied effort. Whether he meant this literally, or more in terms of psychological weight, it is difficult to say.

As you set off from Super-Lioran up the steep 'red' runs of the ski resort you will be crossing the line of the tunnels many feet below. It is exhaustingly up and down for the first four and a half kilometres to the Col de la Rombière. I was there on the kind of morning when the air is frozen and the sun burns through it. The old snow under the trees, littered with needles, and with the consistency of sorbet underfoot, is blue in the shadows until, as you emerge above the tree line, it smacks back into whiteness. Here, skirting the Puy Griou to the south, you are in the basalt heart of the old volcano. The Puy itself is the worn down stump of magma which solidified in the neck on the way up, and the deep valley you meet at the Col de la Rombière has been excavated in the softer andesites which formed the body of the cone. On the far side of it, the ridge between the two mountains of Peyre Arse to the right and Puy Mary, sharp beyond it, is again in the basalt which erupted and began to flow westwards from the vent.

From the Col de la Rombière the path makes a wide S-bend for eight kilometres as far as the Pas de Peyrol, beyond the Puy Mary. You can see the path from the col, making its steady ascent under Peyre Arse (the unfortunate name means the burnt rock) and then curving round the head of the valley to reach and crest the ridge leading to Puy Mary itself. At the Col de Cabre, where one valley stretches northeast of you and another south-west, you will see a remarkable demonstration of how in the last Ice Age the Auvergne lay exactly on the limit of glaciation, where the micro-climate of each valley was more important than the overall temperature. The valley to the north, despite its scoring by many newer streams, preserves the rounded, deeper profile given it by a glacier, with the earlier ridges and side valleys sheared off half-way through. The one to the south continues to look something like its neighbour did before the ice came, finely cut by streams and never scoured by ice. The difference is the result of one valley facing south and getting more sun than its neighbour. Only to the north was snow able to accumulate sufficiently to build the beginnings of a glacier.

The final arrival at the ridge (there are red kites up here with deeply forked tails and crooked wings) is an entrance into an ice-cream world. Here the second limb of the S begins its wide curve along the length of a ridge thickened with snow blown into a wide and fragile cornice. Keep well away from the edges and you will enjoy a fine, elevated mile or two around the head of yet another valley, with the Monts Dore floating over the broken grasslands to the north and the Matterhorn image of Puy Mary ahead. A small break in the ridge, the Brèche de Rolland, means hands as well as feet for a short scramble through thigh-deep snow. The end is a crisp white repetition of the Plomb du Cantal; coming down is like an astronaut walking on the moon, the snow softening each landing and the steep slope making each take-off easy.

A short four and a half kilometres along the road and then a grassy track finally takes you away from these mountains to the welcome of a small restaurant and souvenir shop on the Col de Serres. (It would be the ugliest building you had ever seen if you had arrived by car.) There you can get sandwiches of *pain de seigle, jambon cru*, the raw ham which has become food *typique* in these places, and *fromage de Cantal*, the very plain cheese which is said to be the oldest in the world (Pliny mentions it) and with which the first French astronaut was provided when he went up in a Soyuz rocket in June 1982. The owner of the restaurant lives in Murat. If you are lucky he will have seen you there the day before (he had seen me) and will be amazed at your *courage*. No *alpiniste* himself, he has seen both boars and chamois here, but not often. Enjoy the delicious dry cider he will sell you: it is the last liquid you will get for nearly eighteen hot kilometres and from now until the Monts Dore there will be no snow for refreshment *en route*.

Col de Serres to Lac Chauvet

48 kilometres

The first movement is over; you are now on to a broad long interval. Beyond the Col de Serres the Puy de Niermont rises steadily to the north-east, climbing 300 metres in three kilometres, no craggier than the Malverns. The climb has no surprises. Only a small pool of frost-churned rocks near the summit breaks through the grass. From the top you can again look north over the wide yellow pampa, terminated in the distance by a short block of Andes, a Continental prospect unknown in England. The path runs straight over this featureless moor, the only sign of progress being the slow greening of the grasses as you descend, and the increase again in the flowers. Buttercups line the streams, which are not the bright cold refreshment they were near the

149

Puy Mary (1,787 metres, 5,806 feet) from the Col d'Eylac.

ABOVE *The Monts Dore from the Plateau du Limon:
an epic and flattering movement from mountain over
meadow to mountain.*

TOP *Looking back to Puy Mary and Peyre Arse from
the Plateau du Limon.*

snow-line but warm brown trickles. Above all, the number of summer houses scattered on the grassland, the *burons*, begins to increase. This is the classic country of transhumance, the twice-yearly tide of animals and men who have been coming up from the valleys in the early summer and going back down in the autumn at least since the late Bronze Age, about 3,000 years ago. Here, I met a man from Murat who was checking his fences in preparation for the cows he was about to bring up from their winter pasture. With a brown, lined face and white hair *en brosse* he exactly fulfilled my idea of a mountain man and spoke with great clarity and gentleness. He had eighty-five cows and this year sixty calves, with only six born dead. I congratulated him but he said it was usual to have so many, and that once they were on to summer pastures it was even possible for one cow to mother two calves. They would be suckled for nine months and then sold to beef producers. These were the Salers cattle, with slightly curly mahogany-red coats which, it was said, were once like the Ferrandaises, covered in

A buron on the Plateau du Limon covered in the fish-scale lauzes more suited to flooring than roofing. Around it, a marine horizon impossible in England.

white blotches, but God had lavished special care on them, scrubbing them clean with pumice from the volcanoes.

As you sink gradually over the Plateau du Limon, the Monts du Cantal become no more than piping along the moor behind you, while the Monts Dore gradually begin to differentiate themselves, emerging from a whitened mass into a system of gullies and ridges. Immediately around you, the *burons*, singularly and systematically arranged one every few hundred metres, demonstrate how the people who had been gathered tightly all winter in their lowland village could spread themselves individually on to summer pastures. One would imagine that the Auvergne – and the Massif Central as a whole – was an obstacle which prehistoric currents would have been forced to flow around. But this annual mechanism of ascent and return made the mountains a sort of cultural exchange, and the many Bronze and Iron Age sherds found along the drove-roads indicate that as the herdsmen moved in from every side with summer they encountered each other at the passes, and each winter returned with any news to their own more distant valleys. Paradoxically, it made the mountains more coherent and integrated than the fertile and static width of lowlands around them.

You cross the D3 thirteen and a half kilometres from the Col de Serres, and four and a half kilometres beyond it, along a grassy and stone-walled lane, you arrive at La Griffoul, the first village with a sense of place to it since Murat. You are well down now, and in May a large herd of Salers – with a Charolais bull – was browsing next to the path, their bells knocking like a steel band. I was burnt and thirsty when I arrived here, and there are few balms as good for a burnt face as pressing it into the cold grass of a field. But this was not enough, and I asked at one of the farms in the hamlet for a drink. The woman there reacted in a typically Auvergnat way. She did not offer me a drink herself but carefully and courteously told me where I could find the village pump. It was all that I needed.

It is thirteen kilometres from La Griffoul to Condat-en-Féniers, the capital of this part of the Auvergne. The way there is through fields thick with dandelions and through farms where the dogs claim ownership. You pass through Lugarde, where the railway from Bort-les-Orgues was finally carried through on a high viaduct in 1908. There had been strong opposition from the Church, which feared that the railway's sophisticated influence and the new kind of person it would bring into these remote communities might have a detrimental effect on the morals and faith of the villagers. Certainly it made the process of depopulation easier.

Snow melts on the Monts Dore ahead while great lumps of basalt stick up through the fields. Here more than ever the birds of prey swing or hover in the air above you, buzzards and kites, peregrines and kestrels, and the pale and buoyant Montagu's harrier. All these are beautiful and extraordinary birds. The peregrine, for example, can spot a still pigeon 1,000 metres away, and a pigeon in flight more than half as far away again. On the hunt it can travel three times as fast as its prey (up to 300 kilometres/190 miles an hour) and can knock the head off its victim in mid-flight. A buzzard can distinguish an object half a centimetre long at 100 metres, or a mouse from a kilometre above it. They are at the top end of the food chain and as a result are subject to

Roger Moins in Laquérie above Condat.

poison entering that chain at any link. The disastrous drop in their populations all over Europe since the war is largely the result of DDT – an insecticide which is chemically stable and dissolves in fat. It built up in their bodies and fatally weakened the shells of the eggs that they laid. The spectacular abundance of birds of prey in the Auvergne is evidence that here is an ecological system working almost without interference.

Most of the trees on the plateau are either ash or oak, neither of which is in leaf by mid-May, but as you begin to drop into the valley of Condat the air warms up and large chestnuts and beeches in fresh leaf appear, with foxgloves beneath them. The small village of Laquérie is half-way down the valley, roofed entirely in bright new corrugated sheeting. Here M. Roger Moins, sitting in front of his house mending a child's chair, stopped me and asked if there was still some snow on the Monts du Cantal. I was amazed by the question, as if he had asked me if the sky was still blue. But looking back I realized the mountains were now hidden, and that since he could walk only on crutches his knowledge of them depended on the reports of people from beyond his own horizon.

Condat is just below. Its name comes from the Celtic word for confluence, as here the river Santoire, from the Monts du Cantal, meets the Rhue, from the Monts Dore. It was once a town of weavers, their looms driven by the two streams, but it is now full of villas built by people who have made their money elsewhere (often as cloth merchants) and have come back to retire where they were born. Condat is a pale grey town and on a hot day, when all the French windows are thrown open, has an ingenuously available air.

Eleven kilometres out of the valley and on

Puy Ferrand and Puy de Sancy in the Monts Dore.
The source of the Dordogne is in those snows.

Condat, the first place with a sense of place since Murat.

to the brown plateau will bring you to Egliseneuve. It is the most epic few hours of the walk, in which you cross the departmental boundary between Cantal and Puy-de-Dôme on a grassy yellow track, with the sensation of enormous transition from mountain to mountain across the plateau. There are red-backed shrikes here and many buzzards, suspended quite still on the air below them, bending upwards on their breadth of wing with every change in the draught. Crows mob them and cows stand in the bogs of ponds. You cross the occasional patch of peat, the residue of small pools that gathered in depressions after the end of the last Ice Age, which occurred here about 12,000 years ago. In the cold, acid environment decomposition was slow and the sphagnum moss which colonized these depressions accumulated to form deep tracts of peat, some of which is still cut by the Auvergnats for burning.

Egliseneuve on a May afternoon was defunct with heat. Dogs and people all lay in the shade, with no curiosity and with no tension in bodies that followed every contour of the ground they lay on. Major refreshment is necessary and available here, and you will find yourself eating too many peaches and drinking too many beers. The church after which this slumped place is named is of quite exceptional ugliness and, extraordinarily for a town that calls itself Newchurch, claims to be Romanesque in origin.

A grinding six kilometres, all on hot stony paths, lie between Egliseneuve and Lac Chauvet. The way passes through Les Chauds, whose name is probably derived from the pre-Celtic language and whose true meaning is unknown. Along a small stream full of tiny freshwater shrimps and through a lovely beech wood you eventually emerge to find the Monts Dore suddenly closer, as if you had woken from a night on the Atlantic to find Iceland in front of you. All haze has gone and the snow and brown grass are quite distinct

The first of the Monts Dore from the end of the Plateau du Limon. As you progress towards them, the haze dilutes and the snow whitens.

from each other. It is only a kilometre or two to the lake, which is almost perfectly round and about a kilometre across. It is eighty-six metres deep and was never a crater but the product of underground subsidence related to the volcanic eruptions. The water is still and cold, tasteless and transparent. Hundreds of little fish rest in its warmer edges and the temptation to swim is impossible to resist. Walk over the first few stones, fleshy with weed, and then throw yourself off where it deepens sharply into blackness. The sudden knowledge of the eighty-six metres and its monsters beneath you, and the violent contractions of warm flesh subjected to the cold, will force you out within seconds, where you can then sit quietly warming on the shore watching the frogs copulate in the shallows and the occasional trout sifting past beyond them.

Lac Chauvet to Saulzet-le-Froid

31 kilometres

From above Lac Chauvet the ski-resort of Super-Besse is visible just over six kilometres away under the mountains that it serves. It consists of a black and brown skyscraper and a fuzz of triangular chalets. Of these the skyscraper is incomparably the better — almost the only form of modern architecture that can stand up to mountains. Next to the Puy de Sancy, the highest in the Massif Central, it at least looks like a statement, and the chalets mere blemishes.

The way makes straight for it, at one point through a prairie covered in a stubble of wild daffodils, passing through the tiny hamlet of Vassivière, which is no more than a farm and the buildings attached to its chapel of Notre Dame. Every year, this is the scene of an ancient ceremony related to the most primitive forms of nature and earth religion. Spread throughout France are small statues of the

The Puy-de-Dôme, extinct for 40,000 years, trails
cloud like smoke from an active volcano. A television
mast occupies the summit where the Romans built a
temple to Mercury.

Virgin Mary known as Black Virgins from the wood they are made of, darkened with age. In the Auvergne there is a myth that they were discovered underground at some unapproachably distant time, and ever since have been the object of veneration. These Black Virgins are effigies of the earth goddess which every pastoral and agricultural society has worshipped since the invention of farming. In a place where the coming of summer is represented by the ascent of men and cattle to the mountains it is not surprising to learn that every 2 July a Black Virgin is solemnly transported by sixty men from Besse-en-Chandesse, about four kilometres below to the east, to her summer resting place in Vassivière. There she stays until 21 September, when equally solemnly she is brought back down. It is said that one year the Bessois forgot to perform the ceremony and that the Virgin had herself carried up on the horns of the cows.

Super-Besse is a universe apart. In spring cable-cars are stacked unused at the bottom of their lifts. Gravelly debris lies around the bars, most of which are shut. Food and drink in those that are open cost twice the price charged elsewhere and are sold with less than half the charm. Like every ski-resort at the wrong time of year Super-Besse wears the unalterable moroseness of the morning – or the season – after. If you need somewhere to stay or eat, get a lift down to Besse itself, where life is more congenial.

Twenty-four of the hardest kilometres in this book lie between Super-Besse and Saulzet-le-Froid. It is essential to provide yourself with a full bottle of water before

ABOVE *Super-Besse, a dazzling insertion in the mountain landscape.*

LEFT *Near Vassivière.*

embarking on them, since, except for the cattle trough in Pessade, there is no water to be had. From Super-Besse you begin on a 427-metre climb towards the summit of the Puy de Sancy, up a hillside littered with piste-markers and lift-pylons. It is a gruelling climb and the only way is to take it slowly. The top will reward you with a massive new view, the first since the Plomb du Cantal. Immediately to the west is the Puy de Sancy. Its snows are the source of the Dordogne (the name, like the river Douro in Spain, essentially means 'waters') which begins its life by flowing down a glacier trough to the north. There the small town of Le Mont-Dore is crammed into a slot where the valley narrows, even from up here looking like a rather precious town famous for its *pâtisseries*. *Curistes*, as afficionados of the waters are called, have been coming here since pre-Roman times. The arrival of a good road and the post-Rousseau health fad in the eighteenth century vastly increased the clientèle. The waters are volcanically heated to between 38° and 44°C and are saturated with silica, arsenic and carbonic

On the summer meadows below the first of the Monts Dore.

acid. The faithful can drink them, bathe in them, enjoy thoracic affusions, nasal douches or the snorting of thermal gas through pipettes. They can undergo *'insufflation tubotympanique, nébulisation d'aérosols, douches filiformes et crénotherapie esthétique'* all of which is said to improve singing voices, and to be useful in the treatment of asthma, respiratory ailments and rheumatism. (Alarmingly, in these cases, the subcutaneous injection of thermal gases is recommended.) All of it is available on the French national health service.

The hydros and hotels will all lie below you as you make your way north along the east side of the valley. After the climb from Super-Besse you may feel in need of one or other of the treatments available below, in which case there is an alternative route via the spa. Otherwise you keep high above it on a track that curiously resembles a coast path, along the rim of a massive landslip where thawing

Below the Puy de l'Angle at the Col de la Croix Saint Robert: deceptively gentle profiles to heart-draining climbs.

ground-water has disturbed the earth on the scale of a quarry, and in which a fragile dyke of volcanic rock still stands clear of the stony rubble around it.

After five kilometres the path crosses the D36. The following five have none of the spiky outlines of the Puy de Sancy and its neighbours, but in the heat of a May morning they are no less of a challenge, made worse by their deceptive downy roundness. They succeed each other: Puy de l'Angle, Puy du Barbier, Puy de Monne, Puy de la Tâche, arriving at last at the Col de la Croix Morand, which is said to claim at least one death a year. Unless you are well prepared, this part of the walk, for all the astonishing beauty of the snow patterns on the hills, will be purgatory. It is only a small consolation to look back at mountains already climbed now many miles away. What matters more are the plagues of flies in any wind-shadow, the discomfort of the path itself, the absence of any real shade, and the inevitability with which a down is followed by an up. Worst of all will be the discovery at the Col de la Croix Morand that

both cafés are shut. The six kilometres to Pessade stretch ahead like an ocean. The constant resort to snow on the summits leaves nothing but stomach cramps and a general, unlocalized sickness. It is an old, straight track to Pessade, the eighteenth-century road which brought sherbets and sorbets to Le Mont-Dore. Many birds of prey scout here, but the vultures are in your imagination. You will see a stoat running over the field next to you, like a drop of water on wax. There is no cool in the shadows and no moisture in your mouth or sweat on your body. The unmistakable outline of the Puy de Dôme itself, a stubby, flat-topped cone with a slight lip on the eastern side like the small ridge of tissue on a scar, sits permanently ahead. No spit means little conversation with any companion. The fields on the volcanic soil ahead are coated in the yellow of rape-flower. The roofs of Pessade appear and time stretches as

Patriotic propaganda in Saulzet-le-Froid, where local allegiance counts for more than national.

you make for them. A *crêperie* is hidden among the farmyards but is shut on Fridays. Instead, find a pair of troughs fed from spouts that pour water so cold that flesh aches in it. There is nothing to do but lie in these baths and drink by osmosis through every pore of your body. Such fountains, fed from sources beyond the sun's influence, are magical relief in a personal drought.

Three straight kilometres bring you to Saulzet-le-Froid where food and more drink can be had in the café. Its owner makes a speciality of selling cheese, and you can have St Nectaire, which is crusty, with a smooth, rather bland paste, various blues called Fourme, Montagne and the famous Bleu d'Auvergne, a cheese according to Bryan Morgan 'veined as thinly as a Victorian belle and as mildly blue as a March sky' – that is if you catch it in its youth. Inevitably there are goat cheeses and, king of them all, Cantal, rather like a bleached cheddar, which is made in forty kilogram blocks.

There is one other object of interest in Saulzet: the elaborate war memorial in which a soldier holds the tricolour of the Republic to his lips. This is more than mere convention, since local resistance to national service was nowhere more stubborn than in the Auvergne. It had become common practice in these villages during the nineteenth century to register sons on birth as daughters, to hire widows' wedding rings, said to be an effective charm against a 'bad' draft number, and more drastically and more rarely, for men to cut off trigger fingers to disqualify themselves from military service. It was as much a practical and financial objection as anything. A son was an investment and his disappearance to the army a damaging theft. A low proportion of the men

who had been called up – in some places less than a third – ever returned to their homes. The emotionalism of the memorial in Saulzet and of so many like it is a conscious effort of the central authorities – of the French rather than the Auvergnat point of view – to substitute loyalty to *patrie* for the older and deeper attachment to *pays*.

Saulzet-le-Froid to Volvic

47 kilometres

Between Saulzet-le-Froid and Volvic the Auvergne undergoes its final transformation. Here you are on the edge of a newer volcano country. They are all quite small, most about 300 metres high and none more than 500, a string of popped bubbles on the earth's surface. There are two kinds, both named after more gigantic examples in other parts of the world: the Strombolian (after Stromboli near Sicily) and the Pelean (after Mont Pelée on Martinique in the French West Indies.) The difference in the kinds of eruption depends on the liquidity of the lava, which itself depends on the volume of gas contained in the molten rock, most of which is steam. The great majority of the Auvergnat volcanoes are of the Strombolian type. When these were active there would have been a fairly constant, or at least rhythmic, emission of light rocky material, something between ashes and pebbles, which would have gathered around the vent itself to form the cone. The final shape of the volcano would be entirely dictated by the steepness of slope which particles of this size are physically able to maintain. Almost all of the Auvergnat scoria cones, as they are called, have a slope of about one in three.

No one has witnessed the birth of a volcano here, but scoria cones appear in other parts of the world, and the brief history of Paricutin, a volcano in Mexico, is almost certainly typical of what happened here. Paricutin was born in the small field of a Mexican farmer in the night of 20 February 1943. By the morning it was nine metres high, by the end of the week 157 metres and at the end of six months 350 metres. It was then that the lava emerged, very liquid and buoyed up and lubricated by the massive quantities of steam it contained. Very quickly it flowed the ten kilometres to the town of San Juan Parangaricuto which it enveloped and destroyed. It is important to realize that lava does not emerge, as we all think, from the top of a cone, but at its base, either tunnelling under the mass of scoria or, as often happened in the Auvergne, removing one side of the cone and leaving the rest curled round like a recumbent cow. Paricutin was active for nine years, in which it produced 1,300 cubic metres of scoria and 700 cubic metres of lava. At the same time it emitted the astonishing figure of 52 million tonnes of water, enough to fill a round lake one and a half kilometres across and five metres deep. It is this huge and constant steam blast which turns the scoria red, as the iron in it oxidizes in a hot, wet environment.

This scoria is ideal for the manufacture of porous concretes, which are light, resistant and good insulators against heat and noise. Many of the tracks in this part of the Auvergne are made of this red, grainy material.

Pelean volcanoes are much rarer in the Auvergne. The Puy-de-Dôme itself is the best example. Here the lava is much more viscous and volcanic activity is both more spasmodic and more violent when it occurs. Lava can only ooze from the vent and accumulate on the spot either as a roundish lump or as a needle like the famous *suc* at Le Puy in Vélay.

The gas in the rock has no regular means of escape, and from time to time is forced out sideways in terrifying and unpredictable spurts of immeasurably intense heat. In the eruption of Mont Pelée in 1902 one of these clouds killed 30,000 people in a matter of moments, passing so quickly that the victims' clothes were not even scorched. These clouds would have rolled off the Puy-de-Dôme about 30,000 years ago, but the only evidence that remains of the scale of the eruptions is in the discovery of their ashes in places as widely dispersed as St Rémy in Provence, Lucerne in Switzerland and, furthest of all, Arlon in the Belgian Ardennes, nearly 500 kilometres away.

The walk through the chain of volcanoes turns around the Puy-de-Dôme, which is by far the largest and dominates the landscape. Until you arrive there it is all uphill; once past it, you are coasting to the end. From Saulzet

La Garandie. Few experiences are better than arriving at a village fountain on a hot day and gorging on its miraculously cold water.

you move off past the Puy de l'Enfer, a cone entirely breached on its southern side, and after the small village of La Garandie you squeeze between two more, covered in woods, to find yet another ahead of you across a small juniper-scattered basin. It is strange how quickly you come to accept these extraordinary hills as normal. They are domesticated by their woodland, all of which is nineteenth-century plantation, and by the cows and dandelion carpets.

La Garandie is in the commune of Aydat, a village and a lake about two kilometres to the east. It was the home of Sidonius Apollinaris, one of the most extraordinary Auvergnats who ever lived. He was born in 431 and died in Clermont in 489, his life thus bridging the end of the Roman Empire in France. He was an exact contemporary of Attila and was twenty-four when the Vandals first pillaged Rome. As a brilliant young politician in Rome he had been engaged in the difficult politics of decline, and as President of the Roman Senate in buying off the leaders of the foreign peoples – Franks, Burgundians, Goths and Visigoths – who were already in northern Gaul. At forty, he was made to retire after a scandal at court and for a while, as he wrote to a friend, did nothing except 'gently perspire in light silks and linens' at his villa on the lake at Aydat. But for him the rural life, as he says in another letter, slackened the mind, and he soon had himself made Bishop of Clermont, passing from baptism to the episcopate in under a week. It was no sinecure. Sidonius passionately believed in the Roman way of life (with which Christianity was now closely identified) and when the Auvergne was *given* to Euric the Visigoth in 475 no voice was louder than his in protest at the betrayal. For the last few years of his life he lived in Theocritean retirement – and maybe disillusionment – at Aydat.

As source material his letters have been described as a literary Herculaneum, and for their illumination of life at one of the hinges of history they are invaluable. Unfortunately, he was no Pepys and in many ways they are conventional, precious and unobservant, but their mere existence is enough. What they reveal above all else is that the idea of a dark pall of barbarity falling over the sunlit corridors of Roman Europe is sheer nonsense. Sidonius cannot help sneering at the 'skinned barbarians' but there is no sense at all that a way of life was coming to an end. If anything,

The landscape of volcanic downland in the Monts Dômes. The path drops from the Puy-de-Dôme itself towards Le Grand Suchet and the Puy de Côme.

one could better rely on Visigoth princelings than on Gallo-Roman officials because the level of corruption in the new monarchy was so much lower. The leisured, civilized style of the villa at Aydat was for Sidonius permanent, unthreatened, and unprotected. He loved the Auvergne, 'the land of which a single glimpse is enough to make a stranger forget his own country', and Aydat above all. Here on divans in his whitewashed rooms, with no frescoes and no foreign marbles, with a natural spring piped into fountains and a dining-room with a view of the trout-filled lake, he pursued in a curiously *imagiste* way, the fugitive impressions of his estate: 'It is delightful to sit here and listen to the shrill cicada at noon, the croak of frogs at dusk, the clangour of swans and geese in the early part of the night or the crow of cocks in the dead of it, the ominous voice of rooks saluting the dawn in chorus or, in the half-light, nightingales fluting in the bushes and swallows twittering under the eaves.'

After the Col de la Ventouse, eight and a half kilometres from Saulzet-le-Froid, the path crosses one of the longest lava flows in the Auvergne, called Les Cheires Hautes. It emerged from the Puys de Lassolas and de la Vache to flow eastwards for about fifteen kilometres to the village of St Amant-Tallende, south of Clermont-Ferrand. It is this lava which blocked the outlet of a stream at Aydat and formed the lake there.

A lava flow is unique among rock formations in that a liquid process created it and that once created and cooled it is extremely resistant to erosion. This poured landscape is a chaos, nowhere smooth, but full of rock lumps and hollows, and if you stray from the path, orientation within it is almost impossible. The only elements of structure are two parallel 'ribbes' marked on the map and easily discovered on the ground either as steep embankments or in one place as a low cliff. These are the result of the outside of the lava flow cooling while the inside was still molten. The core continued to flow eastwards while its now rigid casing stayed in place, leaving a tunnel down the middle of the flow. The tunnel collapsed, the ground subsided and these *ribbes* were left standing on either side.

Six and a half kilometres through a red, dry and dusty valley under the open gape of the Puys de Lassolas and de la Vache, and past the more complete and wooded Puy de la Mercoeur, will bring you to the village of Laschamp. The Puy-de-Dôme, with a white TV mast and the hotel on its summit, stands up like a right angle across the fields. It is a daunting prospect and, after a passage

through a green, cool beech wood full of butterflies and the smell of fox-must, the last exhausting climb of the walk begins. A toll road on the line of an old funicular spirals the mountain and takes hundreds of people to the top by car. On your way up, which is shorter, steeper and zig-zagged, you will meet family parties, retirement expeditions and many teenage girls coming gaily *down*. Deny it as you will, the need to make oneself appear tough in front of them is irresistible. Not a drop of sweat will you wipe from your brow until you reach the summit, with its welcome and elegant hotel.

From the top of the Puy-de-Dôme you can see, it is said, an eighth of France and eleven *départements*. All the morning's craters line out to the south, with the afternoon's on the other side, all of them looking artificial. Until the eighteenth century people thought they were Roman fortifications. More astonishing than either is the appearance in its rectangular modernity of Clermont-Ferrand, immediately below to the east. Only the black Gothic spike of the cathedral (built from Volvic stone) stands out against the new white freshness.

On top of the hill there was a temple to the Celtic God Lugh, who was all-skilful and whose name is at the root of both Carlisle and Lyon. The Romans transformed him into Mercury, to whom they built an enormous temple here, of which you can see the rather low-level remains. Most of the statues that have been found of Mercury in the Auvergne have been the traditionally nude young man with wings and so on, but one has been discovered at Lezoux, just east of Clermont, in which he is wearing a long dress and a beard. It is a measure of Roman imperialism that this figure, who is probably Lugh, was so blithely stripped and shaved to become Mercury.

From the Puy it is only twenty kilometres to the end at Volvic. The volcanoes form a kind of infernal downland here, mostly covered in the comforting green and yellow turf, but here and there breaking out into a terrible dry red rash that reveals their true nature. Some of the most perfectly formed cones are here, the Puy de Pariou and the Puy de Côme in particular. I climbed the Puy de Côme, which is famous for its double crater. It is, unfortunately, more beautiful from aerial photographs. I reached the top to find a Frenchman lying in the very pit of the central crater with his arms outstretched as if crucified on the earth, and without a stitch of clothing on him. Simply walking up and down volcanoes suddenly became rather prosaic by comparison.

Forms repeat themselves. The path leads

The door of the school of architecture in Volvic is made in the fine-grained weather-resistant lava known as Volvic stone.

A scene from the memorial to the Resistance outside Volvic. The Auvergne was the heartland of the Resistance and in few places are its memories so strong.

over, round and below the final few cones, some woody, some heathery and some bare, before you come to the last, the Puy-de-la-Nugère. It is one of the most complicated and superimposed structures of all, where several vents have produced a number of interlocking cones. The final descent to Volvic is on its lava flow, which has been widely quarried to reveal the clammy grey rock, the colour of cheap chocolate blancmange. Just short of Volvic itself you come to an immensely powerful source of mineral water emerging from a tunnel between the flows. There is a fountain where you can taste it, surrounded by giant stacks of water bottles, some of the 130 million which are produced each year in the Auvergne.

Volvic is on the very edge of the fertile lowland that borders the mountains all the way from Murat. Like Murat it is a market town on the junction between the two. Arriving here on a Sunday morning, as the cheese and clothes markets were beginning to gather momentum, staffed by short fat men, each of whom was twice as wide as any of the people in the mountains, it felt like a true end and a movement completed.

DISTANCES (in kilometres)
From Murat to:
Col de Prat de Bouc 14; Plomb du Cantal 3; Super-Lioran 5; Col de la Rombière 4.5; Col de Cabre 2.5; Pas de Peyrol 5.2; Col de Serres 4.5; La Griffoul 18; Lugarde 4; Condat-en-Féniers 9; Egliseneuve 11; Lac Chauvet 6; Vassivière 5.5; Super-Besse 1; Col de Cabane de Sancy 5.5; Col de la Croix Morand 10; Pessade 6; Saulzet-le-Froid 3; Col de la Ventouse 8.5; Laschamp 8.5; Puy-de-Dôme 4.5; Puy de la Nugère 14; Volvic 6

MAPS
I.G.N. 1:50,000 Numbers: 2435 (Murat), 2434 (Riom-es-Montagnes), 2433 (La Tour d'Auvergne), 2432 (Bourg-Lastic), 2532 (Veyre-Monton), 2531 (Clermont-Ferrand)

GUIDE
Topo-Guide du Sentier de Grande Randonnée No. 4 Méditerranée-Océan. Tronçon Auvergne. C.N.S.G.R. Paris 1980

AUVERGNE BOOKS
A.N.Brangham, *History, People and Places in the Auvergne*, Spurbooks 1977
Robert Brousse and Serge Paul, *Le Volcanisme Récent de la Chaine des Puys*, G.de Bussac 1973
Teilhard de Chardin, *The Heart of Matter* (1950, many editions)
Peter Gorham, *Portrait of the Auvergne*, Robert Hale 1975
Gilles Lévy and François Cordet, *A Nous Auvergne!*, Presses de la Cité 1981
A.G.Manry (editor), *Histoire de l'Auvergne*, Privat 1974
Bryan Morgan, *Fastness of France*, Cleaver-Hume 1962
Robert Speaight, *Teilhard de Chardin*, Collins 1967

The Cévennes

Le Monastier to St Jean-du-Gard

187 kilometres

To an American painter called Fanny Vandegriff Osbourne we owe one of the sweetest travel books ever written and one of the most alluring invitations to a walk that I know. In the late summer of 1878, when she was thirty-eight years old, Fanny returned to California from a bohemian colony near Paris, where for several years she had been experimenting with a new life (without her husband) and where, two years before, she had fallen in love with Robert Louis Stevenson. He too had exchanged a home country (where he had felt 'like a weevil in a biscuit') for the stimulus and freedom of Fontainebleau. She was a strong, staunch woman with a substantial kind of beauty – her jaw reminded Sidney Colvin of Napoleon – while he was ten years her junior, an extraordinary mixture of vitality and physical weakness, of charm and naughtiness.

Fanny's sudden departure left Stevenson bereft. Partly for consolation, and partly with an eye on the mountain air as well as the prospect of cash from any book he might write, he went south to the Cévennes, an area he had originally become interested in through George Sand's novel *Le Marquis de Villemer*. After a month of rather purposeless ambling around Le Monastier he set off on a journey through the mountains lasting twelve days. The journal he wrote became the basis for *Travels with a Donkey in the Cévennes*. It was published in London the following year.

Stevenson, like the rest of us, loathed baggage; he took with him a donkey (christened Modestine immediately on purchase), loaded with the odd assortment of a thick pilot coat, a bottle of Beaujolais, joints of cooked meat, other edibles and plenty of money all wrapped in a sack made of 'green waterproof cart-cloth without and blue sheep's fur within.' It doubled as a sleeping bag. Modestine, his 'self-acting bedstead on four castors', was a terrible encumbrance. A scholarly edition of the original notebook, preserved in California, makes it clear how it

The rainwater that comes into this tributary of the Chassezac will run east from here to the Rhône and eventually to the Mediterranean. Had it fallen a few hundred metres to the north, it would have reached the Atlantic with the Loire. In the distance is Le Goulet, the first big hill of the walk.

is Modestine's book as much as Stevenson's. She was almost certainly on heat for the first half of the journey, and it was this, not indolence or homesickness, that made her at first so hopeless a companion. Stevenson, exasperated by her slowness, treated her even more abominably than the published book admits. One of the most shocking moments in the book is when the insides of Modestine's legs are revealed to be in a state of 'raw beef'. In the journal that remark hardly stands out from its context of indifference. Stevenson knew to temper or remove these references to his cruelty, while for the book-buying public he added a final farewell (tears included) to the she-ass he was able to look on with affection only in her absence.

Stevenson had no doubt that he was an author, not a geographer. There is very little that is objective about his book; it is the singular account of one idiosyncratic journey through what he chooses to call the Cévennes, but which only arrives at the Cévennes proper about half-way through. His love or hatred of a place is almost entirely dependent on the weather. He exaggerates the remoteness of villages and shrinks them, usually leaving out Baedeker information entirely. Towards the end exhaustion leads to brevity and a tangible lack of literary effort. But for all that it is a lovely book, though not a great one: Stevenson was once famously accused of weaving lace when it should have been broadcloth, and *Travels with a Donkey* bears that out. Like the best travel books it plays in and out of the sharpened phrase, and includes small essays and sudden generalizations. It shares experience and then becomes diffident. These various contours of the book recreate the impression of travel itself, especially on foot — its cramming of event and stimulus after page-long lacunas of tedium, its sudden sense of impatience after days of irrelevance and indulgence, its disappearance into distance and looming transformation of detail.

All this has established the reputation of *Travels with a Donkey*, nowhere more so than in the Cévennes themselves. A Stevenson society from Edinburgh has signposted the route with small white boards emblazoned with the cross of St Andrew, which are distributed through the mountains with a charming sense of the random. Stevenson is heard of in most places. In Le Monastier itself the name of *le grand écrivain anglais* (occasionally amended to *écossais* by some pedant or partisan) is spread around the town. A marble plinth given in 1967 by an American, Mrs Gladstone, marks the place where he began his journey. (The memory of Mrs Gladstone —

known throughout the Cévennes simply as 'Betty' — is almost as inescapable as Stevenson's itself.) The Syndicat d'Initiative has signposted a memorial to Stevenson from a few strategic points. It turns out to be in the Mairie, and is nothing but a rope trailed down a wall with the names of places attached at various points. A rather smart Bar le Stevenson completes the homage. The myth in Le Monastier is that Stevenson came here for *une amie* — a fascinating distortion of the truth — and the very house where the local lovely dwelt will be pointed out to you. But perhaps better than any of these official monuments, and more suitable to the memory of the man himself, was the question put to me by a farmhand as he poked at the road with a stick. '*Faîtes-vous*,' he asked, as though referring to a new kind of skiing, '*le Stévenson?*'

Le Monastier to Landos

31 kilometres

Le Monastier is stitched to a road that runs on the steep side of the Gazeille valley. Often enough the houses have entrances on different floors, one uphill, the other down. There are gaps in the street on the southern side, opening out over the valley of the Gazeille, which is roughened here and there by the bare fluff of pine woods. In low light every slight dip and ridge between these patches is revealed in harlequin. Above the town the hillside hardens to a squat basalt edge, in some places columnar, in others shattered. To the far north the mountains in late November were coated in a half-transparent emulsion of snow. Lower to the west the wide, farmed landscape rises occasionally to knolls darkened by trees. The meniscus plains between them give way to the surface roughness of many villages.

Caught between mountain and valley, Le Monastier, if not quite the 'mere mountain Poland' Stevenson found it, is no place of luxury. Dogs retreat with the afternoon sun across the squares, finally pushing themselves all into the one lit corner, and there, when the light finally goes, shiver or squabble for warmth. Stevenson did not mention even one of the town's three extraordinary buildings — a château in black basalt fragments, with four corner towers and two in the middle of each side, each of them capped with Chinaman's hats, or cockles, in red tile; next to it the Hôtel de Ville in grey granite, a strictly arcaded building quite out of place in its provincial surroundings; and third, its neighbour and the origin of Le Monastier's existence, the

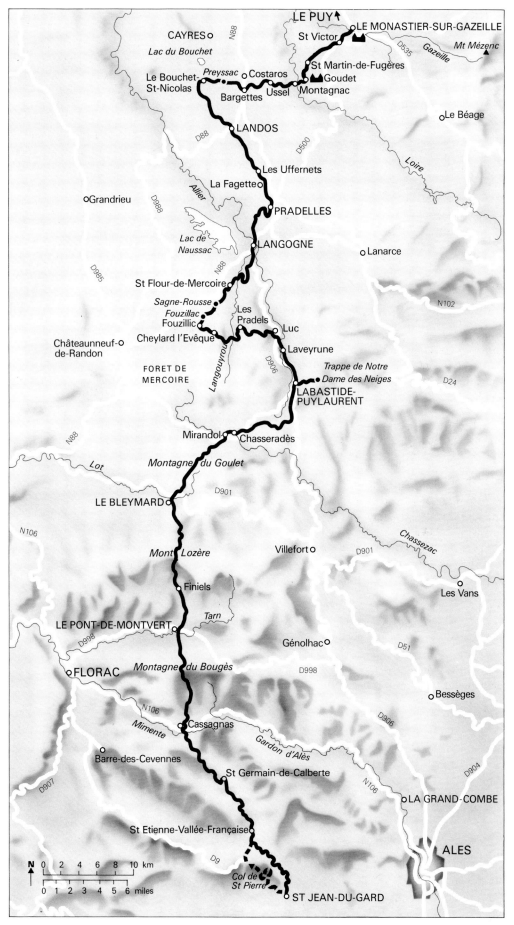

LE PUY↑

LE MONASTIER-SUR-GAZEILLE

St Victor

Mt Mézenc

CAYRES

Lac du Bouchet

St Martin-de-Fugères

Gazeille

Le Béage

Le Bouchet-
St-Nicolas

Preyssac Costaros
Bargettes Ussel

Goudet

Montagnac

LANDOS

Les Uffernets

La Fagette

Grandrieu

Allier

PRADELLES

Lanarce

*Lac de
Naussac*

LANGOGNE

St Flour-de-Mercoire

Sagne-Rousse
Fouzillac
Fouzillic

Les
Pradels

Luc

Cheylard l'Evêque

Laveyrune

Châteauneuf-
de-Randon

Langouyrou

*Trappe de Notre
Dame des Neiges*

FORET DE
MERCOIRE

LABASTIDE-
PUYLAURENT

Mirandol

Chasseradès

Lot

Montagne du Goulet

LE BLEYMARD

Villefort

Mont Lozère

Les Vans

Finiels

Tarn

LE PONT-DE-MONTVERT

Génolhac

FLORAC

Montagne du Bougès

Bessèges

Mimente

Cassagnas

Gardon d'Alès

Barre-des-Cevennes

St Germain-de-Calberte

LA GRAND-COMBE

St Etienne-Vallée-Française

ALES

N 0 2 4 6 8 10 km
▲   0 1 2 3 4 5 6 miles

*Col de
St Pierre*

ST JEAN-DU-GARD

173

The toy-like château in Le Monastier is made of basalt, the bitterest and most intractable of rocks.

marzipan and pasteboard church, its west front in black and red chequerboards of stone, with animals climbing the pedimental frieze. 'Here are the monuments of Le Monastier,' the hotel-keeper showed me and guffawed, half in contempt and half in embarrassment.

When Stevenson was here, the men of the town were famed for drunkenness. Dinner in the hotel reveals that this at least has not changed. The dining room on a Saturday night fills from seven o'clock onwards with men between the ages of nineteen and thirty-five, about fifty of them at the peak, with a small knot of girls cooped in one corner and ignored. A great deal is drunk. Twice, as I ate, a young man swept past me to the window without apology and emptied his evening's consumption into the street, only to return to the table for more. After a few half-fights – no more than a clutched jacket and a straight look – and many bellows of '*Ta gueule!*' the evening

ended as gently as it had begun.

To start off from Le Monastier is no great departure. Its lack of distinction, with an air of a temporary camp, makes leaving it easy. Besides, the wide view is to the west, and all you can see to the south – our direction – is the other side of the Gazeille valley, about a kilometre away. But curiously a cut-off prospect is as much of an invitation as an open one, and for the seven and a half kilometres to St Martin-de-Fugères, as the sun gradually returns the colour to the frost-blanched fields, the sensation is of peering over tops and round edges to find what lies ahead. You begin by dropping to the Gazeille, a trenching-tool of a river that has taken away the far bank on a bend, with the trees all gee-gaw in the stony and earthy waste. The water as you ford it is so cold that you feel no pain, only immediate numbness. Stevenson makes no mention of having wet shoes for the rest of the morning; perhaps he hitched a lift on Modestine.

After a steep climb up the far bank, with all the pain of blood returning, the way con-

ABOVE *and* RIGHT *Ways of life as old as the place itself persist in St Victor near Le Monastier.*

tinues along a level lane for almost all the way, through the hamlet of St Victor, to St Martin. The province of Velay is spread around the road, with its basalt villages and little volcanic peaks. It is over 900 metres above sea level and the living scratched here is not a rich one. Farming is on a garden-scale, with arbitrary plots ploughed or planted like patches of rust on a second-hand car. The only living animals I saw were a pair of heavy, moth-like buzzards. All the rabbits have been shot and all the small birds have long since been packed into *pâté de grives*.

In the middle of St Martin-de-Fugères, its effect heightened by the rustic situation, is the granite-fronted church, with the drama of a single geometrical feature on its plain façade. This is a seven-ribbed surround to the main west door, which retreats in stages into the granite, a beautifully articulated entrance, like the layers of skin revealed in an anatomical drawing.

It is little more than three kilometres to Goudet. You leave St Martin past a staircase of stone troughs made from single blocks, each

The church in St Martin-de-Fugères is faced in a pale granite that can take finer detail than the basalt of which the surrounding houses are made.

with a notch in the lower lip through which the water runs to fill the next. As you come down to Goudet on a path lined with sloes and rosehips, tapping out footprints in the crust of frost like letters on a new page, the ruin of a medieval castle appears in the irregular and piney gorge. It is the broken cap to one volcanic plug and the village is arranged around the skirts of another. Stevenson's description of Goudet's position makes it sound far more shut-away in a hole of a valley, and the river far smaller, than either of them really is. Maybe, however unconsciously, he wanted to increase the adventurousness of his adventure, or perhaps his longing for Fanny made him feel more at the end of the world than he actually was. Later in his book he confesses that although he enjoyed being alone he longed for 'a fellowship more quiet than solitude and which, rightly understood, is solitude made perfect.'

You cross the river on a narrow bridge. In late November it was iced over, with a silent underflow of occasional bubbles and a bed three times the width of its shrunken winter stream. In the banks are little twisted basalt columns, their arrangement and contortion like a decadent Staffa. It may sound ridiculous to call this mountain stream by the name of France's great lowland artery, but this little trickle is in fact the Loire.

Your way now climbs the far side of the valley on a path which soon changes to a milky granite underfoot, the material of the *mairie* in Le Monastier and of the church façade in St Martin. This granite is the foundation of the whole region, a block of solidified magma that was thrust upwards about 250 million years ago and which is only revealed now through erosion. Above it, coating it like a great tubercular gob spat up by the earth much later, is the black basalt which poured out of the now dead vents standing around the plain of Velay. It makes it a two-level, Neapolitan earth.

As you climb, the castle above Goudet becomes more and more like a garden incident, with gently graded fairways zig-zagging up the hill. In thematic opposition a tower in almost total ruin balances on the other side a second tower, almost complete, the passage between them a sermon on decay. From Goudet another four kilometres, up beyond the lip of the Loire gorge, will bring you to Ussel where the café can provide you with an enormous lunch. You pass through Montagnac, where black arches lead into black basalt houses, and where the habit, as in much of southern France, is to build hangar-like barns with a ramp to the first floor and a byre below. Any village, however small, is given immediate substance by these huge buildings, like faculties standing around a modern campus, but it works the other way too, as though an important place had been taken over by a peculiarly untidy farmer to serve as his extended farmyard. I imagine Montagnac and Ussel to be a miniature version of Bath or York after the Romans left Britain and a few unwashed Saxons had taken their place, but I know that is only kindergarten history.

Stevenson made a wide detour to the west from Ussel, intending to visit the great explosion crater now filled by the Lac du Bouchet, but his map was not good enough, or his reading of it incompetent, as he never got there. Instead he arrived at the village of Le Bouchet-St-Nicolas, a kilometre or two south of it and ten from Ussel. To walk there after Ussel's lunch is a long, loping, hazy afternoon,

with gentle rhythms and easy stages. This wide basalt plain – the exact terrestrial equivalent of the seas on the moon – is, in a way, a heightened Hampshire, with the same near monochrome in the browns and blues around you and the same thickness of population in patches. Only the day-long frost in darker hollows reveals the height of it all as over 3,000 feet, rising to 4,000 and more. You bypass Costaros with its red roofs, unmentioned by Stevenson, since its growth occurred only after the arrival of the railway in the early years of this century. The difference between Costaros, whitened with the plaster brought in by new riches, and any of the older black basalt villages around it, is a peculiarly visual piece of evidence of the general failure to integrate the development of rural France. The railway and the towns clamped to it have remained a ribbon of wealth beading a country which, in parts, is only now arriving in the twentieth century. The carts, the tractors, the fields, in fact the whole conception of most of the farming here is all too small to compete with the large-scale efficiencies of northern France, Denmark or East Anglia. This is the kind of country where survival depends on regular maintenance by the Common Agricultural Policy.

As you make your way through the hamlet of Bargettes and on to Le Bouchet the thick earthen slopes of the hills that rise about you in round and regular tumescences are here and there roughly stepped in what can only be called lynchets. This small and accidental terracing, caused by the gradual slipping of earth downhill over hundreds of years of ploughing, is used only as an archaeological term in Britain, where modern farming has long since smoothed out all but a few of such nuisances. But here in the Haute Loire there is a continuity not only of cultivation, but of the same style of cultivation for thousands of years until the present day.

It is a beautiful country. The earth under a brilliant mountain sky has certain rhythms. The slight round hills are skirted by fields, their various browns arranged, like tweeds in a draper's, in casual and slight chromatic variation. On the horizon the higher mountains come to regular peaks.

You reach the hamlet of Pressac, a weird arrangement of five or six manse-like farms, as arbitrarily arranged as if an encampment had simply stiffened into buildings overnight. No sense, it seems, of coherence or even of place has intervened.

At the top of a hill, past a quarry with yellow diggers burrowing into the raw-veal-pink rock, I came to a vision of cows and, on

the far side of a long meadow, the houses of Le Bouchet-St-Nicolas, gathered around the spire of the church. The buildings speak in a kind of patois, every one with stacked wood under an outside staircase and with an almost cloistral yard in front of them. Here, in amazement and reluctance to stare, I saw a dung-cart approach, pulled by a heifer and a bullock yoked across their brows in an ancient image forgotten in England. After exchanging gentle greetings with the old man tending them, I went into the café for a drink. This new bar has been fitted out with the latest in electronic jet-games and is full of conscious rural-rustic references, in the carefully gnarled wood around the bar, the lanterns, wrought-iron brackets and deliberate gloom. As I looked out to the dung cart and its bullocks parked outside, the whole history of Europe for the past two centuries seemed to close up like a fan.

It is six and a half kilometres to Landos on a Roman road, painful with little stones, like walking on marbles. Landos is visible far away down a wide vista, exaggerated by a line of telegraph poles across the yellowing sheep-nipped grass. This is an enormous landscape, Spanish in its breadth, with the feeling that beyond the visible edge it will fold out again in the same pattern. No single feature dictates and none need be filtered by a selective intelligence or touristic wish. Here is a country operating in unaffected beauty. Past a ruined farm (almost the first since Le Monastier) and the roofs of Charbonnier, in the same sloped order as the patchy hills around them, you come to Landos, to its only hotel (des Voyageurs) and finally to its *patronne*, Madame Adam, a fine hostess and a talented painter.

Landos to Cheylard l'Evêque

31 kilometres

Landos, on the same railway as Costaros, is a white place too. Beyond it the landscape repeats itself, with the shallow ballerina skirts of fields around the hills and with the wind-protection and resource of the woods on top of them. There are no rapid transitions or cliff-like ruptures, only a smooth brown extension, wherever you look, of here into there. It is a landscape of certainty, with no need for enterprise or change, and the dates incised on archways in the farm buildings are the only sign that time has passed. From the seven-

The ruined castle at Goudet caps a volcanic plug in the valley of the Loire.

179

The sharp edge of town and country at Pradelles demonstrates decay. The hill-town was the object of pilgrimage in the Middle Ages, but Langogne, its neighbour in the valley below, has drained the life away and left it a place of faded dereliction.

teenth century to the twentieth, barns here have been built in the same way, relying of necessity on local materials and local techniques. Hay is still gathered in pony-tail stooks, while beautiful ill-bred cocks stalk around the roads and farms.

Past Les Uffernets, five and a half kilometres from Landos, with its crowds of dogs and hint of decay – there are no children and broken windows are patched with wood – you arrive above Pradelles, a single street piped along a ridge with smoke hanging over it in back-lit wreaths. This sharp edge of a town, where fields run straight up without interruption to the backs of the houses, is a rarity now and means little growth in the past hundred years. The town has the air of a Home for Distressed Gentlefolk, living in an enervated way on the greatness it once had. Pradelles, possesses a miracle-working image of the Virgin which once brought enormous wealth to the town from the armies of pilgrims it attracted. The cafés now have names like 'Bar Univers' and 'Café du Siècle', but this is only whistling in the dark. There seems to

have been a competition at one stage between burghers as to who could have the most layers to the hood-mouldings around his windows. The deeper a window was recessed, the game went, the smarter the face that looked out from it. In Pradelles those with the most layers are in the main square, which is slightly tipped on the hillside and surrounded by stocky, irregular arcades, in an image of flawed and provincial urbanity. Very little appears to happen in Pradelles, and in the cobbled, straw-strewn back-streets, mottled with dung, many houses are now roofless derelicts.

It is six kilometres downhill to Langogne, a modern town on the railway and the river Allier, which has drained the life from Pradelles. You leave Pradelles' main square and drop down through the dark little streets,

A kind of brittle delicacy coats the moory hillsides above St Flour de Mercoire.

at one point passing under a church which bridges one of them. It is joined to a hospice and houses the famous wooden Virgin. Brought back by a crusader, she now stands at the far end of the church clothed in a stiff white dress.

The hospice is a handsome new building in a conservative style. I talked to one of the inmates who was dressed in blue overalls as flimsy as pyjamas. He could not believe that I did not already know the answers to the questions I asked him. Of course the hospice was only for the province. Of course both men and women were admitted – what on earth did I imagine? And what did I think they would be unless they were old? His sense of boredom, which prefaced every possible line of enquiry, was eroded only once. The magical catalyst that worked this transformation was the word *couples.* Yes, it was true, he admitted, with a glint he was only half embarrassed of, that the hospice had now provided married quarters where there had only been single accommodation before.

With his vision of an Elysium for the aged I left him and descended gradually on a good, frost-stiffened track through turfy fields to Langogne. The semi-industrial town appears around a corner, one chimney dominating it and with a massive timber yard between the railway and the river, the Allier itself an unnatural khaki green. Langogne can offer hotels and banks but little else.

Beyond it the landscape toughens. You have passed now from the old province of Velay into Gévaudan and from the department of Haute-Loire into Lozère. For many kilometres now, without any increase in the number of incidents, there is a sensation of growing hostility – in the absence of prospect, in an eternally uncomfortable gradient, either too steeply down or too slowly up. Nothing ahead beckons and the immediate surroundings of flowerless fields of broom grow tedious. At times it is as though the landscape has become a clamp, its grip tightening the more you struggle within it.

Five kilometres from Langogne, you come to the village of St Flour-de-Mercoire. At the top of it is a memorial to the local men (or boys) who died in the First World War. Little round sepia photographs of them are arranged behind glass in dice-fives on the marble. There could be few more eloquent testimonies than this to the gap between the rhetoric and the actuality of war. Their death was only questionably *pro patria*; there are no heroics and no decorum here, just the stupid memory of a bullet through the ill-fitting tunic, or more likely of disease inside it, faces disfigured by malnutrition in childhood, their minds on other matters, on local girls.

In a granite country of pines and thin, straggly beech trees, the way is now as remote as it will ever be. Stevenson was hopelessly lost here, and even if you do know where you are that knowledge seems scarcely important. You can follow his uncertain way to Cheylard l'Evêque by the tiny hamlets of Sagnerousse, Fouzillac and Fouzillic. Great granite planks fence the way through a wood, from which you emerge to Sagnerousse, three and a half kilometres from St Flour. This is an Aran Island place of unforgiving stone, a collection of hardness, mess and cowering dogs. The rounded hummocks of the rocks bulge hippo-like in the fields. Only the fish-scale slates on the roof of one building show a sense of decoration beyond use. Otherwise it is application and struggle here.

Fouzillac and Fouzillic, two kilometres further and half a kilometre apart, are on the edge of existence. Most buildings are empty, their roofs gone, their walls going. This is the face of depopulation, in Fouzillic softened only by the blue gingham curtains and occasional air of a holiday home. Apart from that, the place is nearly a memory.

Beyond the ruins, wandering lost, I came on two farmers, one with a tractor, the other with a shotgun. In the way that only foreigners have, I gaily hailed them as fellows of the road, to be answered by nothing but a slow and simultaneous turning of two heads. Did they, by any chance, know the way to Cheylard? A long arm swung out from the body riding the tractor, revolved and came to rest in laconic contempt, pointing east at a track into the wood. I effused and was foreign and followed his advice down an obvious lane, deep in crisp beech leaves, to arrive eventually high above the sharp valley that cups Cheylard in a hollow. Smoke hangs above Cheylard like steam over a herd of cows on a cold morning, and the arrival in the village is sweet. The spaces between the houses are paved with wide granite flags and

there is a modest café where you can get a drink but not much else. The famous Betty of California and Le Monastier stayed here for three days with her donkey and children, put up out of kindness in a barn. The old woman in the café remembers her well, but even better the presence of the Germans here during the war when they shot four young men from this village, members of the *Maquis*, at a nearby farm. As always in the remoter parts of France this account of occupation and humiliation is more moving than any Blitz tale could ever be.

Cheylard l'Evêque to Le Bleymard
54 kilometres

The way out of Cheylard is up a road through the forest of Mercoire, a tiny lane which was being surfaced for cars when I was there. The eleven kilometres from Cheylard to Luc are almost all on a sad, dull hill, so ghastly that Stevenson was forced to this now famous piece of philosophy: 'I travel not to go anywhere,' he announced to his journal, 'but to go; I travel for travel's sake. And to write about it afterwards, if only the public will be so condescending as to read. But the great affair is to move; to feel the needs and hitches of life a little more nearly, to get down off this featherbed of civilization, and to find the globe granite underfoot and strewn with cutting flints.' Not surprisingly the disarming (or is it sneering?) admission of his intention to write about this pure experience afterwards was omitted from the published version.

As you descend towards Luc, back down to the trough of the Allier, on the old road half-blocked by springy boughs of broom, a great white statue of the Virgin rises up towards you, head-first, from the top of the castle. Stevenson learned that it weighed fifty quintals, or five metric tonnes. It may seem extraordinary to measure a statue's worth by its weight, but when I asked a man in the village if it really was that heavy, he confirmed that it was and did not appear surprised that sheer mass should be a cause for enquiry or a source of pride. It is true, however, that the monster Virgin has few other characteristics to recommend her. Apart from its white goddess, Luc, though quite a big place and near the railway, is on the verge of disintegration – the old story of empty houses occasionally filled for holidays.

A tramp for nearly eight kilometres along the banks of the Allier will bring you to Labastide Puylaurent. The road is big but never busy, the river entertaining. Your feet might well, like Modestine's knees, be raw beef by now, but the steady metronome beat of each step as it drops on to the level road will carry you through. In November the Allier runs rough and full between meadows yellow with the husks of dried grass. You follow the valley through Pranlac and Laveyrune, and on past the mill at Rogleton, no longer turning.

Few experiences are more disappointing than arriving at a place where your expectation is of welcome and the reality is *fermeture annuelle*. Only one hotel out of many, Les Pins, was open in Labastide in late November and the tone of the whole place was one of blasé indifference. Perhaps this is simply the style of a tourist spot out of season (or between them: Labastide is also a centre for *ski randonnée*). Certainly it is a universe away from Cheylard.

Four and a half kilometres uphill from the village is a place far more receptive to visitors. This is the Trappist monastery of Notre Dame des Neiges, where Stevenson spent a night. His rigidly Protestant background had taught him to look on Catholic monks as warily as 'a boy might look on a lion or an alligator' and he greatly enjoyed the *frisson* of his enclosure with them. The building he lodged in was burnt down in 1912 but an exact replica with various extensions has been built on the spot. As you climb to the monastery a big stack of mountain is revealed to the south. This is the first glimpse of the High Cévennes which the way crosses for the next few days, but the growing view is overshadowed by the emergence over a brow of the monastery itself. It appears proud and substantial, more of a château than an abbey, and more the seat of power than a place of retreat.

The abbey charmingly occupies the crutch of two valleys running together, surrounded by fine stands of beech trees, with an established air of prosperity. In the efficiently run souvenir shop (part of the new complex housing an audio-visual unit) I talked for a long time to a Belgian lay brother attached to the fringes of the monastery. The rule of silence, which defined the Trappists when they splintered from the Cistercians in the mid-seventeenth century, has been modified here, if not dropped entirely. The principal reason, I was told, is that the brothers now have matters to handle that the old Trappist sign-language cannot deal with. As evidence of the problem I was shown computer printouts that displayed and arranged the sales and stock figures of the souvenir shop, as well as the wine business that the monks run.

The layman offered me one of his cigarettes as he reckoned out the bill for my guide-book and postcards. The phrase 'Thank God' spattered his conversation with a strange mixture of worldliness and theological exactitude. I tried it myself when referring to the mildness of the weather but he just looked at me through the cigarette smoke with narrowed eyes. At that moment a monk came out of the Zone of Silence into the shop. At last, I thought, here is a man for whom a venture into the verbal is a rarity, but it was not so and the French that followed was all too ordinarily fluent.

Souvenirs are a handy sideline, but the main money-spinner for the abbey is a form of wine-shipping. The monks buy in bulk, mostly from the Hérault to the south but also from Germany, and expose the wine to the high-altitude air at the abbey, which, it is said, reduces the level of acid in it. This process, called *bonification*, raises the price of the wine which is then bottled and labelled with the valuable name of Notre Dame des Neiges.

Profits from this enterprise have financed the building, amongst other things, of an enormous new hostelry. Priests and relations of the monks come here on retreat from the real world and, as the guide-book says, every guest is received as if he were Christ. In practical terms this means a private bathroom and telephone in each room and five star comfort throughout – the envy, in fact, of all the Labastide hoteliers labouring in unenlightened secularity down in the valley below.

The stage from Labastide to Le Bleymard is the hinge of the walk. At Pont de Bon Dieu, five kilometres from Labastide, you pass the half-way mark and soon afterwards a far more important and quite unmarked juncture. The road leaves the Allier, now dwindled to a mountain stream, and between this point and Chasseradès, twelve kilometres from Labastide, you cross the slightest of hills. It is the principal watershed of northern Europe. The Allier flows from one side of it into the Loire at Nevers and eventually into the Atlantic, while the water in the boggy little stream that runs through Chasseradès will eventually join the Rhône and with it the Mediterranean. On the hill to the north the headsprings of the Allier and the Chassezac (the river that runs down to the Rhône) are only 150 metres apart. The waters heading for the Mediterranean have 150 kilometres to reach sea-level, while those destined for the Atlantic have over 1,000. The gradient (and so the erosive force) of one is six or seven times fiercer than the other, and there

In an upland country, the stone inside the
Romanesque church at Chasseradès becomes
significant, an object of veneration in itself.

is no doubt that the upper reaches of the Allier
will soon be 'captured' by the Chassezac. The
water in them will at an instant reverse its
flow to run down to the sea 600 kilometres
south-east of where, a day before, it would
have joined the Atlantic.

For all the future Armageddon, there is
little to divert you here now. Rowan trees –
thicker and older than any you find in
England – and the occasional ash line the road.
In the woods there is a muddled mixture of
pine, beech and broom, and below them in the
pools of the stream thick piles of dead leaves
like dream faces have accumulated. High in
front is Le Goulet, the first big hill of the walk.

Chasseradès is hidden until you get there. It
is broken in two by a large scab of roughness
around the stream that runs down through it.
At the top, at the point of unity, is the church,
attached to its large Romanesque tower, and
laid directly on the slaty rock which surfaces

in the streets around it. Inside, the rusty
brown stone is exposed in all its roughness, an
outward sign of inward grace, with capitals
carved on to the pilasters under an obvious
Burgundian influence, which has been pro-
foundly muddied and debased in its passage
south.

It is thirteen and a half kilometres from
Chasseradès to Le Bleymard over the hill of Le
Goulet. All the way from Labastide the
walking has been too smooth for comfort. Just
beyond Chasseradès, the gorge of the Chassezac breaks roughly through. This abrasive,
quarrying river, destined for the Mediterranean, is the first sign of the south that we
have come to. Packed into the gorge, hidden
and almost hooded by it, is the small village of
Mirandol, dominated by a curving railway
viaduct that bridges the gap. A maze of lanes
leads down into Mirandol, but it is easier
simply to walk along the viaduct. You get an
aerial look at the roofs of the village blotched
in yellow lichens below you. The slates on
them meet at the ridge in a crossing of stubs,
slotting into each other like the bottom of a

In Mirandol.

The roofs of Mirandol testify to a rural technology of skill and endless labour. Each of the ridge-slates interlocks with its neighbours in a pattern that needs cement to make it waterproof. In the background, the railway viaduct bridges the valley with ease.

box. This way, there is no need for what can be the most expensive part of a roof, the ridge-pieces themselves, which are triangular in cross-section and which need to be sawn out of solid blocks. Even so, there can be no doubt that this kind of crossed-stub roof, though cheaper, is much less effective at keeping out the weather.

As I began to climb the lane leading towards the serrated skyline of Le Goulet, about 300 metres above me and three kilometres away, I was joined by a great, shaggy, big-footed hound who purred when I stroked him. He was immediately christened Albert (it was the name that sounded most like the noises he made) and without invitation or encouragement accompanied me all day to Le Bleymard, padding backwards and forwards with a fine, tail-waving wag that signalled as friendly, sure and calm a spirit as one could ever meet. I trudged and he lolled up through l'Estampe, where there is a hostel run by the French Ramblers, over high cropped meadows and

into the woods on a track deep in mast. The 1,000-foot climb ends at a rather disappointing non-summit where the modern forestry plantations ensure that from no single point can one see past, present and future. Le Goulet is well over 4,000 feet above sea level, but this bulbous hill is really nothing more than a yeasty down.

The mountain ahead, seen for the first time from the top of Le Goulet, is different. It is the great granite intrusion of Mont Lozère, at 1,700 metres the summit of the walk, and, with the sun behind it, a block of blackness in the sky. As you go down on a slightly damp and elastic track towards Le Bleymard, the foothills of Lozère are revealed in the valley mist with the bells of cows and the crowing of cocks above them. This beautiful valley and the mountain fronting it make it seem as

Maison à Vendre, *Les Alpiers: a modest attempt at real estate in a slate hamlet exhausted by depopulation.*

though between Landos and here you have
not been meeting the Cévennes face to face,
but have somehow been padded from the
direct experience of them. It is as if you have
been restricted to a map of too small a scale,
without the actualities of detail and contour,
and now in full-bodied profile the true nature
of the place is revealed. There is a need for
shape and a certain obviousness of direction
in a landscape if you are to see yourself as
significant within it. Only if you can organize
the landscape around you, if you can change it
into surroundings, will the dispiriting sense of
being just another incidental disappear.

You will come down in an aesthetic
euphoria to Le Bleymard, and if the sun is
shining the light will be catching the mica
chips in the slates that roof the town, as
though they were banks of solar panels. But
out of the glare you will find it a poor country.
The way runs straight through a half-deserted
hamlet called Les Alpiers, where everything is
made of slate, from the rock underfoot and the
fence-posts to the walls of the houses and the
roofs. Then out into the poor fields beyond it
scarecrows stand crucified and irrelevant in a
soil that is too thin and whose only yield was
taken long ago. There are few women to be
seen in Les Alpiers now, since it is they, I was
told, who lead the exodus towards the cities,
which the men can only follow. The geographical and the human process are the same;
it is all a slow sedimentary settling down from
the mountains towards the valleys and the
plain.

At the bottom of the hill, on the edge of Le
Bleymard, you cross a thin stream, nothing
more than might once have driven a Kentish
hammer mill. It is the river Lot, only a
kilometre or two from its source and the origin
of that marvellous unstoppable trunk of water
to be found deep in its limestone gorges many
miles to the west. This is a country of river
creation, and even here in their insignificant
youth the streams of the Loire, the Lot and the
Tarn are the lines that dictate the major shapes
of the terrain.

At Le Bleymard Albert and I had to part. It
became obvious that I could neither keep him
until the end at St Jean-du-Gard nor hope
simply that he would find his own way back. I
hired a taxi for him, he bounded in, and the
last thing I saw, as the car drove off up the
road round Le Goulet, was Albert sitting in
the back as comfortably settled as the vice-
president of a bank.

Le Bleymard to St Jean du Gard
59 kilometres

Le Bleymard is hunched below its mountain
which begins to rise immediately to the south,
reaching the summit of the Pic des Finiels in
about eight kilometres. For Stevenson the
600-metre climb to the top and the arrival
there was a period of great expectation and
then of revelation, as, in a series of water-
colour washes, the mountains, 'the Cévennes
with an emphasis, the Cévennes of the
Cévennes' appeared extending forever to the
south. It was foggy when I was there, a
Derbyshire day of closed-down dampness, a
tone reinforced by the Peak District style of
walled tracks on the lower slopes of the
mountain. After about 300 metres climbing
they emerge on to a slight shelf occupied by
some rough buildings known collectively as
the Chalet de Mont Lozère. It is a ski centre
where you can stay in season.

When I was there a strong south wind was
blowing over the ridge. This warm air, made
to rise by the mountain, was full of cloud as it
came over the top. Dropping in billows of
drinkable vapour like the dry-ice rush of
stage-fog, it was the most theatrical piece of
atmospherics that I have ever seen. A moving
coat of cushion stuffing, it came to a comfortable halt in the valley of the Lot to the
north, where it was rapidly filling a reservoir
of mist.

The chalet area was as unfinished as ski
resorts can always afford to be, in the sure
knowledge that snow when it comes will
smooth over whatever looks untidy. A
thousand feet of climbing lie between the
chalet and the summit, a steady easy tramp on
a compass-bearing in fog, past the occasional
ski-lift stilled like a production line at night,
and with one or two of the stone posts that
once guided Stevenson and Modestine on
their way. The washed-out yellow of the
dummocky grass, interspersed with a few
blocks of granite and some buttons of heather
like flattened hedgehogs, are all in the colours
of an infra-red photograph, their relative
values recognizable, but the whole spectrum
shifted by fog into strangeness. Patches of old
snow, seen from Le Goulet the afternoon
before, cross your path, dimpled like an
orange skin, hard and icy. The sense of
progress weakens in the fog, in an endlessness
tempered only by a gradual thinning of the
vegetation underfoot, until you arrive at the
ridge top where granite sticks up almost clear
of it. The only vegetable life viable here (it is
over 1700 metres above sea level and unpro-

tected by anything higher nearby) is a kind of bright green, submarine lichen which clings to the rocks. There was no sight of future mountains, let alone of the Mediterranean, which is said to be visible from here on the best of days.

You come down off the hostile top through a small steep pine wood and then out into the fields above the village of Finiels. Your hands will smell of the pines you have clutched at on the way down. Just outside Finiels I met an old man with his cows and a black dog that was spattered with white hairs as if with paint. He was dressed in rather the same way. He asked where I had just come from and looked skyward in amazement when I told him. 'But that's not the right way at all,' he said and pointed out the road to le Bleymard that skirted the mountain. I began explaining about the Sommet des Finiels, about conquest and the urge to be on *top* of things, but he interrupted me: 'And what, tell me, is the point of such a thing on a day like this, when the cloud is next to one's nose?' I changed the subject – his cows, what kind were they? 'Well, most come from here,' he said.

Above Finiels on Mont Lozère, an irreducible solidity of rock.

'Do they have a name at all?'

'No, no name at all, they just come from here. But one of them is a Tarentaise and the rest, the white ones, [*les vlaincs*, he said in a southern distortion], 'are of course Charolais.' We went down to his house, newly built from re-used stones in a traditional design of which his son was the architect. 'The stones are old, aren't they?' I asked him. 'Yes,' he said without puzzlement, 'and they'll get still older.'

Finiels is at the head of a valley that falls steeply for six and a half kilometres to the valley of the Tarn at Pont de Monvert. It is, as Stevenson described it, 'stubbly with rocks like a reaped field of corn, and floored farther down with green meadows.' There is new money here (witness the rebuilding in Finiels) for new barns, new technology, bigger tractors and trailers, far more than in Le Bleymard or villages like Les Alpiers. This side of Mont Lozère, in what is definably the High Cévennes, has been designated a region

where farmers can qualify for improvement grants which their near-equals to the north, caught in a poverty trap, cannot.

For Stevenson his joy at arriving in this new country south of Mont Lozère was more than just aesthetic. This is the country of the Camisards, Protestant rebels dear to his heart, who at the end of the seventeenth century and for ten years at the beginning of the eighteenth held out against the full force of Louis XIV's army and church. Here at Pont de Montvert in 1702 the most explosive event in the intermittent rebellion occurred, when the Catholic Abbé du Chayla, notorious for his persecutions, was hauled from his burning house and stabbed to death in the streets of the town next to the Tarn. The assassins then moved on to release forty Protestant Cévenols from du Chayla's prison.

To understand the revolt – and incidentally to discover more about the people of the High Cévennes – it is necessary to know something of the religious history of these mountains. With the great rise of Protestantism in the sixteenth century, the Cévenols, a mountain people more of choice than of fate, took to the

Finiels, near Le Bleymard: a massiveness in the granite construction to equal the underlying nature of Mont Lozère.

new religion with more enthusiasm than their neighbours in the *pays fromager et drapier* of the plains to the east. At the end of the century the victory of Henry of Navarre, a Protestant, in the Wars of Religion guaranteed the toleration of Protestants, even though he famously became Catholic himself. The proclamation of their freedom to worship in certain specific localities was made at Nantes in 1598.

Throughout the seventeenth century, in an atmosphere of growing absolutism, the provisions of the Edict of Nantes were gradually eroded. The existence of French people who did not participate in the state religion came to be seen as a political anomaly and a weakness in the position of the monarchy. This attitude received the slogan: '*Un seul roi, une seule foi*' and the rhyme and repetition took on the aura of logic, of obviousness and of necessity. For Bossuet, the Burgundian Bishop of Condom and apologist

for the monarchy, it became clear that: 'The truth is unchanging; the Roman church is unchanging; therefore the Roman church is the truth.' It is possible that in personal terms too Louis XIV imagined that if he suppressed Protestantism in France it would in some way make up, in God's eyes, for his more private excesses and sins. In 1685 the Edict of Nantes was revoked and 250,000 Protestants left France. Those who remained were stripped of almost all protection.

It might be surprising that as much as seventeen years elapsed between the revocation of the edict and the eruption of anger in Pont de Montvert, but the years were not empty ones. To begin with, the authorities suffered from a basic misconception about Protestantism, for they assumed that if the pastors and the structure of the church were removed, the faith itself would collapse. But the Huguenot soul and the Cévenol heart were famous for both patience and ardour, and what mattered to them was not ritual but 'la piété agissante et quotidienne.' The hard and, in summer, dried-out landscape of the Cévennes is not very different from the landscapes described in the Bible, in particular those behind the famous scenes of persecution and eventual delivery from servitude. Babylon is a universal experience, and the reflexive translation of life into story and of story back into life became for the Protestant leaders of the Camisards a demonstration of the daily importance and relevance of their faith. The Bible of Jean Cavalier, the most flamboyant of them and Stevenson's hero, is particularly fingered and grubby on those pages which tell of God's anger descending on Nineveh and Babylon.

The attempts at suppression continued. Between 1686 and 1688 24 Cévenols were condemned to death, 40 to the galleys and 300 to deportation. By the end of the century 60 had been executed and 320 were in the galleys. These figures do not include the victims of the *dragonnades*, which were sudden and brutal descents by detachments of dragoons who were billeted on Protestants to punish them. In the official reports to Versailles on the effects of the atrocities, the analogy most frequently used was that of laundering, where it was usually claimed that village after village had been efficiently 'cleaned' of Protestant vermin.

In these extreme circumstances a powerful form of mystical religion broke surface.

An emulsion of snow covers the long back of Mont Lozère above Finiels and the valley of the Tarn.

Apocalyptic prophesies of the fall of Babylon swept through Protestant France, not only in the Cévennes, but in the Dauphiné and Vivarais too. Children spoke in tongues and whole crowds would suddenly be convulsed with paroxysms of weeping. The revolution in England in 1688 and the replacement of the Catholic James II with William III, the standard bearer of Protestant Europe, raised the hopes of a general transformation to come. But William and the rest of the international Protestant community turned their backs on the Camisards and dismissed them as fanatics.

The assassination of du Chayla in Pont de Montvert on 24 July 1702 set loose a riot of revenge. Catholic churches were burnt down and their priests murdered. Esprit Séguier, the leader at the killing, was caught within a few days and burnt alive. Under Jean Cavalier and Rolland, with no more than 5,000 soldiers but with the support of the populace, a sort of Camisard state was set up, defended with arsenals stored in caves. It lasted until October 1703, when the royal commander settled on a policy of extermination. In the following three months 466 villages in the High

The bridge over the Tarn is the only thread holding Le Pont-de-Montvert together, gashed in two by the mountain river.

Cévennes were burnt and their populations put to the sword. In the mirror image of Glencoe, only a few years before, Catholic militiamen were recruited from St Florent to add religious hatred (and consequent efficiency) to what was essentially the removal of a political nuisance.

The revolt straggled on for seven years more, but its back had been broken. The picture of the Camisard rebellion as the repression of a band of saints by an intolerant state is only partly true; the Camisards were quite as brutal as their enemies and the government's motives might have been justifiable politically. Such questions, though, are scarcely what remains in one's mind of the revolt. More vibrant than any political theory is the reply, for instance, of Esprit Séguier at his trial when asked what he had to say of his crimes. 'I have committed none,' he answered. 'My soul is like a garden full of shelter and of fountains.'

Pont de Montvert is roofed in grey-green slates, the colour of Delabole slates in Cornwall, and the small, winding streets are Cornish too, with tight cul-de-sac yards off them, where chickens are fenced in. In the town, facing each other from opposite heights, are the Protestant chapel and the Catholic church, the one geometrical in its austerity, the other, with a spire, plastered in the architecture of hierarchy and elaboration. The domestic intricacy of the town around them, as detailed as a Victorian sampler, reaches to its southern boundary where the whole careful fabric is rent by the wide and uncontrolled gash of the river Tarn and attached only by the thread of a bridge to a smaller continuation on the far side. Under the bridge the waters of the Tarn are the green of a peppermint liqueur diluted to an ink.

At Pont de Montvert Stevenson, exhausted by his journey and his donkey, turned along the new valley road by the Tarn that leads west to Florac. From there he almost doubled back on his track, along another new road in the valley of the Mimente as far as Cassagnas. This is a forty-five-kilometre detour from the

Above the valley of the Mimente: a new look and a new air greets you as you move over the ridges into each successive valley.

direct route south over the mountains and nowadays, on the busy roads, it would be no fun. As it is, the straighter route south over the next mountain, called Le Bougès, is clear enough. It soon climbs up from a small side valley that repeats the morning walk from Finiels into an evergreen wood made Japanese by islands of larches – in November their needles, both on the trees and in the ruts of the path, are a pure lacquer yellow. It is fifteen kilometres to Cassagnas on slaty tracks which harden here and there into quartz blocks dyed blood-red. For many miles this wood is condemned to utter sameness. But then, if you are lucky, you will find a small, mythical beast, like a South American exotic in the wrong continent, wandering slowly over your mountain path. It will be a salamander, its marvellously black, fleshy body with splashes and stripes of bright yellow all over it, declaring of course that it is no good to eat. The salamander was the badge of François I

193

Apparently random patches of ploughed earth chequer the prairie near Landos.

Near Cassagnas in the valley of the Mimente.

and it is not difficult to see why; there can be few European animals that stand out as it does in muddy, damp surroundings so neatly and spectacularly heraldic.

Eventually you arrive above the valley of the Mimente and, on the horseshoe curving road through what Stevenson called 'the chestnut gardens', you will come down to the village of Cassagnas. Only twenty-five people live here throughout the winter and there is no hotel now, no café and no shop. I camped down on the sliver of green in the very bottom of the valley below the village, and to get a cup of coffee the next morning climbed back up and knocked on the door of the first house I came to. It belonged to Madame Viers (the 's' is pronounced) and from deep inside her kitchen she shouted for me to come in. I went in to find her with her daughter and, on the kitchen table, an entire pig. Its little black eye gazed out dead from a mass of fatty blood and its hairy ears, with a blue sticker in one of them, flapped slightly as Mme Viers gouged out a few pieces more for the *fromage de tête*. Her daughter was busy working on the other

end. This was their one pig a year, bought in the market at Alès and the source of an entire winter's *charcuterie*. Mme Viers was a charming woman who kindly made some fresh coffee for me. She asked if I had read the novel that had just been awarded the Prix Goncourt. I had not, and as her knife slipped deftly in and out and her fingers worked on intransigent gristle or clutched at excess fat, she explained to me the rather complex time-scheme of the novel and how the sense of reality conveyed by the narrator was consistently undermined, only to be re-established at the introduction of each new character. I drank her coffee, watched and listened in awe, refused the generous offer of some sausages and, grateful for everything, left.

The last part of the walk, to St Jean-du-Gard, is about thirty-eight kilometres long and just within the limits of a single day. You climb up from the valley of the Mimente through the sprinkle, on a bright day, of light through the pine woods and soon enough reach a level track, which in fourteen kilometres comes to St Germain de Calberte. Despite notices to the effect that nature lovers are trying to reintroduce grouse into these mountain forests, I met many shooters here ready for anything. It was with difficulty and a conscious exorcism of the memory of Mme Viers' kitchen that I did not see the more substantial of these machos as pieces of *charcuterie* in overalls. We said good morning to each other with the mutual suspicion of dogs and I concentrated on the distance. There are abandoned farms and hamlets here on every ridge and the occasional roofless village exposed to the air in plan. Between them, still worked on the steep hillsides, are a few sticking-plaster fields of highlight green, and beyond them all mountains form ridges away into foreign distances. It is a stepped landscape without fluency, as if the earth had stuttered as it came into being. At the Col de la Pierre Plantée, where there is indeed a planted stone, incised and set upright, you begin to drop to St Germain on a slithering path under chestnuts. It finally emerges into the warmth of the valley near the village, arriving at a new neatness of careful terraces, and with a smell of the south, of rosemary and lavender, full on your face. This valley is almost the first place since Le Monastier that *looks* as if it is owned. There is a new density of cultivation and of culture here, the air has thickened and the sense of desperation has gone. Arrival in St Germain itself is like a dunking in Southern Comfort – there are plane trees in the small square and two grocers, a baker and a coiffeur in the village. Bundles of flowers hang from the houses and the the church is graced with a decorated door.

The houses in this valley have changed from the low, tucked buildings of Cassagnas and before, to a high, almost warehouse style. The progression in ridged mountains is measured by successive ratchets, clicking in at each valley to a new way of life; it is gradually left on the climb up the far side where, once over the ridge, you drop again into difference. But at St Germain the last of these transformations is over. It is a valley walk now to the end at St Jean. Stevenson, pining for Fanny and anxious to get the letters waiting for him at Alès, made a final successful effort to reach St Jean from St Germain without rest. You can follow his route now on an easy, graded and signposted track (which the modern road has neglected) along one side of the valley. It is ten and a half kilometres to St Etienne Vallée-Française, with ravens chasing mewing buzzards overhead, until above the village, boxed in by dark pine woods on either side, a Black Forest château appears spiking the sky above the river.

You will be into a rhythm now and swinging on through St Etienne you will soon come to a point of decision which, if you are as exhausted as I was, will not be a difficult one. At the Ste Croix river you can take either a road made since Stevenson's time which follows the valley almost all the way to St Jean, or climb, as he did, for 300 metres up Mont St Pierre and from there corkscrew down to St Jean. I took the valley road. The river is the same bright green as the Tarn at Pont de Montvert, and the gorge it has cut in the hopelessly shaly rock a great, gouged scarification as if torn by an excavator. You will long for a canoe as your feet hurt and burn on the twisting road. You will notice, perhaps, how the rock is so friable that buildings here can be made only of the quartz that marbles the earth in places like fat in pâté, and how it is even inadequate for roofing slates – ceramic tiles are used instead.

If you have come in one day from Cassagnas darkness will probably fall before you have reached St Jean. Mountains expand into it and you will be surprised by the light of a farm in what you thought was the sky. The cold of the night will be welcome as everything becomes subject to an end which persistently stretches further away. From time to time headlights burn a band of the present through the encompassing dark until at last, around a corner, the unspecific sodium light of a town dilutes the sky above you. Soon enough you will be passing the sign at the city limits and arriving at the high, narrow Grande Rue, where you can collapse into a hotel and a bed.

The next morning St Jean-du-Gard, revealed through the haze of exhaustion the

St Jean-du-Gard: a national image foreign to the mountains themselves.

ABOVE *Le Galadet, above Le Pont-de-Montvert.*

TOP *Above Cheylard l'Evêque.*

The High Cévennes ridge away into southern distances, as though the earth had stuttered here as it came into being.

In the valley of the Mimente.

night before as the first place in the Cévennes with neon signs, appears tainted with valley urbanity and satisfaction. There is a Salle Stevenson here to record the passing of our guide and hero, but, more important, there is the sense of an emergence from the mountains into the plain, from a country of Protestant choice that has been yours for a week, into one where decisions are somehow made for you.

MAPS
I.G.N. 1:50,000 Numbers 2836 (Le Monastier), 2736 (Cayres), 2737 (Langogne), 2738 (Le Bleymard), 2739 (Génolhac), 2740 (St André de Valborgne)

GUIDE
Robert Louis Stevenson, *Travels with a Donkey in the Cévennes*, London 1879 (Modern Edition: Everyman, London 1978)

CÉVENNES BOOKS
Jenni Calder, *The Robert Louis Stevenson Companion*, Paul Harris

André Ducasse, *La Guerre des Camisards*, Hachette 1970

James Pope Hennessy, *Robert Louis Stevenson*, Cape 1974

Philippe Joutard, *La Légende des Camisards*, Gallimard 1977

Heather Willings, *A Village in the Cévennes*, Gollancz 1979

P. Wolff (editor), *Documents de l'Histoire de Languedoc*, Privat 1969

DISTANCES (in kilometres)
Le Monastier to:
St Martin de Fugères 7.5; Goudet 3.2; Ussel 4.1; Le Bouchet-St-Nicolas 9.8; Landos 6.3; Pradelles 9.99; Langogne 6.2; St Flour-de-Mercoire 6.0; Cheylard l'Evêque 9.3; Luc 11.0; Labastide Puylaurent 7.7; Notre Dame des Neiges 4.6; Labastide again 4.6; Chasseradès 12.6; Le Bleymard 13.5; Sommet de Finiels 7.8; Finiels 3.8; Pont de Montvert 6.3; Cassagnas 14.7; St Germain de Calberte 14.0; St Etienne 10.5; St Jean-du-Gard 13.7

The Pyrenees

St Jean Pied-de-Port to Arrens

180 kilometres

Frontiers, like birthdays, do no more than calibrate a continuous change. Identity leaks across them, and a border country with its own character comes into being. This walk for 180 kilometres through the western Pyrenees, very near the Spanish border and actually touching it twice, is through just such a country. These mountains are not as high as those in the middle of the range and here at least the Pyrenees are – and always have been – passable. Roman roads (which were admittedly impossible for wheeled traffic) crossed them; the Arab host that was to be defeated by Charles Martel in Touraine in 732 penetrated France by the Vallée d'Aspe, one of the most beautiful and remote of the Béarnais valleys; Charlemagne's army was able to pass south via Roncesvalles to interfere in an eighth-century civil war between the Arabs in Navarre; medieval pilgrims to Santiago de Compostella made their way south over a large number of Pyrenean passes throughout the Middle Ages; and, more recently, refugees from both Fascist Spain and Occupied France used the high mountain passes as their escape routes. But more important than these dramatic and mostly occasional crossings has been the most enduring movement in these mountains, the yearly migration of flocks, herds and men from the valleys on either side to the high forests and pastures between them. This annual and ancient transhumance (it means 'change of ground') is the cement which has bound the Pyrenees into one country. Wild animals, including boars and hares, still move downward at the onset of winter and back up with the spring, recognizing that to go down is the equivalent of a move south into warmth, and that to go back up is to return to a cooler summer.

It is the Basque country, at least as far as the Pic d'Anie, almost exactly half-way – beyond which, until Arrens, the path crosses the old Vicomté of Béarn. The Basques are one of the strangest anomalies in Europe. Their language (and the only reliable definition of a Basque is someone who speaks it) is quite unrelated to

The limestone mass of Le Billare above Lescun in the Vallée d'Aspe. The snow-patched valley to the right of the mountain penetrates to the frontier and the mountain in the distance is in Spain.

The forest of Iraty, clothing the ridges below the Pic d'Orhi, has been cut and cleared to make pasture for 7,000 years. Even so it remains one of the largest natural forests in Europe.

*Lac Olzalureko in the beech and pine forest of Irati.
Nowhere is greener than the eastern Pyrenees.*

any of the Indo-European family of languages. In other words, if the common roots of Indian, Iranian, Armenian, Greek, Latin, Celtic, Slavonic, Albanian and German are all traced, Basque remains outside them. The only languages to which it bears some relation are the collection of dialects gathered round the Caucasus in southern Russia, the language spoken by the Berbers (the pre-Arab population of Morocco) and Estonian. As a measure of its age Basque contains borrowings from both Latin and Celtic, like Americanisms in English, but more strikingly it still bears traces of the world before the great change in climate that overcame Europe in about 800 BC. The lower Pyrenees are now covered in huge and beautiful beech forests which took root at that time, but there is no ancient Basque word for beech, only *fago*, borrowed from the Latin. Before then, as pollen evidence has shown, birch forests made up the climax vegetation, and there *is* an ancient Basque word for birch, though there are now few Pyrenean birches.

Stranger than the vocabulary is the Basque syntax. Every noun has twelve cases, every one of which can occur in the singular, the plural and a form where the number is indeterminate, so that each noun can appear in thirty-six different variations. The verbs conjugate according to both the object (and its gender) and the subject. The 'reality' or 'possibility' of the action, in tenses that are either past, present or eventual, all work further mutations. The personal pronouns (which take the form of both a prefix and a suffix) themselves vary according to the tense of the verb. How any communication is possible with all this, and archaisms, and the variations from the seven different provinces, I do not know. The posters announcing rugby matches or cattle auctions, which are usually the most accessible and intelligible part of any foreign town, are here covered in Xs, Ks and umlauts and are impenetrably and irretrievably strange.

This strange Basque grammar has prevented

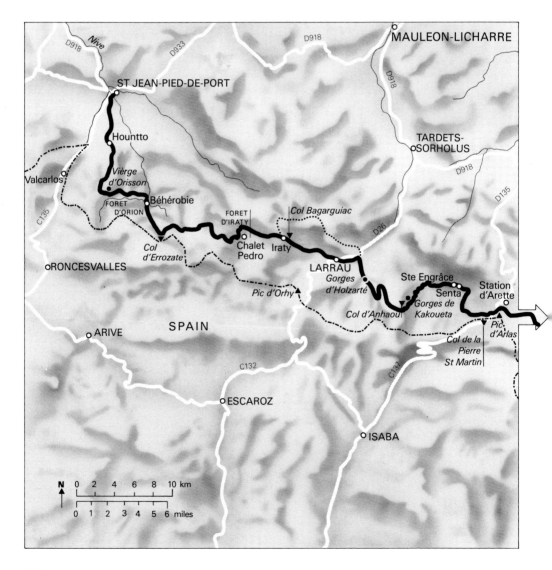

the French penetration of local culture, which has homogenized so much of the rest of France. The Basques have been pushed far back from the territory they once occupied (Gascon and Basque are at root the same word) but within the modern *pays basque* the air is of a French occupation of a foreign country or, as the Basques themselves express it, of people living as foreigners in their own land.

These might be the perfect circumstances for the creation of a ferocious separatist movement, but historical, political and geographical factors have combined so that the Basque terrorist group ETA (*Euskadi Ta Askatasuna*, 'A Basque State and Liberty') has had almost no impact in France. In Spain, on the other hand, where it was founded in Bilbao in 1959, it has maintained a campaign almost as effective as the IRA's in Ulster, reaching its highpoint in December 1973 when Admiral Carrero Blanco, the prime minister, was blown up in a Madrid street. One of the crucial differences between the

Spanish and French Basque countries is that the one is more important to Madrid than the other is to Paris. There are no more than 100,000 Basque-speaking Frenchmen, compared with over 400,000 Basques in Spain, many of whom are concentrated around the important industries of Bilbao and San Sebastian, of which there is no real equivalent on the French side. The Spanish Basques have more to fight for and can exert a greater pressure on their government. Add to this the different histories of France and Spain in this century, and the reasons for the different attitudes on either side of the border become clearer. Near the beginning of the Spanish Civil War, in October 1936, the Popular Front Government gave a large measure of autonomy to the four Spanish Basque provinces, which actually set up a government. This springtime of Basque nationalism was scarred by the *Luftwaffe* raid in April 1937 on Guernica, a sacred place for Basques, and still more deeply by the incarceration of 10,000 of

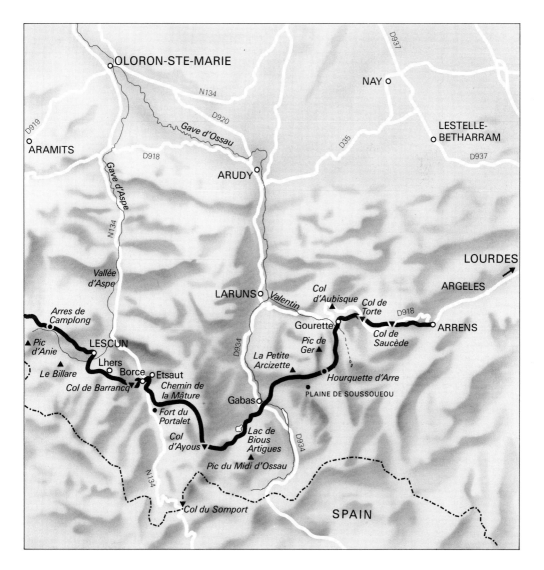

The flowers in the valley of Camplong below the Pic d'Anie are more like an untended garden than a random wild growth. This valley above Lescun is the easternmost place where you might hope to meet the Pyrenean bear.

them in Bilbao after the final surrender of the city to the Fascist forces in June 1937. The French Basques have suffered nothing compared with this experience, nor do they have the urban habits and attitudes necessary for the birth of modern terrorism.

But if France was unable to provide the culture from which an ETA could spring, why should the ETA, once formed, not operate there? The answer, never admitted by the French Ministry of the Interior, which would have to do something about it for the sake of Spanish-French relations, is that the French Basque country actually provides a perfect base of operations for the terrorists. Immediately after the Second World War, before the capitalist countries re-established relations with Franco, the CIA trained Basque guerrillas among these hills and forests, and there is no doubt that ETA High Command is now to be found either in Bayonne or St Jean-de-Luz. Terrorists have given press conferences in France after assassinations in Spain, while the movement back and forth with false papers is facilitated by the volume of holiday traffic between the two countries. Most terrorists pass through the border disguised as tourists, but occasionally the high Pyrenean passes are still used. The *Guardia Civil* gets no recruits from Navarra itself, and the local guides used by ETA easily escape the police in the complex and confusing topography of the border ridges. Radio conferences are held from either side of the border and terrorists on the run are met by reception teams at the designated pass. Wanted and recognizable men escape this way, in commandos of two, three or four men, some of whom are as young as seventeen. It is the only way out after confrontations with the police further south into Spain, and on several occasions regular patrols of the French mountain gendarmerie have found the bodies of men who have been wounded and escaped across the frontier, but who have died before reaching help or safety.

ETA's favourite slogan is the Basque phrase meaning 'Seven is One.' The division of the single Basque nation into seven provinces is disturbing for the nationalists but paradoxically is dear to the hearts of less politicized Basques, for whom loyalty to a particular valley has always mattered more than the wider issue. One nineteenth-century economist wrote that every Pyrenean valley 'is a little world that differs from the neighbouring world as Mercury does from Uranus,' while the graded cosmos of the people of Ste Engrâce, high on the very eastern edge of the *pays basque*, consists of three categories –

those 'below' Ste Engrâce, both physically and morally, the people of the village itself, and those 'above' it, who, since no human being lives above it physically, are necessarily divine. A widespread Basque proverb claims: 'Whoever goes far to marry is either fooled or fooling.'

This attitude has resulted in a fascinating social structure in the valleys, of which you are constantly aware on this walk. Its core, the fixed points around which life revolves, are the huge and solidly built houses, designed to accommodate three and sometimes four generations of the family. Many of them are from the seventeenth or eighteenth century, as the names and dates carved on the lintel show. Man and wife can be found on these inscriptions side by side, since, once inside the door, the woman was in command. The house and all the enclosed land around it always passed to the eldest child, whether boy or girl, even when nineteenth-century laws in both France and Spain forbade it. This served to maintain the small-holdings at a viable size. Younger children had three options: remaining as a paid hand in the family home; entering the Church; or emigrating, either within France or beyond it. About 90,000 Basques emigrated to the Americas during the nineteenth century. In times of exceptional population growth, such as the eighteenth century, when higher food prices made marginal land worth cultivating, new farms were enclosed on the margins between the valley (*terre chaude*) and the upland pastures (*terre froide*). Any place name with the suffix -*berri* (meaning *new*) is probably one of these extensions.

The head of the household was and is known simply by the name of the house, even if he is not the son but the son-in-law of the previous owner, as happens when the oldest child is a daughter and she marries. Other inhabitants of the house are known by their Christian names and the name of the house. When they die they are buried, as you can see in the churchyard at Ste Engrâce, in a communal tomb which also bears the name of the house. This almost suffocatingly intimate association of a person with his particular place would be enough to break up any society, were it not for the equally strong bonds that draw the village back together. These too have a geographical basis. Each house has two, three or four 'first neighbours' (the number depends on the particular valley) to whom each can turn in crisis, and towards whom any of the traditional requests for help must be granted. No house has the same set of 'first neighbours' as any other, and the relationships proceed round the village in a

The bulk of this souletin *farm near Larrau – and its decorative balcony – are signs of the importance of the farmhouse to the Basque way of life. Into this building all the status of the family is concentrated. A Basque surname is not the name of one's father or husband, but of one's house.*

continuous chain of obligation and mutual aid.

On the scale of the valley itself, village is bound to village by the sharing of different pastoral resources. Flocks from the whole community often make a kind of double transhumance each year: to the high pastures in the summer, to the upper valley in the spring and autumn and in severe winters all the way down to the valley mouth. In some mountain communes up to 90% of the land is held, undivided, by the village as a whole. It is accepted that the small houses on the high pastures, *olha* in Basque, *cayolars* in Béarnais, will be unlocked to provide shelter for anyone in a storm. This interdependence and mutual self-sufficiency took formal shape in the valley councils that have been idealized by

ETA and others as the image of democracy. They were in fact more like an oligarchy of property owners. No one but the freeholders had a say, women were excluded, and attempts were often made to prevent an extension of the franchise to any younger sons who had carved a new holding for themselves out of *terre froide*. As democracy it was limited, but nevertheless exceptional in a feudal Europe. There was a sort of aristocracy, but strictly contained. One valley council told its resident noble in 1688: '*Le sieur vicomte d'Echaux n'a point plus de droit que les autres particuliers de la communauté.*' (The Viscount d'Echaux has no more rights than the other individuals in the community.) The whole Basque structure is focused into that one phrase '*les particuliers de la communauté.*'

On this walk, only forest, the inhospitability of the terrain or sheer altitude will remove you from the organized world of shepherd, sheep and cows. In the depths the country is settled, but above them is true wilderness. The mountains' nearness to the Atlantic produces chaotic and unpredictable weather: thick banks of cloud often occupy the valleys, and you have to climb to escape them. This walk does not follow the *Haute Randonnée Pyrénéenne*, a route for heroes only, but nonetheless involves a total of 9,568 metres (31,383 feet) of climbing and 8,870 metres (29,093 feet) of descents. As I was working this out on the long drop down to Lescun from east of the Pic d'Anie and thinking how good it sounded, I was passed by a group of about ten schoolgirls, most of whom were no more than twelve, gaily on their way to the ferrocious Arres de Camplong, which I had just spent a dried-up and desperate two hours in crossing. It should be possible for anyone to do this walk who is fit, patient and equipped. Hilaire Belloc recommended espadrilles, a water-bottle, a compass and a blanket as the only Pyrenean essentials. As you will go well above the line of permanent snow (and at one point over 2,440 metres) espadrilles are probably not a good idea, and as for the blanket, the world of mountain-walking has moved on since 1909.

St Jean Pied-de-Port to Chalet Pedro

37 kilometres

St Jean Pied-de-Port – at the foot of the gate – owes its being to the crossing into Spain, five miles to the south, that runs through Valcarlos to Roncesvalles and Pamplona. It is now one of the most important tourist passes through the Pyrenees, and St Jean caters for the flow. The medieval part of the town is on the right bank of the river Nive. Built and walled in red sandstone, it is steeply cobbled, with the names of burghers carved on lintels. Crowning it is a citadel constructed by Vauban after the Treaty of the Pyrenees in 1659, at a time when he also walled in the suburb on the other bank. The Nive now flows coolly between the two, with wrought-iron balconies looking out from either side and a couple of bridges. The names of the streets – rue de France, rue d'Espagne and rue St Jacques – define the town, since this was the most important staging post on the route to Santiago de Compostella, the place to pause before the crossing of the mountains into Spain. One of the older houses has its door studded with small brass cockle-shells, the usual souvenir from Santiago, which became the badge of pilgrims who had been there, and then of those who were going there and eventually, by the end of the Middle Ages, of any pilgrim at all.

St Jean is full of artisan shops selling sheepskins, berets and Real Shepherd's Umbrellas (blue, enormous and 350 francs each) but every Monday in the stockmarket, held just outside Vauban's wall, an older function of the town appears. It is very well attended: maybe 300 farmers, pale tall men with curly black hair, all of them dressed in black and dark blue, come to watch the auctions – even when there are very few animals for sale, as is the case on most Mondays except during the winter, when the previous spring's lambs and calves are sold. It is exclusively male. Women go to the vegetable market at the other end of town, also held on Monday. I asked one man standing aimlessly at the side of proceedings and not talking to anyone why he bothered to come. '*Il faut sortir*,' ('You've got to get out') he said.

The treatment of the young animals is appalling. Their legs are hobbled so that they can only lie panting and traumatized in the pens or on the scales to which they are transferred with so much carelessness and brutality they might already be deadweight. From there they are put into the two-storey butchers' lorries from Bayonne, St Jean-de-Luz or even Bordeaux. Some writers on the Basques have said that they treat their sheep with great affection and that most shepherds know every one of their ewes by name. This is not the impression you will get at St Jean, and it is significant, I think, that the Basque words for human procreation simply do not make sense when used in an animal context, where a quite different vocabulary applies. Animal life and human life are in this way made quite distinct. In a society that depends so entirely on these animals – the Basque for wealthy, *aberatz*, comes from *abere*, the word for livestock – it may well be a necessary distinction.

St Jean was one of the seats of the Capitaines-Châtelains, royal officers instituted in the seventeenth century to administer the police and justice among the recalcitrant Basques. These pitiable men were notoriously ineffective, their power scarcely spreading beyond the walls of the town itself. As you set off uphill from St Jean and head towards the border the attitudes and preoccupations of the Capitaine-Châtelain and his like very quickly drop away. You strip layers as you climb – of modernity, of institution and of milling people. The gate where the rue d'Espagne formerly made its way through Vauban's wall has been dismantled, and the old Roman road from Dax to Pamplona leads due south, up towards Honto and the Spanish border, the same as when countless pilgrims made use of it over the Pyrenees, the greatest

obstacle between Vézelay and Santiago. Now the way to Roncesvalles uses the valley road to the west, and the official route of the GR 10, the Pyrenean long distance footpath, disliking the fact that the road has recently been tarred, prefers instead to shadow it laboriously a few hundred yards to the west. But the old road is the only way to go.

The first climb is for nearly twelve kilometres up this lane, rising about 920 metres to the Vierge d'Orisson, a modern white statue marking the end of the first big climb for the pilgrims crossing to Roncesvalles. From the start you are among the meadows that carpet these low hills (St Jean is only 180 metres above sea-level) with the huge white farms scattered irregularly over them like an exploded village. Unlike those further east in Soule and Béarn, these Navarrese houses have the human accommodation, the stables for draught animals and the stores for hay and grain all under one roof. As a result they are hangar-like in breadth and length, covered in a low-pitched roof of *tuiles-canales*, which switches roles between *parasol* and *parapluie* in this country of climatic extremes. The walls

The river Nive runs coolly between the two halves of St Jean Pied-de-Port – the medieval city on the left and on the right its suburb, walled by Vauban in the seventeeth century.

A door-knocker in the older half of St Jean is decorated with the cockle-shell of Santiago de Compostella. St Jean Pied de Port is named after the 'gate' by which most pilgrims to Santiago crossed the Pyrenees into Spain.

are plastered and limewashed each year, the alkalinity in this coating acting as a pesticide against any bugs that might burrow in. Immediately around each house is an astonishingly rich and varied culture of vines, figs, even banana trees, and fields of the inevitable maize. This miracle plant arrived here from Spain in the early seventeenth century (where it had come from America) and replaced millet in the peasant diet. It was so much more productive that the population exploded in the following century, and the expansion of Basque communities from small villages like Honto, five and a half kilometres from St Jean, to the dispersed farmsteads you see around you on the climb, probably dates from that time.

The lane mounts between hedges with woven fences embedded in them to make them rigorously sheep-proof, through patches where the smell of the animals makes the air bitter, and past huge-boled oaks and smaller chestnuts – which at one time were a crucial part of the peasant diet for their oil, but were ravaged by blight in the 1860s and replaced by resistant varieties from Japan.

The morning I was on this road the thunder smacked and mumbled among the mountains, but no rain fell from the clouds, which were down to about 700 metres. For a few kilometres I walked up through them until at last, in a miraculous, aeroplane emergence, I broke through to find myself on green and sunny pastures with the cloud sea below me, not under a perfect blue sky, but with another broken layer of clouds above, as though I had simply moved up a floor. There were many small black butterflies with tiny orange spots up here, known by the odd and beautiful name of Amanda's blue. To the west was a flock of about twelve white-headed vultures, circling low and confidently over a flock of sheep. These vultures, common enough

An olha, *or shepherds' summer hut, high on the limestone pastures above St Jean. The summer life of the Basque shepherds, centred on these buildings, is visibly intimate with the land that supports them. The custom is to leave the* olha *open all year round to provide shelter for strangers in storms.*

further south into Spain, are here at the northern limit of their range. They are never to be seen singly, but always in these large and mobile flocks, with their heads slung low in front of floorboard wings.

At the top of the climb you move on to limestone and its perfect turf, patched with thyme (more on the molehills than not) and with ribs of the rock pushing through in places. Here the pilgrims would have had their first rest and planted the leafy crosses they had brought up from the valley – so many that according to one fifteenth-century account there would be a forest of them here at the end of a season, as thick as a harbour-full of masts. This was more than just the most physically demanding stage of the pilgrimage. If one can trust Améry Picaud, the author of a twelfth-century guide-book to it, the Basques themselves made it almost intolerable. 'Here is a barbaric race,' he wrote, 'who deceive every condition of men . . . They are capable of every kind of malice and are depraved, perverse and perfidious.'

It is at this point, before you turn east and make for the High Pyrenees, that you come nearest to the site of the Basques' famous ambush and massacre of the rearguard of Charlemagne's army in 777. The first surviving account of it is from a French chronicle written in 830, but the incident then disappears from recorded history until it resurfaces two hundred years later, wonderfully transmuted into the *Song of Roland*. The Basques have become Saracens and the Pass of Roncesvalles the stage of a great conflict between Islam and Christendom, between Good and Evil. The historical incident is fascinating for its geography. The Frankish army, as strangers, took the lower valley route now used by the tourist road from St Jean to Pamplona. The Basques who ambushed them, however, used the upland tracks such as the one you have just climbed, which are in essence the older ways that flocks had first beaten out with their neolithic shepherds 6,000 years before. This gave them the crucial advantages of height and speed. The *Song of Roland*, in the purity of its opposites, goes far beyond what must have been a rather squalid and brief struggle, but it has kept sight of its place among these green western Pyrenees. When all but a few of the 20,000 knights who had been with him lie dead, Roland, exhausted by the fight, blows weakly on his horn, Olifant. Charlemagne, already in St Jean with the main army, and with little idea that his rearguard has been massacred, suddenly hears the faint sound of Roland's horn coming over the hills. Deeply moved, he tells all

60,000 of his own knights to sound their horns in reply. The Frankish army then turns round and rides to save Roland, but it is too late. The Saracens have fled at the sound of the 60,000 trumpets, and Roland, through the effort of his own exertions, is ready to die:

> Towards Spain he goes, to a wide lawn,
> And climbs a mound where grows a fair tree tall,
> And marble stones beneath it stand by four.
> Face downward on the green grass there he falls.

Then, by the marble stones which mark the frontier, he fights off one last Saracen, and then again:

> The County Roland lay down beneath a pine;
> To land of Spain he turns there as he lies,
> And many things begins to call to mind:
> All the broad lands he conquered in his time,
> And fairest France and the men of his line,
> And Charles his lord, who bred him from a child.
> He cannot help but weep for them and sigh.
> Straightway his head upon his arm declines,
> With folded hands he makes an end and dies.

From the Vierge d'Orisson it is just over eight kilometres to Béhérobie, for a while on the limestone, and then on slaty tracks along the fringes of the beeches in the Forêt d'Orion. These tracks have revolutionized the life of Pyrenean shepherds. After the Second World War hundreds of army surplus jeeps were bought up and they were driven through what had been roadless mountain and forest. Not only did it mean that during the summer the men could move up and down between village and flocks more easily, but also the *fromageries* and Roquefort Societies further north in the plain could make regular collection rounds to buy the ewes' milk direct from the shepherds. Everybody except the conservationists see it as an undiluted good.

Here too you will meet the sheep for the first time. It is best to avoid any direct confrontation with the rams, which you can of course recognize from behind, but which are also bigger overall than their ewes, and some of which have sets of horns that emerge from the head to perform two complete revolutions before finishing up pointing skywards. These animals are affectionately, or contemptuously, known as *Manex*, the Basque for Johnny, since they come from near St Jean. The nickname is also given to the Navarrese people by the Souletins further east, usually with a sneer. The Manex do look ridiculous. They have fine black legs, but above that they are a puff-ball of very long white wool – hair would be the more appropriate word – which economically is the least important part of the animal, but is a good raincoat. What matters is the milk. The 330,000 ewes in the Basque flock produced 14 million litres in 1981.

You will come down to Béhérobie in the valley of the Nive, now a tenth of the size it was at St Jean, and find there a small hotel where you can get a big lunch, including perhaps the famous Basque black pudding which has pig's tongues threaded through it like the egg in pork pie, and almost inevitably some course based on mutton.

As I was eating at Béhérobie the clouds came down still further and it began to rain. 'Never,' the French guide-book said, 'leave in bad weather.' I ignored it and there followed the worst afternoon's walking of my life. Over seventeen kilometres and 1,182 metres of climbing, all of it immediately after lunch, separate you at Béhérobie from the next reasonable habitation at Chalet Pedro, high in the valley of the Iratiko to the east. For the whole five hours nothing was visible beyond the soaking mist around me. On the first climb to the Col d'Errozate, where the path touches the border, the grass is as thick as it would be in a marsh, glazed with rain in almost edible bunches. The air is filled with a constant fine spray, too light actually to fall as rain but suspended as a douche, refreshing at first but which soon enough becomes the prime source of sorrow and self-pity. A sheep-bell rings now and then and the path climbs. Occasionally very white orchids survive among the grasses. As you arrive at the frontier Spain will be damp, grey and invisible. The summer houses of the shepherds, the *olha*, will announce themselves at first by the smell and then by the dogs, which will bark but not bite. The climb continues and you can only retreat into details and self. Where the rock surfaces on the summit (a juncture announced only by a levelling of gradient and by no change of view) it is an extraordinary conglomerate of rounded pebbles in a reddish matrix, collectively called *flysch*. Animals meet you like friends in a dream – sheep of course and the beautiful pale cows of the breed called *Blondes des Pyrénées*. There are pigs up here too. I have little idea what these grey miles are actually like. They must be empty, I suppose, and grassy and relatively level once you are up, with a thick layer of beech forest on the eastern side. More than that I will never know. To go back there on a clear day would be as odd as to return in summer to a ski-resort I knew well only in snow. Lowland places are recognizably the same in different weathers, but in mountains meteorology substitutes for geography, and it is the weather or the season that becomes the constant, and the place which changes. An afternoon in this lonely, damp monochrome is as depressing and even disturbing as any

physical experience could be, and is escapable only by long and continued effort. The calls of rooks are evil within it and I took to singing hymns. For all I know I passed within ten yards of a Basque shepherd roaring out 'Lead kindly light amid the encircling gloom' which alternated for several hours with 'To be a pilgrim.' The arrival at a huge patch of yellow poppies in the forest was as fine an incident in this reduced world as a Renaissance château anywhere else in France. Wet and unhappy, I eventually arrived at Chalet Pedro, with my curses on the meeting of mountain and ocean used up and a deeply embedded wish to subject no one else to this hell. Never leave in bad weather. There is a café but nothing else at Chalet Pedro. The only option is to camp or to call it a day at Béhérobie and then make it one day's journey from there to Larrau, which is about thirty-two kilometres.

Chalet Pedro to Ste Engrâce

43 kilometres

The valley of the Iratiko was quite another place in the early morning. On either side the strong beech forest of Iraty rose from the stream which runs south into Spain and eventually, with the Ebro, into the Mediterranean. This is the border between the two Basque provinces of Basse-Navarre and Soule. As far as the Col Bagarguiac, six and a half kilometres to the east, the path runs through this forest. Typically of the lower Pyrenees, it was once a very complete mixture of beech and pine, but from the beginning of the seventeenth century to the early 1800s the naval dockyards at Bayonne took over 7,000 of the massive forest pines, often 30 metres high and 2 metres in diameter at the base, for the masts of the battleships built there. Suitable pines were exhausted by the beginning of the nineteenth century; there had never been a programme of regeneration and the forest was left as you now find it, much more of beech than it naturally would be.

The shipwrights in need of masts were not the only predators on the forest. The smelters at the iron and copper mines which were spread throughout the mountains needed enormous quantities of charcoal, and it was eventually the exhaustion of suitable wood and not of the ore-bodies themselves that led to the closure of these mines at the end of the last century. But more than either shipwrights or smelters the shepherds are responsible for shrinking the huge areas the forest once occupied. The endless search for new pastures has been helped by the ease with which these

beautiful timber woods can be burnt down when warm, dry winds come over the mountains from the south.

It is a beautiful climb to the Col Bagarguiac, where there are now some holiday chalets and a café, and where the first great revelation of the walk breaks on you. The perfect green valley of Larrau, interrupted by trees and opening into pastures, drops down to the village eight kilometres below you. Above it to the south, cresting the clothed ridges of the Iraty forest at over 2,000 metres, is the Pic d'Orhi, its limestone bands visibly contorted. But far over to the east is the best sight of all, a grey attic of mountains mottled in snow, prominent among them the pyramid of the Pic d'Anie, the fulcrum of the walk, with clouds balanced on its point.

The few miles down to Larrau are some of the best on the whole way. You descend through the communal pastures, grazed by cows, sheep and the famous *pottakak* horses, all of them wearing tiny brass bells with

A Blonde des Pyrénées above the Forêt d'Iraty.

upside-down hearts punched on to them. The bracken which is mown and collected each autumn is stacked in lumps around upright acacia poles, like döner-kebabs planted in the earth. You will notice how even on the scale of the smallest side valleys the southern slopes, which face north, have been left wooded, and the northern slopes (which face south) are the ones that have been cleared for pasture. The value of a piece of land here depends on the amount of sunlight it receives. On the north-facing slopes frosts begin earlier in the winter and continue longer in the spring, while any snow that may fall there will continue to lie when on the other side of the valley it has already melted away. Farms on the shady side are the last to be built and the first to be deserted. There is a story of a Larrau man who married a girl from another village in late October and until 2 February they ate no meat. But as he went out to work that morning he asked his wife to prepare a rabbit, because a good friend was coming to dinner that day. She duly cooked it but was surprised when he reached home at midday to see he was alone. 'Where is your friend then?' she asked rather shortly, and he turned to point at the rays of sunlight just touching the threshold for the first time since the previous autumn.

You come down into the enclosed land, the privately owned part of the commune, where beautifully built barns decorate the pattern of fields, with wooden shingles, and slated roofs at a steeper pitch than those in Navarre. (A steeper roof is more weather-proof, but there is more of it per square foot covered. These slate roofs can afford to be steeper than the tiled ones in Navarre because slate weighs much less than tile.) Here farmhouse and farm buildings, while often connected, are usually separate structurally.

Larrau, with a population of only 500, is like a town. It has two excellent hotels open all the year, a spired church and next to it a pelota court. This famous game, as Basque as the beret, is a nineteenth-century invention. In essence it is a kind of fives, but the court almost never has side-walls. It is usually played with bare hands, although different versions exist, the most famous with a kind of elongated cup that fits over the hand and propels the ball much faster. The balls themselves are encased in leather, for which calf-skin is often used, but the best quality are made of dog-leather.

It is about twenty-five kilometres from Larrau to Ste Engrâce. You move three kilometres down the valley from Larrau, past a continuous series of lamp-posts on every one of which the letters ETA have been sprayed. (It is paradoxical and pitiable that the pun on which the terrorists' name depends for its impact – ETA = état = state – is in the language they hope to banish.) At Logibar turn off the small road on to a track which pushes up the side of the stupendous Gorges d'Holzarte for the next six kilometres, at one point crossing high above the gorge on a 1920 suspension bridge for pedestrians only. The water in the river is grey and opaque with dissolved limestone, and the hands of beech trees that spread out over it vibrate in the cold air sucked down above the stream. These great canyons owe their being to events at the end of the last Ice Age. The normal volume of flow is not enough to incise them and, as happens so often in limestone, these streams would have found a way, by chemical dissolution, of going underground. It was the massive and rhythmical pattern of floods as

the glaciers melted that had abrasive force and weight enough to erode the gorges.

After a very long climb up, just over 600 metres, you at last reach a level track through the sheep pastures. You are here crossing the bridge between two communes and the border between them is precisely determined. On the map it is drawn in a series of straight lines roughly approximating to the watershed between the two villages, Larrau and Ste Engrâce. This is evidence of the carelessness with which nineteenth-century French administrators walked over the ancient limits and compromises worked out by the people themselves. The actual line would have moved with the country, not least because a ridge is the most recognizable of features on the ground. On each side of this private border there is a small shepherd's house called *Olhaberria* – the new *olha* (the word means 'syndicate' from the group of shepherds who share it). No confusion would have arisen between these neighbouring places of the same name – one is of Larrau, the other of Ste Engrâce. The Larrau Olhaberria, incidentally, bears the date 1718.

As the clouds build and collapse on the pastures and in the valleys, you will arrive at the Col d'Anhaou, where the distant grey and white mountains you saw from the Col Bagarguiac appear closer, more accessible and more separate. The sheep themselves drift and gather on the grass like clouds as you drop towards Ste Engrâce. When I was there a white-winged and pale-breasted harrier eased around the sky above me. Along the lip of another gorge, the famous Kakoueta, stony paths lead you down towards the valley bottom through fields in which the hay has been gathered into dumplings, each one with its own protective tarpaulin, across the dammed turquoise water of the river (there is a hydroelectric plant just down stream) and on to the road.

To visit the inside of Kakoueta gorge you have to pay a small entrance fee at the mouth, and you can then make your way along its floor on a series of footbridges to the point where the stream emerges as a waterfall from a hole in the cliff. This is one of the exits (there is another that bubbles up in the river bed itself) of what is claimed as the largest underground system of limestone tunnels in the world. The water that emerges here has percolated through the rock from at least as far as the Col de Pierre-St-Martin and maybe from beyond the Pic d'Anie. The tunnels have been explored to enormous depth from the top end but the exact ways in which the water travels are still unknown. In November 1937 250 millimetres (about 10 inches) of rain fell in 36 hours on the mountains that feed Kakoueta. The volume of water in the fall increased enormously, so much so that the first measurement of it could not physically be made until the following August, nine months later, when it was still flowing at a metre a second more than was normal for that time of year. This implied a storage capacity within the mountains of at least 25,000,000 cubic metres and maybe as much as double that – the equivalent of a reservoir 95 metres deep, 370 wide and almost one and a half kilometres long.

It is nearly four kilometres along the valley road to the end of the community of Ste Engrâce at Senta, where there is a fine Romanesque church. The way is through the dispersed village, every house with bright green or red shutters and new jeep tracks made in the 1960s and '70s curling up to them. In the late 1970s this commune was the subject of a study by Sandra Ott, an Oxford anthropologist. Her book is called *A Circle of Mountains*, because the people of Ste Engrâce do not conceive of it as a valley, but as a continuous ring of mountains on whose lower slopes they live. The idea of circularity, and even more of rotation, in the two senses of a continuous revolution (such as the stirring of rennet into the milk to make cheese) and of replacement in a continuous linked series (like the 'first neighbour' relationships) are the guiding conceptions of life here. They have no proper words for the points of the compass (which would divide up the ring of mountains) and the stream, which cuts the valley in two and so would emphasize its uncircular characteristics, plays no part in their conception of the place, for example when describing where their farms are.

The attachment to the community is intense. While very little interest is shown either in national or in cantonal elections, the average vote in the municipal elections of the commune itself is 96.54% of the electorate. Each household, apart from its 'first neighbour' relations in time of difficulty and during harvest, is nonetheless a self-contained unit. It is not done to broadcast domestic quarrels. 'Cover the fire of the house,' a village proverb goes, 'with the ashes of the house.' This self-reliance dissolves at the coming of summer when the shepherds sort themselves into *olhas* of six men each to take the 4,000 sheep of the commune to the summer pasture. Until the early 1970s all six would spend the period of the ewes' heavy lactation up in the *olha* together, each man in turn rotating through the various household and pastoral chores, but now only two of them would be there at any one time, although the system of rotation is still worked.

Each man makes eight to ten cheeses during the mountain period. His skill at producing a cheese with a dry, rough and unpunctured rind, and a good, white heart which is low in acidity but has 'body', becomes the barometer of his status in the village. Each cheese takes five months to mature and the earliest are ready when, at the maize harvest in the autumn, the 'first neighbours' who have helped with the crop are given a meal in the house. It is not done on these occasions for them to eat all the precious cheese that is laid out, but this must be finely judged. If the cheese is a good one enough must be eaten to demonstrate relish.

The making of cheese is more than just a technical achievement. The word for 'curdle' (and this is true only in Ste Engrâce) is the same as the word for 'make pregnant.' It is accepted that if a man can make a good cheese he is skilled, as Sandra Ott puts it, 'at both causing and preventing the pregnancy of his wife.' The parallelism of the cheese world of the *olha* and the reproductive world of the house in the valley is elaborate and complete. Given that 'red blood' plays the part of the ovum in Ste Engrâce gynaecology, the cosmic and embracing system is: as rennet is to milk, cheese, the *olha* and male procreativity, semen is to red blood, an infant, the house and female procreativity. The people of Ste Engrâce have created a structure that embraces heaven and earth from the necessary circumstances of their lives. It is significant that although the shepherds are expert midwives they absolutely refuse to perform a Caesarean section on any of their ewes. The idea of breaking open the womb of a living animal, of cutting into the circle, is anathema to them.

Even as Sandra Ott was working on her thesis Ste Engrâce was changing, as the older generation realized that their children would not be repeating what had been repeated for infinities. The idea of strangers having holiday homes in the village, once met with alarm and distrust, now became accepted. It is better to have strangers as neighbours than no neighbours at all. In 1977, as the flocks were about to set off in spring, and Sandra Ott was observing it, a woman came out of her house to bless the sheep with a sprig of laurel and some holy water. She was doing it with all conviction until she saw the anthropologist watching her. She then stopped, blushed deeply and hid the sacred objects away. In that boundary of confidence and doubt there is evidence, surely, of a culture coming to its end.

Ste Engrâce to Lescun

24 kilometres

From the church at Senta it is nearly eight kilometres to the Col de Pierre St Martin, 1,130 metres above. Soon after leaving the church you pass the foot of the Ravin d'Arpidia and, crossing from the commune of Ste Engrâce into Arette, you leave Soule for Béarn. Here you move out of the Basque country for good, even though the historical and symbolic limit, the Pic d'Anie, is still several miles to the east. After a very stiff climb you emerge from the forest and cloud into a super-lunary world of clarity and brightness. All the lower hills to the west appear dark and whalebacked above the cloud poured like a sauce around them. The limestone turf is dotted with flowers – yellow orchids and green hellebore, giant buttercups and, best of all, the two sorts of gentian, spring and alpine, both pulling a rich bright blue from the earth around them. The alpine is a kind of elongated bell, like the bottom half of a saxophone, with black specks spotted down its long white throat.

These are details. The place as a whole does not flourish: looking east and south the Pyrenees have been stripped. Here the limestone is fissured and faulted with only the hook needle pines growing on the apparently soilless rock. It is as though the austerity of the mountain sky has reached down and blighted the earth below it, parching the lush greenness out of the mountains. It is of course a combination of altitude and rock that achieves this puritan conversion. All around you here are the gathering funnels for the rainwater which drains into the great underground reservoirs and conduits that feed the Kakoueta falls. It is one of the classic sites of French speleology. The mouths of the *gouffres* gape between the outcrops and the occasional yellow-legged chough clatters in and out of them. In the 1950s the system was first plumbed to a depth of 450 metres, and after the death of Marcel Loubens in 1952, caused by the fraying of his rope, the team he had led continued, to discover the Salle de la Verna, a cave 230 metres long, 180 wide and 150 high. The system has now been plumbed to a depth of 1,332 metres below the pass.

Here, too, for the second time on the walk the path touches the frontier with Spain. A motorable road was built across the pass in 1973, but most of the year it is closed with a chain, saying on the one side *Route Barrée* and on the other *Via Cerrada*. As I was looking out over my first conscious sight of Spain a squad

of Spanish cyclists climbed laboriously and agonizingly up the last few hundred metres to the pass where, with a look of communal and dazed achievement, they sat back on their saddles and slid like liquid into France.

It is the scene every 13 July of a ceremony of great antiquity. It was usual for adjoining communes, both across the frontier and in parallel valleys on each side of it, to make careful agreements, called *faceries*, over the exact demarcation of their grazing rights, often compromising with border zones where grazing was held in common. When the international frontier was at last made precise, between 1856 and 1866, the surveyors spent as long as ten years on the task because they took into account all the details of these local agreements, which rarely and only by chance coincided with the natural watershed. The July ceremony at the Col de Pierre-St-Martin is the annual re-establishment of one of these *faceries* between the people of Barétous in Béarn and Roncal in Navarra. By it the Barétous cows can spend twenty-eight days before 10 July in the zone of common grazing, and the Roncalese cows can occupy it after that. The people of Barétous have to give three unblemished two-year-old heifers to Roncal every year, either as rent or to expiate a murder done by some Barétous shepherds in the fourteenth century. The two delegations join hands over the boundary stone and with the words '*Patz abant*' swear eternal peace. It has worked continuously since 1375, except for a disastrous interval when in 1612 the Roncalese refused two of the cows offered them. The bitterness lasted for decades. In 1635, 120 Roncalese rustled 4,000 head of cattle from the Barétous, who in return stole 5,000 sheep and four shepherds, along with all their capes, loaves, cheeses and socks. Not until 1642 was peace regained, when the Roncalese finally paid 21,000 *reales* in compensation.

From the pass it is nearly seventeen kilometres to Lescun in the Vallée d'Aspe, and for the first time the journey has the air of high mountain walking. Having escaped the mess of the new ski-resort of Arette-Pierre-St-Martin, you set off over the fields of barren limestone to the east. Here and there you will find rocks scraped by the edges of skis when the snow was thinning, and occasionally a straw bale wrapped incongruously around a pine tree to soften collisions. Such traces of civilization apart, nothing could be more demanding than this dry and chaotic country where the rock reflects all heat back up at your face. It is a graveyard of a landscape, where no growth seems possible and all flesh has been reduced to bone. There is no rhythm in these *arres*, as they are called (the word means 'stone'), and you stumble from step to step. You will meet your first patches of grainy snow as the mountains rise in ever emptier harshness around you. It is a supremely conservative world where nothing changes. No plant that grows here can afford the lowland extravagance of annual death and life: those organisms that do survive are hardy perennials, the reliable and unadventurous structures which have been found fossilized in rock tens of millions of years old.

You eventually come to the Pas de l'Osque, where the formless world suddenly takes shape. Across the valley a whole series of striped, layered and channelled cliffs is revealed, reddening in the evening light, while over to the south the great buttresses of Anie itself appear above you. There, according to the people of Lescun, is where the Devil manufactured storms.

The path now crosses the low Pas d'Azuns, and you drop into a valley where flowers cover the ground in sheets – of forget-me-nots, orchids, buttercups, globeflowers, miniature primroses, gentians and violets – surrounding a stream that runs with the meltwater from the Pic d'Anie, and is bridged in the hollows with old snow. It is the westernmost place where the Pyrenean brown bear can still be seen. Sightings of them are now very rare – there are probably no more than fifteen left alive – but you will be expecting one at every turn. Their disappearance would be a tragedy, and great efforts are being made to keep the population alive. Apple trees have been planted, piles of chestnuts laid out, hives set up, ponds dug and filled with frogs, but it is too early to know if the policy is working. The bear, which is not naturally a mountain animal but has been driven up here, has always been persecuted by the shepherds. At one time an active export trade in bears for circuses was maintained. The male can be a terrifying beast, up to 8 feet long and weighing 62 stone,

Le Billare dominates the buttercup meadows above Lescun in a Dolomite image of denuded Limestone.

capable of killing a donkey with one blow. Pyrenean farmers told Arthur Young in 1787 that bears, 'the original tenants of this range of mountains, the first in point of dignity,' used to attack unguarded cattle 'by leaping on their back, forcing the head to the ground and thrusting their paws into the body in the violence of a dreadful hug.'

From the flowery valley it is about eight kilometres to Lescun – down through the beech wood, where the crocuses are deep purple and the black slugs enormous – before emerging through meadows of clover, scabious and cowslip hay to reach the village, where a small hotel will provide all comforts.

Lescun to Gabas

40 kilometres

The whole stage from Lescun to Gabas can be done in one mammoth day, 40 kilometres long with 2,440 metres of climbing and 2,288 of descent: it is just within the limits of pleasure and might take 11 or 12 hours in all. Mountains fill the end of every Lescun street. Leave it by the war memorial, which bears the appalling total of forty-six names from the First World War (300 people now live in the commune). After crossing the stream below the village, move on through the meadows against a backdrop of limestone cliffs looking like the Dolomites. After the first climb the track is easy and level as far as Lhers, six kilometres from Lescun. It runs between farms which are the smallest I have ever seen, one of them consisting of a single one-storey building no more than four metres long and three metres wide. Each of them has two or three dogs, one of which will always be a so-called Pyrenean sheepdog, an enormous woolly white animal with tragic black eyes. These were in fact bred to protect the sheep from bears and wolves, of which the last was shot in the 1930s. The others will be grey dogs called *labrits des Pyrénées*, smaller, wirier and more sprightly, which perform all the more usual tasks of a sheepdog.

Lhers is another perfectly distributed village of farms, each in its own piece of land dotted with small groups of grey suede cows. You gravitate around its edges and begin the first major climb of the day. The Col de Barrancq is only 2.3 kilometres away on the map, 604 metres above you. It is the kind of hill that leaves you with the veins on your temples standing out like drainpipes. When

Borce in the Vallée d'Aspe.

you eventually get to the top you look out east between the branches to see the sky ahead filled with the huge white block of mountains that separates the Vallée d'Aspe from the Vallée d'Ossau, where the day's destination lies.

From the pass the way drops 950 metres to Borce, via a track which makes a wide and steady S-loop. The temptation, to which I succumbed, is to cut out the loops and to slide steeply down through the rich, damp, disintegrating woodland until you reach the enclosed fields around the village. It *is* possible but it is very steep and very dirty and scarcely quicker, even if more exciting, than the proper path. The track is cobbled as you approach the village which, as the Michelin guide says, is *sans coquetterie*. It has a few old and flaking houses and a church whose bells ring every hour twice, once on the hour and once about five minutes later. This is common all over southern France but I have never known the reason for it. I asked the woman in the grocer's. She looked at the woodland filth that covered my trousers and said: 'Because it

The nineteenth-century Fort du Portalet commands the road from Spain over the Col du Somport, taken by the Arab invasion under Abd-er-Rahman in 732. The fort was used as a prison for Resistance fighters in the Second World War.

always has.' I asked why it always had, but for this she had to go round the back to ask her husband. Several minutes elapsed until at last she emerged with the answer. 'It rings twice,' she said, looking not at my face but at my trousers, 'in case you miss it the first time.'

From Borce you cross the Gave d'Aspe over to its smarter twin Etsaut, where there are hotels, restaurants and a hint of *coquetterie*. The way then follows the main road up the valley towards the Col du Somport. This is the route the Arab army under Abd-er-Rahman took in 732, only to be defeated on the Landes de Charlemagne outside Tours by Charles Martel. At the point where the path leaves the road, just before the nineteenth-century Fort du Portalet, look up at the cliff on the left: on the rock ledges there is a large and growing colony of one of the rarer and most beautiful of mountain flowers, the Pyrenean saxifrage. Its base is a silvery green rosette, from which a single cone springs, about a foot long, made up of hundreds of small white flowers.

Take your time in gazing at it, since purgatory begins here. The next twelve kilometres are uphill, climbing 1,588 metres to the Col d'Ayous. Made in the eighteenth century by the naval engineers and known as the *chemin de mâture*, the mastage track, it is merciless on a hot day. It proceeds uphill at an unchanging and scientific gradient, cut for a long stretch half-way up a sheer cliff in a kind of unwalled tunnel. The line on the map moves effortlessly up towards the pass, but for you the shadeless constancy of the slope will drain all life-juices. I took to counting steps and stopping, used up, every hundred. You will find asylum in the shade of a single dwarf oak tree for a while, but duty takes over and will drive you out of it. The water is disgustingly warm and plastic in its bottle.

At last some shade and level ground is reached, as you begin to make better progress and no longer suffer the humiliating subjection of the cliff path. You pass two *cayolars*, one ruined, one occupied, with the Arcadian image of shepherd, dog and sheep on the hillside above them. It is never quiet here; the streams from the ridge of mountains pour continuously and roaringly down night and day. The climb begins again, through astonishingly dense patches of flowers, like a garden run wild. Best of them all is the asphodel, a three-foot-high mace of a plant, whose head is a gathering of fine white trumpets.

As you move up through the climatic layers the flowers reduce, until you emerge from buttercups on to pure grass. You trace the floor of a valley towards its rounded head. Back into the snow patches the rock changes from red to blue – the one a sign of iron, the other of copper – and then to a conglomerate of them both. This last climb from the valley head to the pass is the most demanding of all. You will know you are tired when your feet consistently slip on the snow slopes. Your pace drops still slower until you find yourself almost involuntarily at the pass. It is worth pushing yourself to this limit to know why photographs of mountaineers on real summits always show them with mouth agape in a kind of smile that bridges the inane and the divine, like a child with an unexpected present. Back to the west all the summits you have already passed appear spiky and confused, while to the east you are confronted with the monumental Pic du Midi d'Ossau (2,884 metres), a black hulk with two blunt summits. It is the solidified core of a massive volcano that erupted about 230 million years ago. Its slopes are the most famous refuge of the *isards*, a wild goat like a chamois.

From the pass it is six and a half kilometres down to the Lac de Bious Artigues. The first part is on snow and you can glide sylph-like down it, coming to fields of wild daffodils around three black ice-lakes. You should by now be mindless with exhaustion, and by far the least tiring way of getting down a mountain is to run, for the last part along a wild grey river which eventually crashes its meltwater into the lake. Four and a half kilometres down the forest road is Gabas, with several hotels. I had expected to make my way easily down the road, but it had been blocked by an avalanche which many weeks before had planed its way down the valleyside and still had the twisted and broken remains of trees sticking out of its filthy snow. The stream had bored a hole under the block of ice and cold mist like smoke was emerging from it into the evening air.

Gabas to Arrens

35 kilometres

Finishing lifts you, and the last day's walk is always less effort than it would be on any other day. From Gabas (which unfortunately combines indifference to tourists with innate mountain hostility) you climb the road for a few hundred yards to a hydroelectric plant before turning off on to a track leading through the forest. Gabas was the last place in the Pyrenees to supply the French navy with masts, and some of the trees standing here today would now be big enough, but it is 160 years since the last was cut. The path continues over large pale outcrops of granite and along another corniche cut into a cliff like the one above the Fort du Portalet. You cross the Eau de Soussouéou, where the water clings to the rock, carefully filling in every curve of the bed.

The first climb of the day now follows, zigzagging up a steeply built path which was originally the way down for the copper ore from the mines below the Hourquette d'Arre, the summit of the day and of the walk. After long and steady application on the upward grind you will come out on to the level path – in Yorkshire it would be called a trod – that leads to the mines. It is a beautiful morning's walk once you are up on this elevated promenade. The mountains are dark and serrated around you, except for the nearby Petite Arcizette, whose limestone layers are

folded in what geologists call a nappe, where layers have been entirely turned back on themselves like bedcovers.

It is quite dry here, with no habitation or refreshment between Gabas and Gourette, twenty-two kilometres away. But underneath the Arcizette, just as the water bottle is squeezed for its last drop, you will come on a lovely spring of stone-cold water welling from between the layers of limestone. Sit here drinking while the sound of cowbells drifts up from the Plaine de Soussouéou, oddly like conversation snatched at and broken in a draught.

Rust appears in the rocks, and the pass ahead, the Hourquette d'Arre (2,465 metres), comes into view, a snowy col looped between two outcrops of rock. Above it, as the weather accumulates and thickens with the passage of the day, the sky revolves and darkens. Unseen snow bridges over streams will collapse beneath you until you begin the steep final climb to the pass. In the distance the Pic Midi d'Ossau prods its weird profile into the Pyrenean skyline, and underfoot beetles and ants lie frozen in the ice beside the odd brown beech leaf blown up from many miles below. Boulders lying on the snow create their own shadow, so that as the snowfields melt around them they are left capping their own small ice-columns like giant mushrooms. Again it comes to the counting of steps. When you are walking, most horizons reveal what is beyond them in a bobbing way, with the natural movement of your head at each step, but my

ABOVE *Asphodels, the emperor of Pyrenean flowers, on the Col de Torte.*

LEFT *Le Valentin, full of the meltwater from the Hourquette d'Arre, the highpoint of the walk, falls below Gourette. The noise of water means it is never quiet below the snowline.*

225

Lescun is high on the western side of the Vallée d'Aspe, which is bounded on the east by the mountains in the distance. The GR 10 crosses them before coming down to Gabas in the Vallée d'Ossau on the far side.

Near Lescun.

Pyrenean flowers: Alpine gentian (top left), Welsh poppy (top right), elder orchid (above left), aquilegia (above right) and Pyrenean saxifrage.

progress up to this col was so slow that the next series of mountains appeared whole and uninterrupted with the one step that brought my head level with the pass.

I leant exhausted against the red rock and immediately sank up to my head in the snow. The rock had conducted the heat under the surface and had melted all but a frail crust. I could not have cared less and set off running down the mountain towards Gourette, seven kilometres away, slaloming in and out of the careful cramponned tracks of the only previous walker since the last snow had fallen. The way runs down past the Lac d'Anglas, blue with ice like a disease, and then off the snow on a shaly track to the constant noise of branched cascades.

Gourette was as desolate and dusty as an empty stadium, with all the despair of a *salon* between functions. None of its hotels or cafés was open and the only people there were repairing the button lifts. I was sitting in hunger, summoning the effort for the final push to Arrens, now only thirteen kilometres away, when between the boot-hire shops and

Grazing on the view from the Col d'Aubisque.

the shuttered *coiffeurs* a herd of Pyrenean Blondes was slowly encouraged – driven would be too hard a word – to make their way from pasture to dairy, as they had done before a single lift was built here.

Gourette to Arrens is a tailpiece. Clouds had been rising in their fragile plumes all afternoon and they finally enveloped this end of the world on the last few miles. The aquilegias and the best asphodels and the wild antirrhinums all came to mean more than the big views which these grassy mountains must present on sunny days. Some climbing is involved, but nothing too sustained, and after a short stretch on the N618 and the last climb you coast down towards the end. The last part is on a stony lane with ruined barns all around it, through clouds that gradually darken as they thicken above you, to Arrens, a place of balconies and roses on the route to Lourdes. Here I met M. Pierre Pome, the seventh of seven children, who lived in the same house

A barn door below the Col de Saucède.

Pierre Pome, the seventh of seven children, still lives in the house his family built in Arrens in the seventeenth century.

229

his family had lived in since they built it in the seventeenth century. It was thick black inside with the tar and smoke from the woodfire, which helps prevent beetle. His own balcony faced south-west, as most do, and we went out on to it to stare into the mist together. He explained that it was orientated that way to catch the afternoon sun, should there be any ever again, and with his finger drew the outlines of each of the mountains against the afternoon fog.

DISTANCES (in kilometres)
From St Jean Pied-de-Port to:
Honto 5.5; Vierge d'Orisson 6.3; Béhérobie 8.2; Col d'Errozate 5.2; Chalet Pedro 12.1; Col Bagarguiac 6.5; Larrau 7.8; Logibar 3.2; Col d'Anhaou 14.0; Kakoueta Mouth 7.9; Senta 3.7; Pierre-Saint-Martin 7.9; Station d' Arette 2.2; Pas d'Azuns 5.9; Lescun 8.8; Lhers 6.2; Col Barrancq 2.3; Borce 5.9; Etsaut 1.4; Col d'Ayous 13.4; Lac de Bious Artigues 6.3; Gabas 4.4; Hourquette d'Arre 14.5; Gourette 7.2; RN 618 4.3; Arrens 9.1

MAPS
I.G.N. 1:50,000 Numbers: 1346 (St Jean Pied-de-Port), 1447 (Larrau), 1547 (Laruns Somport), 1647 (Argelès-Gazost)

GUIDES
Topo-Guide du Sentier de Grande Randonnée No 10, Troncon du Pays Basque C.N.S.G.R., Paris 1979
Topo-Guide du Sentier de Grande Randonnée No 10, Troncon du Béarn C.N.S.G.R., Paris 1979

PYRENEES BOOKS
Jacques Allières, *Les Basques*, Presses Universitaires de France 1977
Hilaire Belloc, *The Pyrenees*, Methuen 1909
Claude Dendaletche, *Guide de la Naturaliste dans les Pyrénées occidentales*, Delachaux and Niestle 1973
Daniel Alexander Gomez–Ibañez, *The Western Pyrenees*, Clarendon Press 1975
Jacques Kaufmann, *Mourir au Pays Basque*, Plon 1976
Jean Louberge, *La maison rurale en pays basque*, Creer 1981
Sandra Ott, *The Circle of Mountains*, Clarendon Press 1981
Dorothy L. Sayers (translator), *Song of Roland*, Penguin 1957
Georges Viers, *Le Pays Basque*, Privat 1975

Below the Pointe de Surgatte, within a few kilometres of Arrens, the clouds and sheep move together and apart in reflecting, complementary patterns.

Provence

Aix-en-Provence to St Tropez

177 kilometres

As you slide down towards Provence on the Autoroute du Soleil the towns and sights you bypass in such fluent ease are announced and described on large brown billboards as something to divert the drivers in their tedious luxury. 'Montélimar (Nougat)' rises up and slips past in effortless absurdity; and an hour or so later you will reach the frontiers of Vaucluse, the first department of Provence, where a wordless placard greets you with the double image of a pair of cherries like headphones and a diagrammatic peach. 'Les Fruits de Provence', reads the caption several hundred metres later. There, in stark reduction, is the governing myth of Provence as a zone of exclusive pleasure, where fruit is the morning and evening of an Elysian existence. It is the myth of the south that northerners will always cherish, using it as a sump to drain off our nostalgia for an Eden that we hope is no more than half-lost. Auden wrote in the 1930s:

Again and again we sigh for an ancient South,
For the warm nude ages of instinctive poise,
For the taste of joy in the innocent mouth.

It is this Gauguin impulse that the holiday machine has mobilized, allowing millions the annual attempt to leave the prosaic for the polychrome. It is this too that has resulted in a wall of villas around the Côte d'Azur – as propagandist a name as you could look for, invented by a poet called Stéphen Liégeard in 1887.

But Provence is not like its pleasure-rind. As this walk from Aix to St Tropez will show, the heart of Provence, except for the occasional crack of a valley, is a place of only grudging fertility, where, to exist at all, fecundity must be engineered from terraces. It is a country of desiccated hardness where the sun, far from instilling health into the limbs and land it soaks, inflicts the annual disasters of drought and forest fire. The winds of Provence have the subtlety and charm of mallets, without edge or sharpness, simply air moving past houses as it does past the open

Belgentier. You will come over the saddle-back dip in the horizon, arrive at Belgentier for lunch and afterwards move on up through the vineyards and olive trees in the foreground, a pattern of effort and reward which is the definition of pleasure.

233

BELOW *Plane trees at Le Tholonet.*

BOTTOM *Mont Sainte Victoire.*

*Mont Sainte Victoire. The path runs along the
horizon.*

windows of a train. The love of nature could never have been invented here, nor the realization that landscape and garden might benefit from a gentle fusion one with the other. Here the gardens one finds in the villages must always be, as they once were in the north, a denial of the reckless nature outside them. Beyond their tight enclaves of cultivated control the landscape is dry and uncompromising. Its mountains swank a solid and inelastic grandeur, mass-produced features like the mass-produced statuary one finds in garden centres. Seasons, like night and day, arrive and depart with exactness. There is nothing twilit about this country, and nuance hardly matters. Its life is chiselled, not sanded.

For the writers of Provence, like Henri Bosco and Jean Giono, their paternal landscape is blunt and obvious, a prosaic and rational presence that is cynically made use of at its weaker spots and more susceptible moments and which can never be loved. In Bosco's *l'Enfant et la Rivière*, an ungenerous country of utter banality is tempered only by the river of the title. Its *'eaux glissantes et silencieuses'* are marvellous and tempting to the child for their variation and reed-hidden secrecy. Apart from that, as the boy repeatedly admits, *'ce paysage m'attristait'*. In Giono's novels his people, with 'a courage as placid as a jar of olive oil' and the 'sun-stretched skins of drums' suffer a heartless nature with patience. For a moment in *Regain*

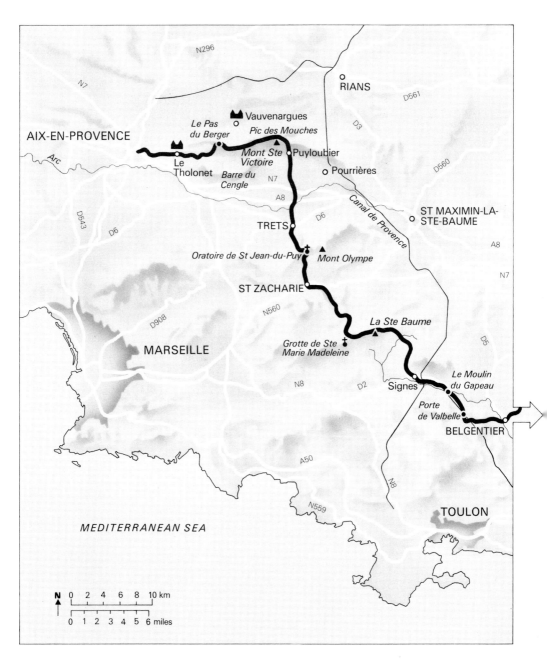

the fountain in the village square becomes the focus of it all: 'During the summer, the sun, which drinks like an ass, empties its bowl in three easy gulps; the wind washes its feet under the spout and then splashes the water into the dust. In winter the fountain is frozen to the core. Like the rest of this country, it doesn't get a chance.'

Aix-en-Provence to Puyloubier

37 kilometres

To begin in Aix is to start at the head; the rest is a working down. The best parts of Provence are distilled into its streets. More often than not it is market-day, when the dun, one-coloured squares bulge with the produce of the richer lands around it. Here the ground-swell of lowland fertility from the Bouches-du-Rhône slops over the bounds of usual decency. In billowing stalls one finds, imported and unimported, the fruits of the earth: pineapples from the Côte d'Ivoire, Mexican hat mushrooms called *lactaires*, figs, muscatel grapes, red peppers, Spanish oranges, and Golden Delicious apples. It is the inside of an American supermarket exposed to the open air and stripped of the sense of stylized, hygienic creation. Here the endives, garlic and potatoes, the turnips, courgettes and wrist-thick celery, the haricots, chestnuts

Leeks in the market in Aix-en-Provence – vegetables with a satiated, tycoon air.

and walnuts from Grenoble are all the elements of a Provençal burp. Gladioli and dahlias become the natural, crowning effusion of a spectacular earth.

You can have no doubt that this is a Mediterranean place. In between the market stalls, in black robes, thick tartan scarves and heavy black woollen coats, move one or two very black Africans drawn here, as to so many towns in Provence, by the market and its opportunities. Algerian faces are as common as French, and you will realize sharply that what matters most about Aix and the

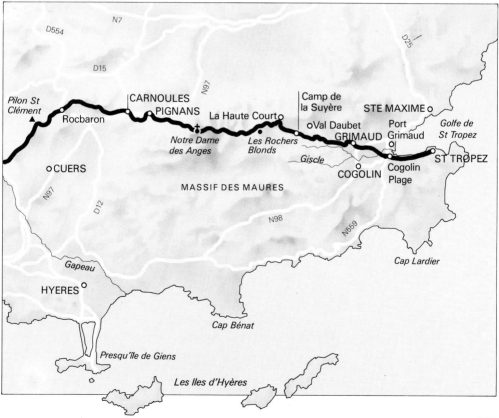

Near Trets, with Mont Sainte Victoire in the distance. Patches of limy soil appear regularly in the fields of the plain.

The stupendous November of the oak forest below La Sainte Baume.

The chemical colours of the
Provençal autumn near the
Moulin du Gapeau.

The Maures, the last obstacle
before reaching the
Mediterranean at St Tropez.
The path climbs and
descends each of these ridges
and valleys.

239

Aix-en-Provence is inescapably civilized and too refined to notice its tatty edges or broken balustrades.

One of the dolphins with spiral eyes that decorate the Place des Quatre Dauphins in Aix.

surrounding country is that it is on the edge of the same sea as Naples, Palermo, Izmir, Tel Aviv, Alexandria and Algiers. Its mere geographical links with a France dominated by its northern capital scarcely matter. It is not odd that the Greeks should have colonized Marseille, Nice and Antibes, nor that the name of Aix itself is derived from an imperialist naming of its many waters – Aix is only *aquas* compressed. Inevitably the English town it is twinned with is Bath, and the names say it all. Even if Bath does have far more interesting Roman remains, it is the Provençal not the Somerset town which has remained more Roman. Northern invasions have never obliterated the past here.

James Pope-Hennessy thought that the constant gurgling of the fountains and the deep, shady streets of Aix made it like being at the bottom of a tank. Perhaps on long, late Sunday afternoons that is how lugubrious the place becomes, but on a weekday morning Aix is much gayer. Its prestigious past as capital of an independent state that was never subjected by France but voluntarily allied itself to her, as the former seat of a *Parlement* and great university (only a couple of faculties now remain), as the birthplace of Mirabeau and his chosen constituency in 1789 – all this becomes a disregarded, slightly tatty background. Aix does not conform to the serious image that cities like Sienna or Urbino so carefully cultivate, where the historical is cosseted and cleaned at the expense of the present. In Aix there is the near-Venetian and careless paradox of a leprous decay in the buildings, only part-hidden by a bright foreground of innumerable polished limousines and of cafés graded exactly by the fifty centime difference in the price of a *café crème*, by the style of the chairs and their occupants and the stiffness of the starch in the waiters' jackets. Hairy stone heads embedded in the corners of buildings are neglected by the fashionable girls who pass below them. But it is the famous fountains that best represent the eclectic range of the city's styles. At the smart end is the lovely seventeenth-century Dolphin Fountain in the middle of its own small square. On each of its four sides sits a fat little dolphin with spiral eyes, spouting water from between saw-tooth gums. One now moves up through realms of ever-increasing pomposity to the grotesque culmination at the end of the Cours Mirabeau of a massive display, built in 1860, of fossilized gymnastics by various gods and goddesses. Why is it that we never notice the absurdity of human or divine images permanently vomiting what is meant to be pure new

water? But then, as if Aix realized it was going too far, the drive towards grandeur stops and in the middle of the Cours Mirabeau, its grandest, largest, most café-lined street, one finds posing as fountains some hearteningly shapeless, moss-muffled rocks, like *gouffres* transported whole from the limestone hills around. They are coated in weed like a green rust and stand as a kind of anti-monument, ridiculing the Tritons and naiads just down the street.

It is typical of Aix that in the eighteenth century the medieval town wall should have been demolished and the Cours Mirabeau laid out on the site as a stage for indulgence and display (the word *cours* is exact: it is a space pushed beyond the limits of a street, but still too long and thin to be a *place*). It is equally typical that the cathedral should remain a rather lumpish, utilitarian object pushed away in a disorganized and now uncentral area of the city, like an old boiler in the attic: a necessary part of the system which does not need to occupy half the drawing-room. Nonetheless it is worth going up there just to see the statue, high above the main door, of St Michael with his spear vanquishing and puncturing the Devil, who for five centuries now has been emitting a final scream of agony; and, a little more soberly, for the small Romanesque cloister, weather-beaten and partly-restored, attached to the cathedral.

Aix looks at its best in bright light. It is of course Cézanne's city. He was born here in 1839, the illegitimate son of a hatter whose shop was in the Cours Mirabeau and who later became a banker and one of Aix's solider citizens. Although it is understandable that the fashionable people of Aix should have had little sympathy with the socially incompetent and temperamental painter, it is equally possible to detect, I think, the constructional source of Cézanne's final vision in the hard, shafted light that one finds in these streets. There is no glow to it; it is all edge, compressed into a kind of petrified clarity that highlights shape and structure in any object that it strikes. There is a knowledge that things in this light have a back to them – their third dimension is in some way revealed. However, there is unavoidable prejudice – Cézanne's way of seeing will automatically make you look for, and prize, what you expect to find. But in the reaction of Van Gogh to this southern light (an outlook as different from Cézanne's as one could think of) it becomes plain that the light has an objective quality, not just in the eyes of a particular painter. Van Gogh wrote to his brother from Provence: 'When I had done those sunflowers, I looked

for the opposite and yet the equivalent – it is the cypress.' That is a hardened habit of eye and mind, and although it could scarcely be further from Cézanne's admitted search for the essential grey, the two painters share at least a commitment to the heightened nuance, to the intensified actuality of a world made more solid by this unsubtle light of Provence.

The way to St Tropez leaves Aix on the D17, which the commune has decided to call the Route Cézanne. Almost the only accolade he gets from his mother city is in leaving it, but nothing could be more appropriate. It is fringed on both sides by villas, with drives disappearing down to them, many of them closed off with wrought-iron gates, in the recurrent Cézanne image of the dwindling lane going nowhere or round a corner, a half-invitation into the picture. This country too was the one Cézanne explored again and again as a boy with Zola, almost his only friend and the son of a Venetian engineer working on a dam project near Le Tholonet. To the south, as you walk on the easy tarmac switchback of the road, a few dark valleys are revealed clothed in Mediterranean woodland, quite

An image, made familiar by Cézanne, of the allée *lined with plane trees, going nowhere in particular and, like the painting, existing for itself.*

different in outline from a northern wood. There is nothing here of the automatic density of tree-cover you find in temperate forest. Instead there is an arbitrariness in the way a particular tree has found its pocket of sustenance. The skyline is broken and the individual trees, nearly all evergreen, only just hold together as a wood at all. Here and there in autumn a poplar stands out as a single flame in this evergreen world.

A bank of ancient plane trees above a brown vineyard marks the edge of Le Tholonet, six kilometres from Aix. They are great duchesses of trees, tawny in autumn, whose massively cylindrical bodies lean slightly out of true from age. They form a double avenue that filters all light into a haze, and their pale, stately procession leads to a disappointing château with windows framed by turquoise blinds. Just beyond the trees in the Relais Cézanne you can get a good lunch for a few francs, regularly interrupted by a

On the roadside near Le Tholonet.

then emerge from the trees, and having shed the lower layer, the face of the limestone mountain again confronts you, exaggeratedly ridged in the low light, buttresses shading the bays between them. The sun here has a sharpened heat and laser-like directness, so that even with no wind you create your own shadow to cool one side of your body. The warmth you might expect to blot the general atmosphere behaves as if it were thickly viscous and unable to flow around corners. As you move in and out of the pockets of shadow you feel that the rim of the air inside them is beaded with drops of condensation: progress through them is delicious, like regular sips at dry cider.

To find the route to the ridge top you must aim almost for the point where the high voltage line from the power-station at Gardanne crosses the mountain to the north. This old way, called the Pas du Berger, is no stroll but a steep sharp cleft, possible for a shepherd but surely not his sheep, in which hands and feet are all necessary. The roots of the few trees pushed into it have been highly polished and their grain revealed by repeated sweaty use as banisters. You emerge on to the cold, open top, above the belt of heat-dense air, and to the north you will see the spine of limestone called *les costes chaudes* protruding from the vegetable fungus around it. To the south the chimneys of Gardanne and to the west an emptied reservoir called the Lac du Bimont are the two distinguishable features in a country of low hills whose presence is signalled only by a darker darkness in the earth-haze.

It may take as much as two hours to climb the 600 metres to the top of Ste Victoire, the last part of which is more gentle on the northern backslope of this limestone wedge, which was bumped up about 40 million years ago as part of the Provençal side-show to the major Alpine collisions. As incongruous miniature box bushes brush against your legs, you approach the first summit crowned by a piece of nineteenth-century religiosity, the enormous Croix de Provence that dominates the whole plain of Trets to the south. Before reaching it you arrive at something far sweeter and less strident. Notched into the very ridge and quite unexpected is a tiny courtyard framed by simple buildings – a chapel, a dormitory – making a little lagoon of civilization in the open, crushing expanse of the mountain. (The name Ste Victoire is said by some to record an important Roman victory in 102 BC over the Teutons who were marching on Italy. More likely it is a corruption of a pre-Roman Celtic wind god, Ventura, and this hill-

breezy *bon appétit* from every stranger that walks in. The proprietors when I was there imagined that writing notes as I ate could only mean I was a food inspector. Several generations of the family, including a rather testy dachshund, ringed my table in slightly threatening anxiety to ask if everything was all right. I assured them it was, smiles appeared and the dachshund's tail was allowed to wag.

Beyond the village the same lane pushes on eastwards through a country of habitual drought, in which the smartness and wealth of fenced-off villas is quite alien to the land from which they have been cut out. Heat gauzes the distance. In it, unannounced and hardly darker than the thickened air that shrouds it, appears the great grey block of Mont Ste Victoire, no more than a ghost of a mountain. Its bulk becomes more real as you approach its foot over the next five kilometres. By the time you arrive there its unyielding austerity has shed all softness and with it all allure. Here and there thin streamers of dark vegetation are pinned to its sides. The honest bareness, which they exaggerate, has nothing attractive or vulnerable about it.

The mountain was the one Cézanne regularly painted as a flattened backdrop to the lusher surroundings of Aix. For the fourteen kilometres and several hours it takes to walk the length of it you will enjoy the strange and rare experience of being able to clamber all over an art object. The climb itself starts off on gravelly tracks through groups of Aleppo pines, lovely lime-juice-green trees with needles in clusters like upturned hands, and past a hut called Refuge Cézanne (what else?) with the roof fallen in and the walls sprayed with separatist remarks – *OC* simply in capitals and *Français = Etranger*. The paths

top hermitage may well be the transformed survival of an earlier temple, its back turned against the north wind it is here to assuage.) Attempts have been made to give the buildings some classical vocabulary but the shallowness and politeness of it all shows the impulse to be hollow. There is a round well in the middle of the courtyard with a chicken-wire grill over it. *Potable sous Réserve* it says, but any *réserve* you might have had you will have lost on the climb and there is no need to hesitate before drinking from it. The water you can raise from thirty feet below in a wire-dangled mug is clean, cold and delicious.

The ridge continues for nine kilometres east of the cross. To the south above the brown plain the mountain tops float over the haze, as if the sky and clouds were below them. In the north the endless spotty, untidy, unfinished ridges increase the lack of definition in the landscape. The effect is curiously isolating and unsettling. It is more difficult to establish one's own coordinates when the scales themselves appear so unreliable. More definite below, at the foot of Ste Victoire to the

The limestone plates of Mont Ste Victoire stand up as fins through the scrubby Mediterranean forest.

north, is the village of Vauvenargues, with a castle on its southern edge where Picasso lived his last years and where his body was buried. This place was also the home of Luc de Clapiers, Marquis de Vauvenargues, an eighteenth-century writer of maxims. His most famous and guiding idea was that 'Great thoughts come from the heart', which sounds as if it did.

The encompassing quiet and the haze will turn your attention to things close to you. The limestone flakes underfoot are almost intolerably sharp. There are sparrow-hawks and ravens up here and pretty brown crickets, practically invisible when sitting on the ground but which display bright apricot flashes in flight. In places vertical layers of harder limestone stand out as walls where more friable rock has been eroded away from between them. After the Pic des Mouches, the summit of the mountain, 1,011 metres high, you drop gradually with the ridge, later entering a low scrubby wood of small oak bushes and myrtle. Eventually you slither on a sliding path, with the ground moving under you like a down escalator, between small bushes bright in autumn with the chemical yellow of decay, down at last into Puyloubier. The village is nothing much, arranged downhill with washing hanging out into the street, a pizzeria, a café where you can get mountainous sandwiches at any time of day, and a peculiarly belligerent kind of pampered dog. It was somewhere near here that Marius, the Roman general, defeated the Teutons in 102 and slaughtered 100,000 of them. It is said that the next village, Pourrières, is named after the memory of their rotten corpses, but, I am told, the name is more likely something to do with leeks.

Puyloubier to Signes

41 kilometres

At Puyloubier the way (which from now almost until the end follows the *Route de Grande Randonnée No 9*) quits Ste Victoire itself, but for days to come it will feature in the view behind you, behaving like a memory in the waywardness with which it disappears in haze, only to re-emerge the next morning pristine and near. The prism-like look it had from Le Tholonet has now gone. Its whole ruckled length is slumped out before you, gathered in slight bunches like a well-arranged curtain, the watercourses dropping from them marked in the evergreen mass by yellow veins of deciduous trees.

For twelve kilometres you cross the plain to Trets, on dusty bright tracks through vineyards whose fruit will arrive in bottles as Côtes de Provence, almost all of it a light rosé. In November, well after the *vendanges*, some of the vineyards have bunches of grapes still on the browning, dried-up plants. These were unripe at the time of the main harvest and went unpicked. If it were not for you and me they would go to waste unseen. For a few privileged hours across this richer plain (the deposits of seas that invaded the limestone trough about 80 million years ago) 'stumbling on melons as you pass' becomes for once the experience of walking in Provence. The grapes to choose are those with a thick dusk of bloom still on them; the shinier ones are past their best. I tasted some: they were no refreshment, almost without liquid and as sugary as sweets.

The mountains ahead clarify in an evening light and sharpen into darkness. At their foot the dotting of white houses marks the fringes of Trets (in the Provençal way, every one of its letters is pronounced). After crossing the motorway from Marseille to Italy and then the river Arc, which ran red with blood after Marius' victory, you soon arrive, met on the outskirts by the poisonous smoke from the municipal rubbish tip and by something called *La Liberté Enchaînée* given by a Mayor of Trets in 1977 in a moment of misguided modernity. From here Trets can only improve. Its main square is roofed by plane trees with branches like the bouquets that are thrown on to stages, and with their trunks dotted in pools of different bark like an unfinished painting by numbers. This is the modern centre of a town whose past is one of astonishing continuity for any Englishman who is used to the interruptions of history. The Ligurians (the indigenous people of Provence before the Celts – and it is significant that in Britain we have no idea of what our pre-Celtic people were called) lived from at least 3000 BC up on Mont Olympe above the town. The weather in northern Europe quite suddenly got colder and wetter in the eighth century BC. This slight but important change stimulated the series of great folk movements that dictated European history until the Norman invasions at the end of the first millennium AD. Trets acted as a kind of seismograph for these regular and major tremors. In about 750 the Celts arrived, equipped with iron, and somehow co-operated with the Ligurians to move down into the plain. Only 150 years later the Greeks from Phocaea on the east of the Aegean (themselves subject at home to pressure from the north) and the founders of a colony at Marseille (Massilia) set up a trading post on this plain and called it Trittia. In 154 BC the Greeks called in Roman soldiers to help against the Celts, and within fifty years the Romans had established the first province of their empire here. It lasted until AD 576 when Germans invaded and sacked the town. In the ninth century the Saracens took over Provence, incidentally introducing the crocus, from which you get saffron, an ingredient without which *bouillabaisse*, the national dish of Provence, would be nothing. Guillaume, Count of Arles, liberated Trets from the heathen in 950 and set the foundations for a medieval prosperity, which except for a slight lapse in the sixteenth century it has never really lost.

The best part of the town is up behind the Hôtel du Commerce in thin, high streets held together in a tight warp of telephone wires. Moored in the middle of them is the solid, near shapeless church, with a bell-tower that is said to be unfinished but looks no more so than the edifice it is attached to. A proud document inside claims it is on the site of a Christian church dating from the fourth century. On the pier next to it is a slightly wobbly, early medieval inscription that mentions God and Mont Olympe in the same breath, all in a Latin text which, in a kind of linguistic eczema, is breaking out into French all over.

Leave Trets to the south, under one of the fourteenth-century gates through the town wall, and begin to climb the ridge of limestone hills that mirrors – in a reduced way – Ste Victoire across the valley. The way up, paved in places with stone flags, is at least as old as the twelfth century and possibly much older. It could be a Gallic route from hill to valley. In the Middle Ages it became the pilgrims' way from Trets to the oratory of St Jean-du-Puy, nearly five kilometres away on the crest of the ridge, and whose bell-tower can be seen from the valley. Three small shrines mark the way, with branches of fresh ling in all of them, and in the back of one like an advertisement for scent or an incident from Hardy the simple words 'J'attends'. In places where the path narrows between the pines the rock is worn as smooth as cathedral steps, and throughout the climb your own hauling breath will be accompanied by the asthmatic chirr of crickets. They are famous for their camouflage skills but if you look you can find one easily enough. They seem to be the wrong size, less like themselves than the miniaturized versions of some full-size Leviathan. They are more like instruments than animals, with a body slung from weirdly cantilevered legs. The rear of the females is shaped like a scimitar, from which the eggs are laid. Both sexes are locked into plated armour, with a defensive, out-curving neckpiece like something made in Milan in 1480.

The hermitage on the hill-top of St Jean-du-Puy is no more than a few scattered benches and buildings, the overhanging trees forming islands of shady grass and gently conveying a sense of domestic sanctity. This is all that is left of a religious community that was here until 1891 when the last of the hermits left. An inscription that commemorates the members of the Resistance who hid here during the war introduces a different character to the place. It is difficult to imagine this place was ever secret enough, with Trets close by on the one

Down from the sterility of Mont Ste Victoire, the path crosses the richer agricultural plain around Trets.

side and St Zacharie on the other. Even in November, haze blocks off what is said to be the good view north to Mont Ste Victoire, but far more enlightening in the half-mist is the appearance of new hills to the south, dark and layered, the scenes of future revelation. This sudden apparition of a complex, broken topography in a country which until now had been intelligibly plain is like stumbling on the winding medieval quarter of a town principally framed by rational squares and boulevards.

As you drop the four and a half kilometres to St Zacharie you change departments, from Bouches-du-Rhône into Var. This south-facing valley is warm with quiet, the sense of silent heat heightened by the buzz of insects. The air is thick with the must of broom and lavender smoke, and with the sweet alloy of smells released by rosemary when the sun is on it. The stones in the unused path are not worn as they were on the way up, but jagged. You cross and recross the bed of a stream in which the rock has been smoothed by a few days' flow each year for centuries and arrive

by way of a small valley at the village of St Zacharie. Almost the first building you meet is the church. Inside it is almost totally dark, the sun coming through only one window, and casting such a narrow beam that it merely serves to darken the rest of the church. Thoughts of the heightened contrast between the light of the world and the obscurity of God, of the anti-rational south and its remains of pagan worship still to be found in the recesses of caves, all entered my head while I was there, and the message delivered I prepared to leave. The only physical objects I had felt in the dark were the massive Romanesque piers, rebuilt after the departure of the Saracens. But then my eyes, in quite a sudden dawn, grew used to the lightlessness and saw in a moment that the walls and piers were covered in a form of dried mustard masquerading as paint. I left unsure if I was dejected or pleased at this evidence of tastelessness.

Bacchus in St Zacharie, with grapes for curlers and the grin of power.

The rest of the village is sweeter, brightly lit in diluted colours. The only anomaly in these lavender streets with pale blue shutters is a *pâtisserie* in plum and pink glass, a building as edible as its contents. In the next street is a Bacchus head on the keystone above a door, slightly chipped, with grapes in his hair like curlers.

It is fourteen kilometres from St Zacharie to the foot of the Ste Baume massif, the first two and a half along the St Maximin road. You leave it at a restaurant called the Moulin de la Sambre and then plod calmly up the gorge of a half-dry river for nearly five kilometres. The good, gravelly track keeps to about the same level as the gorge gradually deepens around it. As the hills build up without effort on either side, the sensation is like riding a needle pushed slowly under the skin. The woods on the gorge sides are peppered with yellowing oaks in tessellations as regular as wallpaper, and then, suddenly, the great limestone wall of Ste Baume lurches into the sky ahead – a wedding cake of vertical icing.

As I emerged from this narrow valley I sat down on the edge of a small field to write my notes and had hardly begun when a hunter accompanied by his two beagles, with bells around their necks to prevent them being shot at in mistake for a boar, came out from the wood and stopped in front of me. He looked in a curious, rather sniffing way at me, and my notebook, maps and pencil, and his dogs did the same. I smiled at him in official welcome but said nothing. 'Ah,' he finally remarked in slow estimation, separating every syllable as if they were the initials of some arcane and suspect organization, 'In - tel - lect - u - el.' No number of denials could have persuaded him otherwise and he walked off into the wood, with his dogs clinking behind him, to find a boar he could take it out on.

The way up to the foot of the cliff of Ste Baume (the name, from the Provençal word for cave, *baoumo*, is pronounced in a too-many-syllable, Inspector Clouseau way) zigzags steeply along an old road, climbing 200 metres before reaching the easier gradients of the new D80. To the north Mont Ste Victoire appears in the distance like the indented bulwark of a liner. Nearer is Mont Olympe, a spike of mountain, and below in the foreground the wooded dummocks that the gorge wound through in the afternoon, cosy by comparison. Ahead, jets make acute accents in the sky over Ste Baume and the road threads through a little oak wood, which in autumn can look stupendous if a low light is deflected through its yellow leaves, making a kind of bank of light, sustained by black trunks with

patches of blacker moss leopard-dotted on them. It is amazing that the drying up of sap supplied to the leaves of any plant should produce this blaze of colour, but of course it has a purpose. It advertises the tree – far more than in the green days of its prime – at the moment when the fruit, the acorn, is most in need of attention. Such adept publicity is never an accident of nature.

At the foot of the mountain itself is a collection of barn-like buildings. This is the *Bénédictine Centre Culturel et Spirituel* built in the decades after 1859 to cater for the pilgrimage boom that swept France at the time. You can still stay here, if you give advance warning, and there is a café where young men with a just-off-the-mountain air will sell you expensive hot chocolate. But all this is incidental. What will occupy your attention is the great, grubby iceberg of the mountain, its feet wrapped in a muff of northern trees quite alien to Provence. Here there are tall forest stands of lime and beech which would wither in the drought and heat elsewhere in the south. But the north wall of the mountain keeps the wood in permanent shadow, creating a micro-climatic island of the north. This foreign insertion has always been precious; it is now part-owned by the state, and only dead trees can be felled in this wood thought to have been sacred to the Gauls. All this would be beautiful and interesting enough, but as you allow your eyes to wander over the mountain, its ridges caught and reddened in the last light, you will notice on the cliff above the wood a pair of Parisian houses snipped out from their rightful place and slapped on the slope here like a pat of plaster. This is the modern hermitage and chapel at the cave (*la Sainte Baume* after which the whole mountain is named) dedicated to Mary Magdalene. Thirteen years after Christ was crucified she was set adrift in a boat with her brother Lazarus and their sister Martha. They eventually landed after months afloat at Les Saintes-Maries-de-la-Mer in the Camargue. After preaching for a while she went into retirement in this cave and lived there for thirty-three years in total, chaste isolation. Those who approached found their legs turned to lead.

The way up there now winds steeply through the wood on wide steps, the risers made shiny by pilgrims' feet, the treads thickened with leaves. The *grotte* itself is a wide shallow cave, walled off with a façade coated in ivy. Inside the smells of cave-damp, sulphur and candlewax surround stone saints standing around like figures in a rock garden. Sunday morning ramblers, equipped with

mountain boots in untarnished buckskin and with rucksacks with enough straps and buckles to provide ten long nights of entertainment, moon about trying to look pious. The hermitage itself is *de luxe*, with both electricity and a sewage system. As I peered round the corner a vacuum cleaner emerged from one of the windows and had its contents shaken 300 feet down the precipice.

From the shrine you must drop a few hundred feet before climbing steadily to the ridge. From here it is fifteen kilometres to Signes, a good deal of it hard-going along the crest and then down the back-slope of Ste Baume. In places on the ridge nothing softens the armoured crust of the limestone, while immediately below colonies of beech and oak stand out in the autumn wood, the one a brown rosette from above, the other more yellow. The way is almost pathless on the mountain, but as you turn south at the eastern end of it you reach a good track, sometimes crossing a softer layer of dark grey limestone that will be balm to feet bruised and burning from days of rougher paths. A little chapel on

The chapel above Signes is the first building you come to on the way down from La Sainte Baume, the best possible outpost on the edge of the Holy Mountain.

the edge of Signes is the first building for many miles and, as you enter the town, grey terraces stiffen and ridge the valley sides.

Signes to Carnoules

43 kilometres

Signes is not at ease with itself. In the bars middle-aged men, bored on a Sunday afternoon, look into mirrors to check their quiffs are still pert. On the juke box Sylvie Vartan sings 'Love lasts as long as a cigarette'. Boars' heads stick out like baronial relics above the café tables and the expresso machine works only if it is hit. But behind this half-modern place, already showing signs of decay, is an older Signes, less pretentious, less susceptible to rot. The long curving street into which you arrive is grey and introspective, lined with

houses whose shutters are permanently closed. In the main square, where water runs out from the mouths of paraplegic fountain heads, there is a near-picturesque clock-tower (dated 1449 but rebuilt in 1904) and an extraordinary plaque on the wall of an ordinary house commemorating the stay there during the Occupation, not of Louis Lumière, inventor of the cinema, but of his scientific equipment.

For about six kilometres beyond the town you cross a vine-filled plain in an interlude of absolute airfield flatness. Leave Signes by a lane past the grey stone church tower and walk through the vineyards that in November are an unrelieved brown. The year's growth above the vine-stock is left on as thin, twiggy sticks until the leaves have dropped to form a thick winter mulch around the stock. They are then clipped off to leave the root stark and insensible. Past vineyards in which sheep and donkeys are somehow pastured on miserly scraps and edible fragments, you will soon come to a branch of the new Canal de Provence, a motorway of a canal, with a black

Signes, a shuttered and protective air.

The Bauhaus style of the Canal de Provence.

251

The track near Moulin du Gapeau.

and white, Bauhaus style to its curves. Its purpose is to feed the plains near Solliès and Toulon, to provide the irrigation which makes fruit-farming possible there, and to relieve those areas of their dependence on the vine, which only adds each year to the European wine glut and all its problems. In an average year over 300 million gallons of French wine is distilled at CAP expense into industrial alcohol.

The way now begins a long and less interesting climb up the hills, between dry stone walls on the old road from Signes to Revest. After about seven kilometres it arrives at a great field of limestone pillars 9 or 12 metres high, called collectively *Les Aiguilles*, which stand like battered chessmen on a forest board. The way then reaches a plateau and a further dreary three and a half kilometres brings you towards Belgentier. Then, past the ivy-engulfed ruins of a farm, you arrive at the most exciting moment of the walk. From a limestone lip facing east, a deep, terraced valley with hills within it is revealed below,

with the corduroy roofs of Belgentier part-hidden by one of the ridges; over to the south-east, miles away and khaki in the haze, lies the Mediterranean itself. What you thought were dark woods on the plain are ships off Toulon and what you imagined were more hills beyond them are islands. They are the Iles d'Hyères, the southernmost in the series of corrugations of which Ste Victoire and Ste Baume are the northern ridges. This is a transforming arrival. The sight of the sea brings a sudden orientation; from now until St Tropez you will somehow feel hinged to it. That outline, that coast articulates all the mountains inland, and the sense of no progress, which was in danger of swamping this walk, is immediately removed.

Belgentier is an hour away below on a narrow path beneath dipping, circling ravens and to the occasional accompaniment of the clocks of Belgentier, ringing the hours and their divisions eight minutes apart. Nearer the

The olive tree, on the extremes of vegetable existence, is more like a rock made fertile than a fruiting, flowering plant.

Belgentier.

town the path steps up and down the terraces, or *planches* as they are called, which are regularly spaced with olive trees. The large black fruit hanging off them, plum-big and wrinkled, are disgusting to eat: before they are edible they need to be soaked in brine. These olives which so exactly identify Provence are in fact an import from Syria, brought in by the Phoenicians in about 680 BC. An occasional fig tree is planted in among them, and together they represent the whole range of the country. The old boles of the olives are vast and creased, seeming to belong only to the edge of the vegetable world, less like plants than outcrops of rock made fertile by divine intervention. Next to them pose their opposites, the figs, all dangling arms and flaccid leaves. The fig is a Miró tree, all gaiety and tremulous articulation, its fruit embodying the common idea of Provence as squashy, sweet and receptive. But the olive is the more accurate in its discreet, grey suiting, an efficient and business-like executive. Facing each other, a sybarite and a puritan, the fig is the fruit of pleasure, the olive of necessity.

You round a corner to arrive at Belgentier. Its lunchtime streets, full of the clack of stacked food plates, exude the aroma of the south. It is a lovely town, much more itself than Signes and with a notice in the main square which is enough to warm any walker's heart. *'Belgentier,'* it says, *'place exclusivement réservée aux piétons.'* In one of the streets above it water gurgles out of an iron pump below a mass of limestone, taking its place in the street as nonchalantly as any of the neat houses on either side. In such a broken country of isolated valleys it is inevitable that towns even a few kilometres apart should be quite different in tone and style. Probably because Belgentier is on a main road north from Toulon it has been saved from the cul-de-sac decadence which has Signes in its grip.

The climb up from Belgentier is like running the morning's film in reverse, a 370 metre climb made worse by the fact that it is after lunch. Once up (and it is an exhausting process) the way runs along the spine of the

ridge of Canrignon for nearly six kilometres to the Pilon de St Clément, a repetition of the sharp limestone path that hurt so much on Ste Victoire and Ste Baume. The village you are aiming for, Rocbaron, is visible far away to the east, and in the south the wide swathe of the view, accented here and there by cypresses and pylons, fades in layered densities towards the horizon. These graded blues are very beautiful, but I have always wished in real mountains for the jewel-like actuality of the distant landscape that one gets in the background of Renaissance paintings. Instead of the diminished solidity that reduces a distant landscape in reality, there in the artist's panorama the hills, towns, even people, merely turn a little bluer. The sense of where from and where to would be sharper in that kind of world.

From the top of the mountain it is four and a half kilometres to Rocbaron, at first on gravelly paths but then on the smoothed-out luxury of a tarmac track leading through more vines to a wood and a slight hill. I had read in *Var Matin* in the café in Belgentier that on the

Belgentier – exclusively, and reassuringly, reserved for pedestrians.

previous day a man collecting mushrooms had been shot twice, once in the head and once in the arm, when someone hunting had mistaken him for a boar. It was the *twice*, with its hint of indiscriminate enthusiasm, that was worrying and I whistled conspicuously throughout this and every wood afterwards, in the hope that boars did not use the same tactic.

You will find Rocbaron being rapidly smartened. There are several second homes on the edges and an estate agent in the little street. Perhaps the most significant sign of development is the strange sight in this tiny village of a dentist, complete with the familiar green chair and drill, there presumably to catch a new luxury trade.

The eleven kilometres from Rocbaron to Carnoules is over the last block of limestone you will cover. All morning, interrupted by the hoarse, harsh jays, you will skate on the broken crust of limestone, piled on the rock from which it has been separated. The scrub

255

on either side has been cut to allow an average Frenchman to fit down the tunnel in between. For an average Englishman, though, the experience is one of constant ducking. In the occasional gaps one looks down south to the sea at Toulon and the plain behind it, until recently, in geological terms, a bay of the sea.

Soon after passing a bowl of brown fields at Thermes you drop to the valley itself on the edge of Carnoules. A string of new villas defines – rather hazily – the beginning of the town. All of them are carefully Provençal, with cornices made by pushing tiles end on into plaster, with roofed chimneys, balconies, outside staircases and a rigid avoidance of symmetry. Why are they all so dreadful? Maybe it is because of the knowledge of the breeze-blocks under the neatly roughened plaster or the sense of self-satisfaction in their understatement. When one of them goes over the top with its Provençal detailing the honesty of its vulgarity is a great relief. Few things can be worse than discreet kitsch.

More important, though, is the appearance in the red clay from which their patios and driveways have been cut of the tell-tale seams of coppery green and schisty stone, the first rock of the Maures, the metamorphic mountains that wall the Carnoules valley on the far side.

Carnoules to St Tropez

56 kilometres

Through roses, nurseries, greenhouses and more vines the last stage of the walk begins by crossing the plain for seven kilometres, soon leaving Carnoules and edging past Pignans, both places pretty dead. It is fast and flat until you reach the edge of the hills. From there until Grimaud, about thirty-five kilometres away, the path is through the Massif des Maures, a deeply trenched collection of mountains, far older than any of the limestone ridges you have already crossed. These hills once belonged to the island of Tyrrhenia which occupied the western basin of the Mediterranean (in a sea that covered most of France) and of which Corsica, Sardinia and the Balearics are the only other remnants. The various metamorphic rocks – micaschists and amphibolites – are slaty, can be broken in the hand and are easily eroded by streams. The softness has produced the steep, narrow valleys which make this stage so exhausting, but has also meant that underfoot the paths are much smoother and more comfortable than they were on the spiny, brittle limestone. The soil is acid and the thick vegetation is

quite different from anything met so far. There is heather here and many chestnuts and a new sort of pine called the sea pine, with dark blue-green needles and a burgundy bark. Most spectacular of all, though, is the cork oak. The Saracens taught the local people to use the bark from this tree. The trunk of each oak is stripped every nine to twelve years by making two circular incisions around it, top and bottom, and one long cut between. The cork is then peeled off in long strips which are stacked to straighten them. Boiling restores the elasticity and 5,500 tons of springy cork are exported each year from Var and Alpes Maritimes, nearly half the total French harvest. All this seems prosaic enough, but the recently denuded trees are an extraordinary sight. The lower half, where the cork has been taken, is a strong, muddy red, emerging from the rest of the tree like an expanding telescope. Above it the uncut cork is bungy and fissured, long sutures marking the higher branches like a moon-map. Previously I had associated cork only vaguely with any natural process, and to see these trees with cork *instead of* bark around them was as if someone had actually wrapped an ordinary oak tree – for some unfathomable reason – in the remains of his enormous champagne bonanza.

The first climb, up the northern edge of the Maures, is the worst. It is 5 kilometres long and 570 metres high, gradual enough to make rests seem like cheating and steep enough to be utterly sweat-drenching. Oratories punctuate the whole way to the top, where there is the church and hermitage of Notre Dame des Anges. It is a long, long grind up there, with the only possible refreshment to be found in the chestnuts which in places mattress the path. But you have time at least to reflect on the nature of pilgrimage. Near the top one of the oratories is labelled *Notre Dame de la Sainte Espérance*. A few yards away is its secular equivalent, an advertisement for *Bière d'Alsace Chez Youyou*. But, as you will find at the top, where haze hides the views, Youyou has unfortunately closed down. A hermit lives up here still, but no amount of battering on any of the doors I could find would rouse him. He runs a hostel where you can stay with advance warning. His official address is: M. Gilbert, Ermite de N.D. des Anges, 83790 Pignans.

There are five pilgrimages up here every year to venerate the statue of the Virgin believed to have been carved by Nymphe, the sister of St Maximin, both of whom came over in the boat with Mary Magdalene. The main pilgrimage is in July *'sous la présidence de M.*

Val Daubet, a hamlet in the Mauves.

l'Evêque,' according to a notice on the grey church – conveniently, the map shows a heliport only minutes away by church limousine.

For sixteen kilometres from Notre Dame des Anges the way follows a snaking road along the crest of one of the ridges. It is called the Route Marc Robert after a fireman who was killed in a forest fire here in 1971. A thick layer of woodland, complete and unblemished by buildings, fleshes the spine and the ribs of hills that come up to it. A few hives are the only inhabited places, whose bees must surely need to pick with dentist's tools to get the nectar from around them. You will find many mushroom hunters here, whistling assiduously, and a spectacular block of quartz like a Sugar Mountain, known as Les Rochers Blonds. It is very quick along this level road and almost without incident until far in the east you see at last the wide, indented Gulf of St Tropez, the long-looked-for end.

At a point difficult but crucial to find you must turn off the crest road and drop into the Vallon de la Court. Enormous chestnut trees dripping with enormous chestnuts line the path. The production of *marrons glacés* from these woods is one of the main industries of the area. After one and a half kilometres you arrive at La Haute Court, with the sweet, closed-off atmosphere of a remote Provençal village. Many of the houses are empty, almost the first sign since Aix of the rural depopulation which has blighted so many of the less famous areas of France. As you are imagining yourself in the heart of an undiscovered country, you might hear from beyond a patched and battered door, as I did, the opening bars of a Brandenburg concerto, and then above it in a kind of irregular counterpoint the tap-tapping of a typewriter. All that you have stumbled on is an intellectual's retreat.

From La Haute Court to Grimaud is twelve and a half kilometres. In a terminal failure of the imagination the planners of the GR9, which we have followed ever since Mont Ste Victoire, have decided to make it reach the Mediterranean not at St Tropez but at some

Les Rochers Blonds, *a knuckled clot of quartzite pushed into the deformed and ancient rocks that make up the forest massif of the Maures.*

unheard of place called St Pons les Mures. There is no need to succumb to this dull decision, and it is easy enough to find your own unguided way to the place of proper arrival on the coast at St Tropez. I say this, but I managed to get badly lost below La Haute Court in a wood thick with boughy undergrowth when I thought I could take a short cut. It had been burnt in a forest fire a year or two before, and after a frustrating three-quarters of an hour I emerged, smeared in tiger-stripes from the charcoal that coats the trunks and bushes, on to a forest track. I found a *chasseur* immediately opposite where I came out, his whole posture half-cocked in excited anticipation. It turned out he was only one of a large party here for the boar. One would have thought *la chasse* involved some idea of movement, but for these men that is not the case. They get back to nature by putting on green clothes and then try to kill it

by standing next to their Citroen Visas and Renault 5s while the dogs are in the wood attempting to flush the elusive boar. The hunter himself can only wait with his sandwiches. *'Il faut avoir de la patience,'* one of them said to me stoically. Had he ever shot one? 'Good Lord, have I ever shot one! Hundreds, some of them a hundred kilos or more.' Like a few of the more optimistic of his fellows he had a short length of rope attached to his belt. This was to tie the legs of the dead animal together, should one ever appear. When they do emerge they are apparently not frightening at all, but come meekly up to the barrel. Only if the shot is incompetent enough to wound but not kill will the boar turn fierce. The terrible expressions on the heads to be seen in cafés are only the cosmetics of death. The lips are artistically arranged around and over the short tusks in an angry curl that flatters the killer's ego. The sheer number of men who indulge this ever-increasing sport has meant that some protection for the boar has been introduced. The season which used to last until March now ends in December.

A chasseur *for wild boar, engaged in the most sedentary hunting in the world. The only necessary qualities are time on your hands and an index-finger that works.*

A cork-oak part-stripped of its valuable skin and left like an actor without trousers.

Saint Tropez: as pretty as Chelsea, but warmer.

Hunters measured my progress like milestones on the last slopes of the Maures, where great slabs of glistening micaschist stand up like boards, squeezing small cork-oaks sandwich-like between them. The castle above Grimaud dominates the plain and beyond it, above the sea, St Tropez itself appears for the first time, a white blot disintegrating uphill into individual villas. Coming down to the plain you will experience the sensation of wealth, like the pile of a carpet thickening beneath your feet, as the style of houses lifts a few notches, and you catch sight of one or two yellow jeeps driven by twenty-eight-year-old women with manes of hair and sunglasses. As always happens at the end of a walk, places as interesting as Grimaud are neglected in the accelerating rush towards the end. From its main square with palm trees, yachts in the gulf appear large, and the twelve kilometres to the harbour in St Tropez seem nothing that two and a half hours cannot deal with. There is always a Meccan attitude at the end – what pilgrim, for goodness' sake, would dawdle in front of his goal?

Reaching it is rather slow, at first through still more vineyards and then along a busy road almost next to the sea, but shut off from it by villas. When you finally arrive at the harbour itself, the hub of bronzed fashion, you will find yourself an absurd anomaly, brown only to the elbow, with your chest in a ridiculous two-tone, tanned in a V at the neck of a shirt, a style more suitable to governesses than heroes. All this you will conceal by keeping your clothes on in a place famous for the fact that one does not. Or at least that will be your first reaction, imagining the place as it is said to be. But it is not long before another St Tropez shows itself through the mythological haze. There is something of acute sadness in this seaside town, where it becomes more obvious than ever that with all our decisions and our luxuries we have missed the mark. We look here for the people we want to be and find that they have moved off – or at least their successors have. It is in the nature of the sophisticated world to pick up, chew over and spit out places that for a time take its fancy, and our rather melancholy lot is to inspect the remains. There are one or two shreds still to be found, tourist sights as established as nineteenth-century statues anywhere else: a boat with *Liz II, Panama* gilded on the stern; a beautiful couple in their late thirties with the air of unnecessary preoccupation and hurry that people who know they are being stared at – and are used to it – adopt; the absurdly coy and dated risqué postcards. The tone of the whole place is like those old election posters one sees all over France, in which a handsome, well-dressed *député* or presidential candidate is seen through a disfiguring green mist accompanied by a canned message now slightly silly or even unintelligible.

I would not want to represent St Tropez by what these last two decades have done to it, or to pretend that the deserted November beaches, decorated with weed and empty Harpic bottles, are what it has now come to. In the streets and squares above the harbour, where the low winter light ricochets off the saffron walls, where the swags of bougainvillaea have a mineral density of colour, where smokescreens of the aroma of *herbes de Provence* block the narrower passages, it is not difficult to discover still the charm and beauty that first drew foreigners here from the north.

DISTANCES (in kilometres)

From Aix to:
Le Tholonet 6; bottom M. Ste Victoire 5; Croix de Provence 3; Pic des Mouches 7; Puyloubier 3.8; Trets 12; Orat, St Jean-du-Puy 4.7; St Zacharie 4.5; Ste Baume Massif 14; Signes 17.9; sight of Mediterranean 14.5; Belgentier 5; Pilon de St Clément 8.9; Rocbaron 4.5; Carnoules 11; Pignans 4.1; N.D. des Anges 8.5; La Haute Court 18; Grimaud 12.6; St Tropez 12.3

MAPS
I.G.N. 1:50,000 Numbers 3244 (Aix-en-Provence), 3245 (Aubagne), 3345 (Cuers), 3445 (Collobrières), 3545 (St Tropez)

GUIDE
Topo-Guide du Sentier de Grande Randonnée 9–98 (Jura-Côte d'Azur), Tronçon Bouches-du-Rhône et Var. pub. F.F.R.P.-C.N.S.G.R. 1980

PROVENCE BOOKS
A.N.Brangham, *The Naturalist's Riviera*, Phoenix 1962
Henri Bosco, *L'Enfant et la Rivière*, Gallimard 1953
Jean Giono, *Regain*, Bernard Grasset 1930
Lawrence Hanson, *Mountain of Victory* (Cézanne), Secker and Warburg 1960
James Pope Hennessy, *Aspects of Provence*, Longman 1952
W.H.Redfern, *The Private World of Jean Giono*, Basil Blackwell 1967

Bibliography

John Ardagh, *The New France* (3rd edition, Penguin, 1977)

Jacqueline Auriol and others, *Guide de la Nature en France* (Bordas 1976)

M. Bloch, *l'Histoire rurale française* (2 vols, 2nd edition, Colin 1961–4)

Fernand Braudel, *The Structures of Everyday Life* (Collins 1981)

B. Braum and A. Singer, *The Hamlyn Guide to the Birds of Britain and Europe* (Hamlyn 1970)

Sandy Carr, *Pocket Guide to Cheese* (Mitchell Beazley 1981)

Nora K. Chadwick, *The Celts* (Penguin 1970)

Alfred Cobban, *A History of Modern France* (Penguin 1957)

G. Duby and A. Wallon (editors), *Histoire de la France Rurale* (4 vols, Seuil 1975–6)

P.-M. Duval, *La vie quotidienne pendant la paix romaine* (Paris 1953)

Joan Evans, *Life in Medieval France* (Phaidon 1957)

Lucien Febvre, *Life in Renaissance France* (Harvard University Press 1977)

Richard Fitter and others, *The Wild Flowers of Britain and Northern Europe* (Collins 1974)

E. Forster and O. Ranum (editors), *Rural Society in France* (John Hopkins U.P. 1977)

John B. Friend, *Cattle of the World* (Blandford Press 1978)

Francois Gebelin, *The Châteaux of France* (Ernest Benn 1964)

J. Hampden Jackson, *A Short History of France* (Cambridge University Press 1974)

L. G. Higgins and N. D. Riley, *A Field Guide to the Butterflies of Britain and Europe* (4th edition, Collins 1980)

Pierre Lavedan, *French Architecture* (Penguin 1956)

E. Le Roy Ladurie, *L'Histoire de climat depuis l'an mil* (Flammarion 1967)

Alexis Lichine, *Guide to the Wines and Vineyards of France* (Weidenfeld and Nicolson 1979)

Hugh and Pauline Massingham, *The English-man Abroad* (Phoenix 1962)

Jules Michelet, *Tableau de la France* (1833)

Oleg Polunin, *Flowers of Europe: a field guide* (Oxford University Press 1969)

Charles Pomérol, *France Géologique* (Masson 1980)

Mary T. Watts, *Reading the Landscape of Europe* (Harper and Row 1971)

Eugen Weber, *Peasants into Frenchmen* (Chatto and Windus 1977)

Gordon Wright, *Rural Revolution in France* (Oxford University Press 1964)

Arthur Young, *Travels in France*, edited by C. Maxwell (Cambridge University Press 1950)

Addresses and Information

Comité National des Sentiers de Grande Randonnée
92 rue de Clignancourt
75883 Paris CEDEX 18
Telephone: 259–60–40

Institut Géographique National
107 rue la Boétie
75008 Paris
Telephone: 225–87–90

The I.G.N. shop in rue la Boétie is incomparably good. It is arranged like the map of France with the maps you need laid out in the appropriate area. Every conceivable map is on sale here, as well as the all-important *Topo-Guides* which are the essential tools for these walks. They contain a great deal of practical information, including the route and its distances, hotels and their telephone numbers, bus and train details, and the shops where you can buy food and maps. They also have a few paragraphs of background on the walks themselves.

A mass of general information can be had from *Walking in France*, by Rob Hunter (Oxford Illustrated Press, 1982); from *Le Guide du Randonneur*, published by the C.N.S.G.R. and frequently revised; and from the magazine *Randonnée GR, Informations Sentiers*, also published by the C.N.S.G.R. five times a year, and available from the above address. Its most valuable section contains revisions to paths which have been affected by local hostility, new building or the removal of field tracks. A special map showing the complete network of *Sentiers de Grande Randonnée* is published by the I.G.N. and frequently revised.

Index

Numbers in italics refer to illustrations